Perman's new book on productivity goes beyond the how of effectiveness to the why: *Why do anything well?* The answer is found in our theology. Excellence, attention, and care are all ways that we leaders love our God and our neighbors. Drawing on the wisdom of business gurus, neuroscientists, and pastors, Perman has provided a resource for all of us who desire to steward our time, talents, and resources better so that we can live out the gospel more faithfully and fully in the time we've been given.

Getting stuck is frustrating, disruptive, and unavoidable. Getting stuck is also not the way it is supposed to be, suggests Matt Perman in his new book, *How to Get Unstuck.* Gleaning the wisdom from the best of the personal-effectiveness gurus, Perman combines common sense and biblical principles to help you get out of the rut that may have become your new normal. This book will help you joyfully bring more flourishing to the communities God has called you to serve.

I'm a big fan of Matt Perman's work. If you can imagine a cross between theologian Jonathan Edwards and *Getting Things Done* guru David Allen, then you have in your head a picture of Matt Perman. No one combines theological substance with practical and transformative self-management insights like Matt. His *What's Best Next* was hugely helpful—and I couldn't be more excited about his thoughtful and imminently practical new book *How to Get Unstuck.* Nothing faddish or superficial here. This is God-centered and gospel-driven wisdom—the best of self-management insights set within a genuinely Christian framework of flourishing in Christ. Highly recommended!

Christians today need to understand how to live healthy and productive lives, not only in the home but especially in the workplace. Productivity is hardwired into our DNA by God, who created man in his image and likeness. This is why I'm so excited about *How to Get Unstuck* by Matt Perman. I encourage you to pick up a copy of this book and learn how to become even more productive via a Christian worldview.

DAVE JENKINS, executive director, Servants of Grace Ministries, and executive editor, *Theology for Life* magazine

HOW TO GET
UNSTUCK

HOW TO GET
UNSTUCK

BREAKING FREE FROM BARRIERS
TO YOUR PRODUCTIVITY

MATT PERMAN

ZONDERVAN

How to Get Unstuck
Copyright © 2018 by Matthew Perman

This title is also available as a Zondervan ebook.

This title is also available as a Zondervan audio book.

Requests for information should be addressed to:
Zondervan, *3900 Sparks Dr. SE, Grand Rapids, Michigan 49546*

ISBN 978-0-310-52681-0

Published in association with Andrew Wolgemuth of Wolgemuth & Associates, Inc.

Cover design: Derek Thornton, Faceout Studio
Cover art: Shutterstock
Interior design: Kait Lamphere

Printed in the United States of America

18 19 20 21 22 23 24 25 26 /DHV/ 15 14 13 12 11 10 9 8 7 6 5 4 3 2 1

To everyone out there who is trying to make a difference. You can do it.

If the Son sets you free, you will be free indeed.

JOHN 8:36

I am the light of the world. Whoever follows me will not walk in darkness, but will have the light of life.

JOHN 8:12

Truly, I say to you, if you have faith and do not doubt . . . even if you say to this mountain, 'Be taken up and thrown into the sea,' it will happen. And whatever you ask in prayer, you will receive, if you have faith.

MATTHEW 21:21-22

For we were so utterly burdened beyond our strength that we despaired of life itself. Indeed, we felt that we had received the sentence of death. But that was to make us rely not on ourselves but on God who raises the dead. He delivered us from such a deadly peril, and he will deliver us. On him we have set our hope that he will deliver us again.

2 CORINTHIANS 1:8-10

CONTENTS

PART 3. PERSONAL MANAGEMENT:
The Clock

PART 4. SPECIAL OBSTACLES:
The Laser

INTRODUCTION

We All Get Stuck in Some Way

It's okay to be stuck,
but we don't want to stay stuck

So, if money and access and organizational might aren't the foundation of the connected economy, what is? Initiative.
SETH GODIN[1]

If you've ever been stuck, you are in good company. Mark Twain got stuck when writing *The Adventures of Tom Sawyer*, Einstein got stuck when developing the general theory of relativity, and Martin Luther got stuck trying to grasp the doctrine of justification by faith alone.

Even the apostle Paul got stuck on his missionary journeys (Acts 27:20; 1 Thessalonians 2:17–18).

We all hate being stuck. But it happens to everyone in various ways—sometimes in big ways and very often in smaller ways. You can even be stuck in multiple ways at once.

You likely are stuck in some way right now. You might feel like you don't know where you are headed in life, which is certainly one major type of being stuck. Or you might know where you want to go but keep running into obstacles—another way of being stuck.

You might be trying to do something large and important that you just can't push forward. Or the ride to accomplishing your goals is just plain bumpier than it ought to be because of various "sticking points" in your productivity approach, workplace environment, or time-management tools. You know there are ways to do things more effectively, but you just aren't sure what they are.

The encouraging and surprising truth is that it's okay to be stuck. Being stuck can be a mark that you are doing important things, because important things are often hard. And when things are hard, we are likely to get stuck.

Further, God meets us where we are stuck. In fact, it's when we are stuck that he often meets us most deeply. David often prayed things like,

> Rescue me from the mud;
>> don't let me sink any deeper!
> Save me from those who hate me,
>> and pull me from these deep waters.
>> (Ps. 69:14 NLT)

Now that's being stuck.

We've all been there, and all is not lost when we are. It's okay to be stuck. But we don't want to stay stuck.

None of us enjoys being stuck. And it sometimes puts crucial, important things at risk. There are things we want to do, things we need to do, and things that make a difference in the world that won't get done if we stay stuck.

The good news is that it is possible to get unstuck and overcome the obstacles to doing great work and getting the right things done. David prayed for deliverance and got unstuck. Paul never became passive, in spite of his many obstacles. Mark Twain finished *The Adventures of Tom Sawyer* after taking a year off to replenish. And Einstein got the help he needed with the math to bring the theory of relativity all the way through to completion. (Yes, Einstein needed help with math!—of a very advanced sort, of course.)

STUCK IN OUR PRODUCTIVITY

We get stuck in lots of ways. We can get stuck in traffic, stuck in line, even stuck in the mud. You might be stuck in a job you don't like, stuck in your attempt to lose weight, or just plain stuck in a rut.

At root, we are stuck when we really want to do, change, or accomplish something, but something prevents or blocks us from doing it. Those things can be internal (sometimes we are the reason we are stuck!), or they can be external.

One of the biggest ways we get stuck is in our productivity. We'll focus on that in this book because productivity has such an impact on everything we do every day. And it's getting worse. More and more people are noting that being frustrated and stuck in their productivity is one of their biggest pain points in work and life.

It's no surprise that we feel this way. Obstacles to our productivity are everywhere. We often feel frustrated, like we are floundering. We feel overrun with distractions, overloaded with input, stretched by multiple competing demands, exasperated by unrealistic expectations, thrown off track by interruptions, annoyed by incomprehensible snags in the systems we use, trapped by other people's bad productivity, and more and more.

In a nutshell, many of us feel like we are not getting done what really matters to us and what we are truly capable of doing. And even when we are accomplishing things, doing so is a battle that surely must be harder than it really has to be.

THE GOAL OF THIS BOOK

The goal of this book is to get you *unstuck* in your productivity in work and life, do it in the right way—a God-centered, gospel-driven way—and enable you to stay unstuck through obstacles.

In other words, this book is about more than just meeting your own needs. It is about getting unstuck so that you can accomplish

God's purposes more effectively. Getting unstuck from things that don't matter so you can accomplish the things that really do. Ultimately, this is a book about conquering busyness, doing great work, and escaping average for a cause greater than yourself—and doing all this in a holistic way that doesn't sacrifice one area of life for another (such as sacrificing your family for your career).

YOU CAN GET UNSTUCK

One might ask, is getting unstuck really possible? Yes, it is. Since our goal is to get unstuck in our productivity—defining productivity holistically as living a flourishing life, not just doing better at work—we are specifically going to utilize the principles of *personal effectiveness* to get unstuck. We will see a bit more what this means shortly, but for now it is helpful to know that the discipline of personal effectiveness has been shown to, well, be effective.

For example, recent studies have shown that effort and skill trump innate talent.[2] Seth Godin wisely notes: "The myth seems to be that you're born with some magic combination of parents, DNA, and lucky breaks, and they conspire to determine what you accomplish in life. Nonsense. And a good thing, too, because it means that for all of us, there's a wide-open path—if we choose to do something about it."[3]

Even more than this, Stephen Covey notes in *Principle-Centered Leadership* that many managers who have implemented the principles of personal effectiveness that go to the root (addressing paradigms) have seen "gains in human performance of 500 percent."[4] He points out that "quantum change" in performance comes from true personal effectiveness that addresses your paradigms, not just behaviors or even attitudes (which is the kind of effectiveness we will be looking at). And then what really moves the fulcrum is moving from individual contribution to leadership.

And Charles Duhigg, author of the now almost classic *Power of Habit*, writes in his follow-up book on productivity:

There are some people, however, who have figured out how to master this changing world. There are some companies that have discovered how to find advantages amid these rapid shifts. We now know how productivity really functions. We know which choices matter most and bring success within closer reach. We know how to set goals that make the audacious achievable; how to reframe situations so that instead of seeing problems, we notice hidden opportunities; how to open our minds to new, creative connections; how to learn faster by slowing down the data that is speeding past us.[5]

So it is possible to get unstuck. Now, what is our process for doing so?

USING PERSONAL EFFECTIVENESS TO GET UNSTUCK

The following principles can help you get unstuck. They can be organized within the framework of the discipline of personal effectiveness, which will enable you to remember them better and use them more effectively.

What Is Personal Effectiveness?

First, we need to ask: What is personal effectiveness? You may have heard of the term "personal effectiveness," although it isn't often used today. Today it is often just called "productivity." If you are a fan of David Allen's *Getting Things Done*, when you implement your Getting Things Done (GTD) system, you are dealing with personal effectiveness.[6] If, like me, you love the work of 99U, which originates from Scott Belsky's great *Making Ideas Happen* and helps the creative world be more productive, when you read their books and articles, you are reading about personal effectiveness.

The discipline of personal effectiveness was most fully developed by Stephen Covey in the 1980s and '90s. He played a key role in popularizing ideas like "urgency and importance," goals and roles, and mission statements.

Getting Things Done and other more recent productivity approaches and resources are more contemporary versions of this quest for improved productivity. They are very helpful, but what is interesting is that they leave behind some of Covey's key concepts. They don't reject them but leave them in the background.

Personal effectiveness in its best form brings together these two main angles from David Allen and Stephen Covey. It shows you how to process and manage your work across all levels (where GTD excels), but also shows you how to do this from within a center of *correct principles*, reflected in your mission and values. So ultimately principles are central, not methods and tactics. Finally, we then need to add to this explicit God-centeredness, as we've seen, as these principles come ultimately from God and his Word. And so God is at the center of our productivity and gives us the power and direction to do the right things in the right way and for the right reasons.

How Does Unstuck *Relate to* What's Best Next?

In *What's Best Next*, I presented my recommended process for personal effectiveness.[7] I call this process "gospel-driven productivity" (GDP). *What's Best Next* gives the full statement of GDP.

Here in *Unstuck* my aim is not to give the full process but to provide brief insights on how to get unstuck from specific issues surrounding personal effectiveness. All of these principles can be used together very effectively. You may opt to turn to whichever ones seem most relevant to your particular current challenges.

Further, I present some principles that are crucial for effectiveness but that did not fit into *What's Best Next* or that can benefit from an expanded treatment of what I was able to give there.

Unstuck therefore gives you new material focused especially on breaking free from productivity obstacles. But this new material fits with and integrates completely with *What's Best Next*, enabling you to begin with either book.

THE PROCESS FOR GETTING UNSTUCK

The process of personal effectiveness has four parts, and our principles for getting unstuck group into these four areas. As I mentioned, I won't seek to give you a comprehensive system, as the goal here is to get you unstuck as quickly as possible (and I've already outlined a full system in *What's Best Next*). Rather, I will provide brief windows into some especially successful practices for getting unstuck and within those windows focus especially on some powerful but overlooked aspects.

One of the greatest ironies is that sometimes we get stuck in implementing the very systems of productivity that are supposed to help us get unstuck! For example, one aspect of personal effectiveness is to identify our mission. But this can be hard to do, and we often get stuck doing it. Or in setting up our to-do lists, we may find that they end up being complicated or that we never look at them. We will discuss some of these aspects of being stuck as we look at our snapshots.

Here are the four sections of the book that bring together the principles we will look at for getting unstuck.

Part 1. The Problem and the Principles: Foundations

First we will examine the chief problem that gets us stuck in our productivity—busyness—and its roots in the urgency addiction. We will see that urgency versus importance is the fundamental issue in time management. This problem is the root of all the others.

We will see that to be truly effective, you cannot just focus on behaviors. You have to change at the root, which means changing your mind-set and paradigm. That is, you need an entirely different approach to effectiveness that is not based on urgency but is rather based on importance.

As a result, you also will likely find that this is a new approach to personal effectiveness from what you are used to, with these distinctives:

- It is based in the importance paradigm rather than just prioritizing what is urgent.
- It is geared to the knowledge work era rather than the industrial model of work.
- It is God-centered rather than leaving God out and then leaving it to you to integrate the process with your faith on your own.
- It affirms the place of work in your life and finds it exciting rather than something to avoid.

Personal effectiveness in a nutshell is this: operate from a center of sound principles. Use those principles to set your priorities. And then organize and execute your life around those priorities. This section gives you the center of sound principles that you can then use to create your priorities and organize and execute around them.

Part 2. Personal Leadership: The Compass

Part 1 shows that you can't go straight to setting priorities (which most time-management books do); instead, you have to start with what is behind priorities. Otherwise you will not set the right priorities, and you will get stuck.

With that understanding in place, in part 2 you can now begin to develop a vision for your life and determine your priorities. This section touches on the key concept of life planning, which is being discussed more and more. It is about designing your life—but with a twist: doing it in a *God-centered way*.

I call this part "the compass"[8] because it's something that has to precede even having a plan. Your compass is how you find your way even when the map isn't clear. Having a compass by which you can detect "true north" enables you to adapt and create your own maps—which is at the heart of true personal leadership.

Part 3. Personal Management: The Clock

Then you need to be able to implement your vision. You do this by applying discipline, or focus. This step is twofold: saying no to things outside of the vision (and recognizing them as such—a key component of focus) and staying focused on the tasks you select. It involves organizing yourself, motivating yourself, and actually carrying out your plan as well as *controlling to plan* by identifying deviations and correcting them.

The key to time management at the end of the day is simple: you need to know where you are going, and you need to focus on the things that will get you there. The reason it is so hard is that we often don't have a clear vision, and when we do, we aren't aware of how to stay focused on it. By learning these skills, you will gain the ability to manage your life, make change, and get from where you are to where you want to be—that is, to get unstuck.

For readers of *What's Best Next*, you will notice that this strategy aligns with the DARE model. "Define" covers personal leadership. Then "Architect," "Review," and "Execute" focus on personal management.

Part 4. Special Obstacles: The Laser

Finally, I will give quick but powerful solutions to getting unstuck from some of our most common sticking points.

Note that getting unstuck is not just about the laser. It can't be, since we've seen that everything we do needs to be based on a vision, which in turn needs to be based on correct principles. Many people want to go right to the laser, but that won't work. The laser needs to be plugged in to the other components. Then it becomes very powerful.

Use this book to quickly get unstuck from the pitfalls of common challenges, such as developing a vision for your life or organizing your time, and also to find the basic process for productivity. In sum, *Unstuck* is about how to accomplish God's priorities using quick tips for getting unstuck in common time-management dilemmas.

HOW I'VE BEEN STUCK

I've been stuck numerous times in both literal and metaphorical ways.

One time I was stuck in a canyon with my brother after a mountain bike journey gone wrong, and we had to hike up a one-thousand-foot vertical rise to get out—carrying our bikes.

Another time I got my car got stuck in the mud in the middle of nowhere. I was with my two sons and had taken a wrong turn in the country, and the dirt road turned into pure mud at the bottom of a hill. We couldn't gain traction to drive out and had to call a towing company with a large tractor to pull us out. (They were prepared—this apparently happened a lot.)

And I've been stuck in my productivity. Stuck in projects redesigning large websites and in learning large chunks of material for new roles I'd been given. Perhaps most of all, I've been stuck in writing my books. I got stuck writing *What's Best Next* and have heard the joke hundreds of times about how ironic it was that I got stuck writing a book on productivity. (I still find it funny, and I don't begrudge the teasing.) I even got stuck writing this book—the biggest irony of all, stuck in writing a book on getting unstuck!

But writing hasn't been my only, or biggest, area of getting stuck. A few years ago, I encountered a special challenge: something went wrong with my health, and I did not know what it was. I began to have extreme fatigue and muscle pain. My legs and lower back felt heavy and had a throbbing type of pain. I could no longer do what I normally could do, which really threw me off. I would make time estimates and design my workload based on what I could normally do, because that is what I was used to. But when it came time to do these things, the energy just wasn't there. And I didn't know why. At night I often could not fall asleep. Doing anything was so difficult. It felt like I was constantly carrying a fifty-pound weight with me.

I went to doctors and tried all sorts of things. Blood tests came back normal. We could not figure it out. Physically nothing was wrong with me. Nevertheless, I was feeling real physical pain. But when you can't figure out what is causing the pain, how can you fix it? I looked into fibromyalgia, which is a diagnosis of exclusion—basically, if doctors can't figure out anything else, and a few other criteria are met, it might be this.

We finally discovered that what I had was depression. I had battled depression before, but for some reason this time it caught me off guard. At one point, I met with a group of people who wanted to know more about what my depression was like, so I brought part of my weight set from home with me. I had a volunteer carry a bunch of things across the room while also carrying two twenty-five-pound weights. I said, "This is what even the simplest tasks are like for me—returning a voice mail, mowing the lawn, taking a shower. Anything I do is that much harder."

How I got unstuck from depression is somewhat surprising. I share this with you to let you know that while I've read and studied a great deal about personal productivity and time management, I've been stuck myself. And I understand that the reasons why we get stuck can vary, depending on our circumstances. My experiences have taught me that anyone can get stuck for any reason. Even when you are equipped with the latest productivity insights, it can happen. Because I've been stuck so often in my life, I've had to learn how to get unstuck as well. And over the past few years, after much trial and error—as well as help from the latest productivity research—I've become something of an expert at getting unstuck. And fortunately at getting stuck less often.

WHO THIS IS FOR

I've written this book for anyone who is passionate about what they are doing and wants to make change. I want to help you do more of what God calls you to do, and do it better. I want to help you avoid the paths that will get you stuck in the first place and to overcome the barriers that get in your way. And when you do get stuck, I want to help you get unstuck.

Specifically, I hope this book can help both non-Christians and Christians.

This Book Is for Non-Christians

C. S. Lewis said that the most effective books in helping non-Christians come to faith are often those that are not explicitly Christian. I'm breaking that rule. This book is explicitly Christian. There are now many Christians in the field of productivity and leadership that are true experts and are writing for general audiences. What we now also need is an explicitly Christian view—even for non-Christians. I say this because, as Christians, we have useful things to say to the world in general—even when speaking explicitly from our Christian worldview. The things we have to say can be of benefit even to those who don't accept our faith beliefs. Further, they can also help overcome the stereotype that the Christian worldview is superficial.

I want to show that the Christian solution is truly useful and good. I want to show that it provides something essential and doesn't go light and superficial on the best practices and latest research. And I want to present the Christian vision of productivity, but not as an outsider. I am doing it as a participant in the common culture. I have learned from the best secular thinking (that is, thinking that isn't explicitly faith based) and am building on those ideas—not looking down on them or dismissing them because they aren't explicitly Christian. I am living in the same world as the most productive non-Christians, and many of the same things help us both. As Christians, we need to affirm that truth. We also need to show how this truth integrates with a biblical perspective, and how non-Christians can follow biblical principles in their lives that will transform as well as improve many of the things they are already doing and the goals they already have. Thus I believe this book will be of benefit even to those who do not share the faith of Christianity.

This Book Is for Christians: The Growing Movement

And this book is especially for Christians who are passionate about what they are doing and want to make change.

The Christian world has been doing an amazing job of thinking about almost every aspect of life from a gospel-centered perspective. But time management has been frequently neglected—or treated superficially. Now, however, this is changing. There is a growing movement among Christians who care much about getting things done and doing an amazing job. They are especially excited about doing good work and are endowed with remarkable creativity and initiative to make it happen. They are people in both ordinary and extraordinary circumstances who simply have the desire to make something significant happen.

More than ever before, Christians are starting organizations, making a difference where they are, and impacting the world. They are starting churches, getting involved in their communities, and loving their families. This is an extraordinary worldwide movement, and we need to equip it and fuel it. We can see it in the many great conferences that are happening: the Global Leadership Summit, Catalyst, Q, and so many more. And we can see it in the great churches and organizations like Austin Stone, Redeemer NYC, Sojourn Louisville, and so many more.

Yet, sometimes, we get stuck.

I want to help you turn your desire to make a difference and even change the world into real action—and do it in a God-centered way, a way that honors him and is empowered by him.

This book is about accomplishing God's purposes without getting stuck.

THE RESULTS: What Will Happen If You Can Get Unstuck

We already know that by learning personal effectiveness, you will be able to manage your time deliberately; you will have more time, more energy, and more momentum; and you will be able to apply it to accomplish great work.

But there is something beyond these things that for many of us is even more exciting: as we get unstuck, we can change the world. We can advance the common good, tackle large global problems like extreme poverty more effectively, and further the spread of the gospel.

And so, at the end of the day, this book will equip you to make a difference in the world. It starts with the most central, but often overlooked, factor in doing that: learning how to lead yourself. Let's go.

THE UNSTUCK CLINIC

Core Point

We all get stuck at some point, and this is normal. The discipline of personal effectiveness can help us get unstuck from productivity obstacles, but the most important thing is that we do this in a God-centered way.

Exercise

Write out a description of your vision of what it looks like to be unstuck.

Resources That Address Getting Unstuck

Applying scientific research and neuroscience to productivity challenges:

- Charles Duhigg, *Smarter Faster Better: The Transformative Power of Real Productivity*
- David Rock, *Your Brain at Work: Strategies for Overcoming Distraction, Regaining Focus, and Working Smarter All Day Long*

New and great all-around books on productivity and focusing on the core:

- Greg McKeown, *Essentialism: The Disciplined Pursuit of Less*
- Cal Newport: *Deep Work: Rules for Focused Success in a Distracted World*

Getting unstuck emotionally:

- Jennie Allen, *Stuck* (DVD-based study)
- Daniel Goleman, *Emotional Intelligence: Why It Can Matter More Than IQ*
- Christine Jeske and Adam Jeske, *This Ordinary Adventure: Settling Down without Settling*

Taking responsibility and initiative:

- Stephen Covey, "Habit One: Be Proactive," in *The 7 Habits of Highly Effective People*
- Seth Godin, *Poke the Box*

Flourishing:

- Tom Rath and Jim Harter, *Wellbeing: The Five Essential Elements*
- Martin Seligman, *Flourish: A Visionary New Understanding of Happiness and Well-Being*

Virtue and flourishing:

- Aristotle, *Nicomachean Ethics*
- Stephen Covey, *The 7 Habits of Highly Effective People*

Career:
- Jon Acuff, *Do Over: Make Today the First Day of Your New Career*
- Emma Seppälä, *The Happiness Track: How to Apply the Science of Happiness to Accelerate Your Success*

Keeping your faith real:
- Todd Wilson, *Real Christian: Bearing the Marks of Authentic Faith*
- Francis Chan, *Crazy Love*

PART 1

THE PROBLEM AND THE PRINCIPLES

Foundations

CHAPTER 1

HOW WE GET STUCK

There are three ways we get stuck in our productivity

Almost all of us feel torn by the things we want to do, by the demands placed on us, by the many responsibilities we have.
STEPHEN COVEY[1]

I love that Dr. Seuss book *Oh, The Places You'll Go!* The main character is off to great places and doing great things. He has incredible potential, and he is using it. It's an inspiring book, often given to graduates:

> You'll be on your way up!
> You'll be seeing great sights!
> You'll join the high fliers
> Who soar to high heights.

The reason I like this book so much is because it's realistic. It presents both the highs and the lows. For shortly after this, we read:

> Wherever you fly, you'll be best of the best.
> Wherever you go, you will top all the rest.
> Except when you *don't*.
> Because, sometimes, you *won't*.

It goes on:

I'm sorry to say so
but, sadly, it's true
that Bang-ups
and Hang-ups
can happen to you.[2]

That is, we get stuck. Things might be going great. We might be flying high, accomplishing our goals, and doing amazing things. Everything is going our way. But then, suddenly, it isn't. Things that worked for us before stop working. All of a sudden, none of the options before us are appealing. We aren't sure what to do. Nothing we try pans out.

What do we do when that happens? And is there a way to avoid it—or at least make it happen less? Is there a way to get unstuck and maybe even get stuck less?

Here's another angle from which to look at it. The world of work keeps getting more exciting. We have more opportunity than ever now to make an impact because, thanks to the internet, we are all empowered. We don't need to get the approval of gatekeepers (sometimes overly restrictive!) to get our work out to the world. Everyone can speak up, and everyone can get their work out there.

Our aim in this is not to feel good about ourselves but to serve. We want to do work that brings benefit to people in the best way we can. Doing so is important and it matters. It matters because it's part of the most fulfilling life; it's part of God's plan for us for reflecting him in the world; and it's the way he renews our cities socially, economically, and spiritually.

But there is something in the way of doing this kind of work.

Sometimes we get stuck.

Why does that happen? And what can we do to prevent it? To answer these questions and to know what to do when we get stuck, we need to understand a bit more about what it means to be stuck.

WHAT IT MEANS TO BE STUCK

We are stuck when we don't know how to move forward. Or when we try to move forward and our efforts are ineffective. We spin our wheels, and we just can't move ahead. We are stuck when we are not making the impact we are supposed to be making. We are also stuck when our work lives are taking up more of our life than they ought—when work is reducing the amount of time our families deserve, reducing church involvement, reducing our time to recharge, hindering our relationships, and having other ill effects. That is, being *out of balance* is also part of being stuck.

Here's how we talk when we are stuck:

Stuck: "I don't know what to do."
Stuck: "I'm trying to do X, and A keeps getting in the way."
Stuck: "I'm making progress, but the road is bumpy—way bumpier than it should be."

Getting stuck happens to all of us to varying degrees and in multiple ways. We get stuck in our attempts to make change, stuck in our productivity, and stuck in our attempt to get important things done in a balanced way.

BEING STUCK COMES DOWN TO THREE MAIN THINGS

How do we break free from the productivity obstacles that get us stuck? First, we need to understand the causes better. At root, we get stuck in our productivity in three chief ways:

1. We don't know what God wants us to do.
2. We know what God wants us to do, but we don't know how to make it happen.
3. Obstacles in our way are preventing us from doing it.

We Don't Know What God Wants Us to Do

Sometimes we aren't sure what we need to do or want to do at all—with our lives, with our career, with the next project, or even with the next hour. When this happens we may feel disoriented, lacking direction, or just confused (that is, stuck!).

Lack of direction is a very significant—and much overlooked—source of being stuck. For you can't get where you are going if you don't know where you are going!

The problem here is *lack of vision*.

We Don't Know How to Make It Happen

Very often, even when we do know what we need or want to do, we aren't sure how to do it. We aren't sure what the path is—or how to chart the path and move along it. This is like being in the water and seeing your destination, but not knowing how to swim. You know where you want to go but can't move yourself there. This, also, is a much-overlooked cause of being stuck.

Here you can feel trapped, stuck in the most literal sense. Stuck in the mud and immobilized.

The problem here is *lack of planning and execution*.

Obstacles Are in Our Way

Beyond that, even when we do start on the path, obstacles threaten to throw us off. These obstacles often take the form of our being overscheduled, overbusy, and overwhelmed. And, interestingly, sometimes fear is an obstacle. One of the biggest obstacles is fear of risk—or even fear of success.

This is the problem of *obstacles in the way*. We know how to execute and may even be pretty good at it, but our execution has holes. We are more vulnerable to obstacles than we need to be. This is the most recognized cause of getting stuck, and it needs to be addressed. But it can't be addressed first, because often the obstacles are actually symptoms of being stuck in one of the first two ways.

SUMMING IT UP

We are stuck when we don't know what we want or can't accomplish what we want. Not knowing what we want is the problem of lack of vision. Not being able to accomplish what we want breaks down into two subproblems: we don't know how to execute, and obstacles are in the way.

Lack of vision, lack of execution, and obstacles—those are what get us stuck.

THE UNSTUCK CLINIC

Core Point

We get stuck in our productivity when we don't know where we should be going, don't know how to get there, or keep encountering obstacles.

Exercise

What are the biggest ways you are stuck right now? Take a few minutes to reflect, and write them down.

Taking It Deeper: A Quick Survey to Identify If You Are Stuck

VISION

- Are you accomplishing what God wants you to accomplish?
- Do you know what God wants you to accomplish?
- When you accomplish your goals, do you feel they were the right goals?

EXECUTION

- Do you feel prepared for each day?

- Are you completing things on time?
- Are you unhurried?
- Are you making progress toward your goals?
- Do you like the approach you have for managing your work?
- Are you able to get from where you are to where you want to be?
- Are you able to accomplish the things that matter most to you?

Obstacles

- How often do you get in the zone in a typical workweek?
- In your work, are you able to do what you do best every day?

CHAPTER 2

FLOURISHING

What It Means to Be Unstuck

The Bible talks about being unstuck and gives us
great clarity on it; being unstuck also connects
with universal concepts like human flourishing

---

*The Bible is about human flourishing ... [and] the Bible's vision
of human flourishing is God-centered.*

JONATHAN PENNINGTON[1]

I f we are going to get unstuck, having clarity on what it *means* to be
unstuck helps immensely. Lack of clarity on our goal—whatever
the goal happens to be—is one of the biggest reasons we get stuck.
And so it would be ironic if we failed to apply this to the task of
getting unstuck itself!

So what does it mean to be unstuck?

WHAT IT MEANS TO BE UNSTUCK

We all want to do work that matters—that makes a difference. We
want to be getting the right things done in the right way and for the
right reasons. Because we live in a fallen world, we know that obstacles
are inevitable. And so, to begin, we can sum up what it means to be
unstuck like this: getting important work done through obstacles.

Note that this summary statement encompasses all three of the
things we need: vision, execution, and overcoming obstacles.

We see vision in the phrase "important work." You aren't just doing anything. You are doing *important work*—work that stems from and aligns with a vision. It meets needs and utilizes your abilities and capacities.

We see execution in the word "done." You are "getting important work *done*." You aren't just trying (as noble as that is!). You are actually making things happen.

And you are getting this important work done *through obstacles*. Obstacles don't throw you off track or kill your efforts. You persevere and can navigate through them.

Being Unstuck as an Ongoing Capacity

Further, being unstuck doesn't just mean you can get through the current block. It's about something with a much higher rate of return: the ability to get through blocks as an ongoing capacity. It means you can create and get important work done even when the conditions are hostile and even through obstacles—and that you can do it consistently.

To be unstuck is to be getting important work done through obstacles, and to keep doing it—over and over again. That's the master skill we need in our era, a skill we all need. And as things keep getting more challenging, we need this skill now more than ever.

We especially need this skill when we are performing at the edges of our ability—which is what you will have to do sometimes if you seek to make a real, lasting difference in the world. To do important work often takes everything you have.

THE BIBLICAL VISION OF BEING UNSTUCK

We need to go beyond this, however, and have an understanding of being unstuck that is explicitly biblical. For there is no way to truly be unstuck without taking God into account and, beyond that, *making him the center*.

As my pastor once said, "Christ doesn't just want to be another app on your operating system; he *is* the new operating system alto-gether." Christ should not be just one component among many in our lives. He ought to be the center from which everything else flows, because he is Lord of all.

Consider this: if everything in your life was going your way—if your finances were in order, you loved your job, your family was happy, you lived in your dream house, and you had everything you wanted, would you be unstuck?

I suspect the answer could still be no. The reason is that some-thing very important—something essential—may still be missing. And that's Christ.

If God is the most important being in the universe, and if he created us for a relationship with him, then we are not truly "unstuck"—that is, living in line with our purpose—unless he is at the center of our lives.

Too often, personal effectiveness is used as a tool to build the life we want, and God is left out of the picture. This is not a small matter. It is actually very dangerous, for Jesus said, "For what will it profit a man if he gains the whole world and forfeits his soul?" (Matt. 16:26). How do you forfeit your soul? By not seeking God first.

Jesus also spoke of something he called "the deceitfulness of riches" (Matt. 13:22). The typical conceptions of personal effective-ness often play right into this. They teach you how to get everything you want, and you then *think* you are flourishing, living a complete life, and "unstuck." And it is smooth sailing.

But in reality you are smoothly sailing to the wrong destination (cf. Luke 12:13–21). It is comfortable and perhaps even fulfilling for a time. But it does not end well. It does not produce the life God desires and will not lead you to an eternity with him, where you will experience true and perfect flourishing *forever*.

So we aren't truly unstuck unless Christ is at the center of our lives. For Christ to be at the center of our being unstuck means that we do all that we do *for him* and *in his power*. He is the center of our lives that gives us security, guidance, and strength. He is our aim in all things, and we follow his teaching in making every decision about how to live our lives and manage our time.

Christ as our center also means that we look at the Scriptures directly to answer the question "What does it mean to be unstuck?" When we do, we see some interesting things.

THE BIBLICAL VISION OF BEING UNSTUCK IN 1 CORINTHIANS 15:58

The concept of being unstuck is captured very well in 1 Corinthians 15:58: "Therefore, my beloved brothers, be steadfast, immovable, always abounding in the work of the Lord, knowing that in the Lord your labor is not in vain." This is one of the Bible's fundamental passages on being unstuck, and it helps us understand God's vision for our work and life. We see three things about being "unstuck" in this verse.

God Wants Us Unstuck

First, God wants us unstuck! He commands us to be "always abounding in the work of the Lord." Where do I see being "unstuck" there? In the word "abounding." God doesn't want us just to do his work here and there or only a little bit, or simply to endure hard slogs in our attempt. He wants us to *abound* in his work—to do it abundantly.

"Abounding" would also include being energized and whole-hearted (cf. Eph. 6:6–7), and even in some measure being in the zone. It means being motivated, engaged, and making progress with joy on the right goals. So, to be unstuck is to be abounding in the work of the Lord.

Our Way Will Not Be Devoid of All Difficulties and Hard Slogs

Second, though, notice something else. In the second part of the verse, Paul speaks of our "labor." In part, this is another term for work, but Roy Ciampa and Brian Rosner are likely right in their commentary on 1 Corinthians that Paul is going a bit further here.[2] Sometimes our work in the Lord is laborious—difficult, challenging, and hard. In other words, though the goal is to be unstuck, our way won't be all wine and roses. We will face hardship and suffering and agonizing along the way.

Being unstuck is not only about having momentum and moving along with minimum friction. It also has to include the ability to endure difficulties and even hard slogs. We do not want to fall into what Martin Luther called a "theology of glory"—the notion that the Christian life is exclusively one of victories, miracles, and success. We endure crosses and hardship, and the fact that we are experiencing those things does not of itself mean we are doing something wrong.

To Get Unstuck We Need to Get "Stuck" on the Right Things

Third, notice that central to being "unstuck" in the right way is actually being "stuck" in another way. For Paul speaks of us being "steadfast" and "immovable." That's stuck! But stuck in a good sense. Stuck on the right things. Having a sense of purpose, knowing our principles, and being wholly devoted to God. To be unstuck from the wrong things, we need to be fully "stuck" in the right things.

OTHER PLACES THE BIBLE SPEAKS OF BEING UNSTUCK

The Bible speaks of us being unstuck in several other ways as well. The concept of being unstuck is included in these central biblical themes.

Freedom

Jesus says, "If you abide in my word, you are truly my disciples, and you will know the truth, and the truth will set you free" (John 8:31). And Paul tells us that freedom is one of the central gifts of the gospel: "For freedom Christ has set us free; stand firm therefore, and do not submit again to a yoke of slavery" (Gal. 5:1). "So you are no longer a slave, but a son, and if a son, then an heir through God" (Gal. 4:7).

Being free is being unstuck, untangled, able to move. Especially in view here is being free *to follow Christ* and not submitting to unbiblical regulations on our spiritual lives. Following Christ, and him alone, fully. And so freedom is, most of all, the ability to do what we know we ought to do—with joy and not constraint.

John Piper sums up the biblical meaning of freedom in this fullest sense, of being free "indeed," that Jesus and Paul are speaking of: "You are fully free—completely free, free indeed—when you have the desire, the ability, and the opportunity to do what will make you happy in a thousand years. Or we could say, You are fully free when you have the desire, the ability, and the opportunity to do what will leave you no regrets forever."[3]

Shalom

The concept of shalom, or peace, is a central biblical concept that is receiving much more focus today than in the past. We see it throughout the Old and New Testament. One of the core passages on shalom is Jeremiah 29:7: "But seek the welfare of the city where I have sent you into exile, and pray to the LORD on its behalf, for in its welfare you will find your welfare."

The term translated "welfare" here is the Hebrew *shalom*, or peace. It is not just the absence of conflict, but the positive presence of complete well-being—with a right relationship with God at the center. Jesus let his followers know that this peace comes from him in John 14:27: "Peace I leave with you; my peace I give to you."

Joy

Joy—in Christ—is God's ultimate aim for us. John Piper has done the best job in recent decades of unpacking this theme (see the excellent *Desiring God: Meditations of a Christian Hedonist*).[4]

The great news is that our pursuit of joy and God's purpose of glorifying himself are not at odds, because God is most glorified in us precisely when we are most satisfied in him.

Service

Flourishing is not self-centered! Even psychologist Abraham Maslow revised his "hierarchy of needs" later in life, putting self-transcendence—living for a purpose greater than oneself—at the top rather than self-actualization (fulfilling your complete potential).

This is in line with the biblical view, where we are taught that we are to seek God's kingdom above all (Matt. 6:33) and that even our freedom is to be used for the sake of service. "Live as people who are free, not using your freedom as a cover-up for evil, but living as servants of God" (1 Peter 2:16). "For you were called to freedom, brothers. Only do not use your freedom as an opportunity for the flesh, but through love serve one another" (Gal. 5:13).

UNSTUCK AND HUMAN FLOURISHING:
A Positive, Not Just Negative, Concept

So being unstuck is ultimately a positive concept. It's not just about overcoming obstacles; it connects to broader principles of work and life purpose. It is ultimately about the positive side: flourishing.

Simply overcoming the blocks to your productivity does not get you productive. Productivity is something positive. And that is what we are truly after. Interestingly, it is the same with psychology, where especially the discipline of positive psychology has emerged to show that flourishing is not just the absence of problems, but a positive thing in its own right: "Positive mental health is a presence: the presence of positive emotion, the presence of engagement, the presence of meaning, the presence of good relationships, and the presence of accomplishment. Being in a state of mental health is not merely being disorder free; rather it is the presence of flourishing."[5]

What is flourishing? The concept goes back to the Scriptures, as we have seen. We saw above that it is the concept of peace and fulfillment—of being well ordered and everything being well. But let's take a deeper look. In philosophy Aristotle was one of the first to deal with flourishing in depth. He defined flourishing as "the innate potential of each individual to live a life of enduring happiness, penetrating wisdom, optimal well-being, and authentic love and compassion."[6] So flourishing includes in it reaching our potential—and doing it on the basis of character, not mere technique. It includes being a good person.

It also includes having a great and ultimate purpose—and one that is holistic (not just about career). Dostoyevsky is often quoted as saying: "The mystery of human existence lies not just in staying alive but in finding something to live for." Flourishing is not just being successful in your career. It is "a whole life lived to the fullest—a focused and authentic life."[7] It is to live with every ounce of your being and "suck the marrow out of life." It means "to live life to the fullest in an authentic and sustainable way."[8] Flourishing is not just temporary happiness or happiness merely as an emotion.

Most Christians in leadership roles are now familiar with Jim Collins's excellent work on great companies. Interestingly, the coauthor of Collin's first book *Built to Last*, Jerry Porras, continued to research what makes a flourishing life.[9] With two other coauthors, Porras articulated his findings in *Success Built to Last: Creating a Life That Matters*. Here is how they define the path to a meaningful life, or flourishing: "Become consciously aware of what matters to you and then rally your *thought* and *action* to support your definition of *meaning*."[10]

They go on: "For Builders, the real definition of success is a life and work that brings personal fulfillment and lasting relationships and makes a difference in the world in which they live." And "Folks who chase a fantastic but vain hope for fame, wealth, and power—for its own sake—may even achieve it, only to become miserable and pathetic people. . . . [That is] a potentially toxic prescription for your life and work."[11]

So purpose is central—and not a materialistic view of life. In other words, even secular thinking is coming to see—and backing it with research—that traditional views of success as wealth and fame do not fulfill and are not true flourishing. They may be a by-product, but those who are truly content with their lives and have those things found them as a by-product, not the original goal.[12]

Seligman makes the great point that full flourishing, or well-being, has five components: "positive emotion, engagement, meaning, positive relationships, and accomplishment."[13] One of his key insights is that well-being is a result of the integration of these realities, not a single concept. That is, it is not because of just one thing you do; it is from the bringing together of these five realities.

Finally, biblically speaking, the Westminster Catechism gets at flourishing when, in answer to "What is the chief end of man?" it says, "To glorify God, and to enjoy him forever." We are to *enjoy* God. We are to have joy. That's flourishing. And forever. Enduring and sustainable joy is true flourishing. And it comes from God, the true source of joy and ultimate value in the universe.

To sum this up, here's an expanded definition of being unstuck:

To be unstuck is to be making a difference through obstacles in things that matter to you. It's to be accomplishing your goals. More specifically, it's to know how to set the right goals and get them done. It's to know what God's purposes are for you and to make them happen with him and in his power. It's to be able to move and navigate in life and work from where you are to where you want to be—to where *God* wants you to be. It's to be able to say, "I want this to be different," and then be able make it happen.

My goal in this book is to help you find what God wants you to do, and then for you to do it with excellence *and through obstacles.*

WHAT BEING UNSTUCK LOOKS
LIKE IN OUR PRODUCTIVITY

Our goal in getting unstuck is to flourish, while doing so through suffering and obstacles, for the Scriptures teach we will never be away from challenges in this life, but that we can have Christ's shalom through them (John 16:33).

When it comes to our productivity specifically, we can see what we are after with three quotes from the best productivity experts of the last few decades.

First, David Allen summarizes it this way:

> You can train yourself, almost like an athlete, to be faster, more responsive, more proactive, and more focused in knowledge work. You can think more effectively and manage the results with more ease and control. You can minimize the loose ends across the whole spectrum of your work life and personal life and get a lot more done with less effort.[14]

Second, Stephen Covey summarizes it this way:

> Highly effective people carry their agenda with them. Their schedule is their servant, not their master. They organize weekly, adapt daily. However, they are not capricious in changing their plan. They exercise discipline and concentration and do not submit to moods and circumstances. They schedule blocks of prime time for important planning, projects, and creative work. They work on less important and less demanding activities when their fatigue level is higher. They avoid handling paper more than once and avoid touching paperwork unless they plan to take action on it.[15]

Peter Senge writes:

People with a high level of personal mastery are able to consistently realize the results that matter most deeply to them—in effect, they approach their life as an artist would approach a work of art. They do that by becoming committed to their own lifelong learning. . . .

Personal mastery is the discipline of continually clarifying and deepening our personal vision, of focusing our energies, of developing patience, and of seeing reality objectively.[16]

Finally, you are highly productive—unstuck—when you have these skills:

1. *Clarity.* You know what you are there to do at both the high level and *each day*. This allows you to set limits on your work.
2. *Discipline.* You work persistently and do not allow yourself to be distracted.
3. *Focus.* You work on one thing at a time and give it your full attention.
4. *Energy.* You have high capacity.
5. *Speed.* You have a quick turn-around time.
6. *Estimation.* You know how much you can do in a day.
7. *Completion.* You complete your work every day.
8. *Love.* You do your actions from a heart of genuine goodwill toward others and think hard about what their needs really are so you can meet them successfully.

Now we need to know what to *do* once we are unstuck. That's the next chapter: the unstuck cycle.

THE UNSTUCK CLINIC

Core Point

Being unstuck is ultimately a positive concept. It is getting the right things done *through* obstacles again and again for the good of others and the glory of God.

Exercise

How are you doing at obeying the command to be "abounding in the work of the Lord" (1 Cor. 15:58)? Are there things you are not doing that you should start doing, or things you are doing that you should stop doing to carry out the Lord's work?

Further Resources

- Aristotle, *Nicomachean Ethics*
- Stephen Covey, *The 7 Habits of Highly Effective People*
- Martyn Lloyd-Jones, *Studies in the Sermon on the Mount*
- Jonathan Pennington, *The Sermon on the Mount and Human Flourishing: A Theological Commentary*
- Tom Rath and Jim Harter, *Wellbeing: The Five Essential Elements*
- Martin Seligman, *Flourish: A Visionary New Understanding of Happiness and Well-Being*
- Todd Wilson, *Real Christian: Bearing the Marks of Authentic Faith*

CHAPTER 3

THE UNSTUCK CYCLE

What do you do when you get unstuck?
And how do you avoid the willpower fallacy?

---

*Fear not, for I am with you; be not dismayed, for I am your God;
I will strengthen you, I will help you, I will uphold you with my
righteous right hand.*

ISAIAH 41:10

Two mistakes we've especially made as Christians have unfortunately caused us to get stuck more!

THE TWO MISTAKES

The first mistake is understandable, given that it is ultimately *grace*
that gets us unstuck. The second is ironic, for it is the very opposite
of grace! But understanding it also helps us understand better what
God in his grace ultimately wants us to do when we get unstuck.
Getting this right is essential to truly getting unstuck in the way
God wants us to and for the purpose he wants us to.

What are the two mistakes?

Passivity

It would be a mistake to conclude that since God ultimately
gets us unstuck, we should not take action ourselves.

Sometimes, there literally is nothing we can do but wait. In those
cases, waiting is what we must do.[1] But when there is something we

can do, *we are to do it.* Not as a substitute for prayer, but flowing out of our prayers. This is simply a proper understanding of sanctification. We do not stop working because God is working, and neither does God stop working because we are working. Rather, God works in our working. His work is first, but we are to take action to do what is in our power. Then we can rest, knowing that the results are left to God.

Martin Luther captured this perfectly: "Work and let him give the fruits therefore! Rule, and let him prosper it! Battle, and let him give victory! Preach, and let him make hearts devout!"[2] This is why I have often said that one of the big mistakes we've made as Christians is taking a merely devotional approach to productivity. We have often thought that building emotional fervency and comfort is enough. But that by itself is a passive approach. Biblical spirituality is active. We are to run (1 Cor. 9:24, 26; Heb. 12:1), labor (1 Cor. 15:10), press on (Phil. 3:14), work out our salvation (Phil. 2:12–13), strive (Col. 1:29), and pursue righteousness (2 Tim. 2:22).[3]

We need to realize the same thing about our productive action and methods and strategies that J. Gresham Machen said about the use of the intellect: "No conversion was ever wrought by argument. A change of heart is also necessary.... But because intellectual labor is insufficient it does not follow, as is so often assumed, that it is unnecessary."[4]

Judging Others When They Are Stuck

Another mistake we often make as Christians when we see people stuck is that we tend to assume laziness too quickly.

When we see someone struggling with their productivity, we may assume they aren't working hard enough or that they can just fix the problem by deciding to. We hear this type of thinking in phrases like this: "If it really matters to you, you will do it," and "People find time for what really matters to them."

I call this the *willpower fallacy.* Such thinking assumes that change can be made simply by deciding to make change. It fails to recognize that often the causes of the challenge are complex, and that change needs to be *grown* instead of *installed*.

THE SKILL-WILL MATRIX

Two factors may hinder you in a task: lack of will may be one, to be sure; but lack of skill may be another. We can illustrate this with the skill-will matrix. When you plot these two factors on an axis, here is what you get:

	WILL	
S K I L L	High skill, low will *We often wrongly assume this is the problem*	High skill, high will
	Low will, low skill	High will, low skill *This is usually our problem—not laziness*

Some people lack will and skill. Some have the will but lack skill. Some have skill but lack the will. And some have both the will and skill.

With productivity, we tend to assume too quickly that the chief problem people have is lack of will rather than lack of skill. But I propose that our chief problem is actually lack of skill. Productivity requires something more than just the decision to be productive (as important as that alone is!). It requires building the capacity to be productive: the mind-set, skills, and tools. And these are not always taught so well.

This leads us to one of the most important concepts in this book: the unstuck cycle.

THE UNSTUCK CYCLE

We've seen that being stuck is common. You seek to do something important and therefore likely difficult. It might go great at first. But eventually you encounter obstacles. That is, you get stuck.

We've also seen that all is not lost. People who have accomplished historic feats, including Einstein, Mark Twain, and Martin Luther, have experienced being stuck, and they got through it, so you can too. The Bible also talks about being stuck and gives us the encouraging truth that the times when we are stuck are often times when God meets us in a special way. So you look to God, you implement certain methods to help you get unstuck, and with perseverance, hard work, and skill, you get unstuck.

What do you do now that you are unstuck? Is that it?

Obviously, you keep going toward accomplishing your goals. But there is something else you need to do: *you need to help others out of their stuckness.*

Help Others Get Unstuck . . .

The biblical ethic is about glorifying God and serving others. Those who have an advantage are to use it not chiefly for themselves but for the needs of others. As the apostle Paul writes, "I do not mean that others should be eased and you burdened, but that as a matter of fairness your abundance at the present time should supply their need, so that their abundance may supply your need, that there may be fairness. As it is written, 'Whoever gathered much had nothing left over, and whoever gathered little had no lack'" (2 Cor. 8:13–15).

Likewise, both Paul and Peter emphasize that we are to use our freedom (our unstuckness!) to serve: "Live as people who are free, not using your freedom as a cover-up for evil, but living as servants of God" (1 Peter 2:16). "For you were called to freedom, brothers. Only do not use your freedom as an opportunity for the flesh, but through love serve one another" (Gal. 5:13).

God enables us to get unstuck not only so we can flourish in our work and lives but also so we can have the joy and privilege of helping others get unstuck.

. . . And Do It Without Judgment

We need to help others get unstuck in a certain way—namely, without judgment. We should not make others feel bad for being stuck, and we should not assume that it's their fault. Life is simply hard, and we are doing challenging things. People are going to get stuck.

We need to help others get unstuck without judgment because the problem is often lack of skill, not lack of will. And because criticism has been shown to be an ineffective way of motivating people.[5] And because the Scriptures teach us to help others *with gentleness*—even if there is sin behind their problem. "Brothers, if anyone is caught in any transgression, you who are spiritual should restore him *in a spirit of gentleness*" (Gal. 6:1, emphasis added). And, of course, we must not judge because we ourselves have been stuck as well.

Notice also that not being judgmental applies to ourselves. In her excellent book *The Happiness Track: How to Apply the Science of Happiness to Accelerate Your Success*, Emma Seppälä shows that new research confirms that even harsh criticism with ourselves does not work.[6]

So this is the unstuck cycle:

Since getting unstuck is about grace, the grace that we receive from God enables us to get unstuck, and we then extend grace to others to help them get unstuck (cf. 2 Cor. 1:3–7).

THREE TRAPS TO BE CAREFUL OF

Finally, there are three traps to be careful of.

Thinking You're Stuck When You're Not

Sometimes we think we're stuck simply because things are hard. But if you're continuing to make progress and aren't experiencing huge snags, you're not stuck. Rather, you're in a dip.

A dip is a temporary hard slog that you will get through if you keep pushing and don't give up. And pushing through the hard slog is actually the fastest route to the destination. In these cases, you will be especially tempted to bail. Be discerning and able to identify that you're in a legitimate dip and you're not a failure.

Thinking You're Not Stuck When You Are

Some people are stuck and don't know it.

Everything can be going your way, going smoothly, and going quickly. Everything feels and seems wonderful. Yet, as we've seen, you are still headed toward a dead end, a form of getting stuck, if you are leaving God out of the picture.

You are sailing to the wrong destination. This is the worst form of being stuck. That's why this chapter is so essential. We need to keep God central and look to him first at all times.

Stuck Without Knowing It: Depression

Depression takes us beyond the scope of this book, but I need to say something about it because it can be a huge source of getting stuck. It can be especially tough because you may not know that you have it. It doesn't come with the obvious signals that a broken leg or the flu has. Depression can have a devastating effect on your life and productivity without ever announcing itself.

If you are feeling really stuck and have a sense of hopelessness or deep sadness, consider whether there might be something more going on. Depression is treatable. Sometimes getting unstuck can involve the very hard work of counseling and medication. We shouldn't look down on people who have depression, and for some reason depression seems especially common today. For encouragement for those suffering with depression, I would recommend *The Genius of Puritanism*[7] and *Christians Get Depressed Too*.[8]

Now that we know what to do with being unstuck, it's time to start learning *how* to get unstuck.

THE UNSTUCK CLINIC

Core Point

God gets us unstuck so that we can in turn help others get unstuck. Doing so is a manifestation of his grace and unleashes a virtuous spiral of help in the world. And we are to do this without judgment.

Exercise

Who in your life is stuck right now? What can you do to help them get unstuck?

CHAPTER 4

RECOVERING PERSONAL EFFECTIVENESS AS A FORCE FOR GOOD

The need for and the call to personal effectiveness

Be steadfast, immovable, always abounding in the work of the
Lord, knowing that in the Lord your labor is not in vain.
1 CORINTHIANS 15:58

God calls us to always be "abounding in the work of the Lord." As we've seen, that is a type of being unstuck. How are we doing with that? How can we abound in the work of the Lord more fully?

Central to abounding in the work of the Lord is not simply devotional fervency, but also productive skill. Skill in being able to get things done, achieve goals, and make ideas happen. After all, isn't that what Paul is exhorting us to do? He is calling us to accomplish work, and these are the very things that work involves. They are an essential part of work. And note: Paul isn't exhorting us just to try; we are actually to accomplish the work we are called to do. That requires knowing *how* to work, which is the skill of *personal effectiveness*. When used in a God-centered way, it is central to how we get unstuck.

HOW DO WE GET UNSTUCK? PERSONAL EFFECTIVENESS

What is personal effectiveness?

Here's a good summary: personal effectiveness is the skill of leading yourself every day to get the right things done in the right way, for the right reason, and in the shortest possible amount of time. We could say it's knowing how to get things done, make ideas happen, and do great work. It's the skill that goes underneath everything else you do and enables you to do it. It's how you figure out what your mission is, stay on track with your mission, manage your tasks, schedule your activities, keep your stuff organized, and assess problems (such as procrastination and distraction) to find ways around them.

You could call it time management if you want, but it is really about much more than managing your time. Personal effectiveness goes beyond time management. Personal effectiveness includes time management, but the time management has to be based in vision and purpose and principles for our entire lives. In fact, if we conceive of time management apart from the other aspects of personal effectiveness, we will likely end up *mis*managing our time.

We can go further and say that being unstuck is about extraordinary achievement. It is really the science of attaining extraordinary results. It is about excellence, high performance, and flourishing. The greatest writers on effectiveness, from Jim Collins to Stephen Covey, will tell you they are actually writing about unleashing human potential and achieving extraordinary results. This is also one reason why personal effectiveness is central to getting unstuck, for being unstuck is, stated positively, about being personally effective. It is about unleashing extraordinary achievement, excellence, and flourishing.

HOW PERSONAL EFFECTIVENESS SOLVES
THE THREE CAUSES OF BEING STUCK

We saw in chapter 1 that all the ways we get stuck in life and in productivity fall into three categories: we don't know what we want, we don't know how to get there, and obstacles are in the way.

Personal effectiveness has three components, and they actually match up exactly to these three problems.

Personal Leadership

Personal leadership is about developing a vision for your life. It's the ability to know what's most important and to define where you want to go. This addresses the problem of not knowing where you are going—and does it in a God-centered way so that you are really going in the direction God wants you to go.

The way to address the problem of not knowing where you are going is to develop a vision for your life. This involves

- developing your purpose and mission,
- developing your values,
- developing your large life goals, and
- defining your roles.

Personal Management

While personal leadership is about vision, personal management is about discipline. This is essential because vision alone is not enough—you also have to carry it out.

You know *where* you want to go from personal leadership, and personal management is the skills, practices, and focus involved in making that happen. It addresses the problem of knowing where you want to go but not knowing how to get there.

Personal management involves

- determining your intermediate goals,
- choosing the activities to which you will give your time,
- defining and managing your projects,
- determining your next actions,
- managing your schedule, and
- just plain doing the work.

I find it helpful to use the term *time management* here. A lot of people don't seem to like using this term, and I myself try to minimize using it because it seems so mundane: "How can you need to learn more about that?" But it is actually central and not at all redundant—at least not at the pace and with the challenges we have in our day. But if you don't find the term *time management* super helpful, try *maximizing your time* or *getting things done*, or the like.

While time management is central, it is nonetheless only part of the equation. For it doesn't matter how well you are managing your time if you are going in the wrong direction. Hence, time management must always happen in the context of personal leadership.

That's what so many miss. And that's why some people find time management boring—they don't realize it's about executing amazing things, accomplishing dreams. It's the concrete, on-the-ground component of making great things happen.

Overcoming Obstacles

Overcoming obstacles involves strategies for overcoming the challenges to your time management, but it is about more than that. It is about passion and motivation, for passion is a key part of God's power that gets you through the obstacles. It is hard to press through challenges when you are not motivated! On the other hand, being motivated and passionate not only gives you energy to do more than you otherwise could but also yields fresh insight for overcoming future obstacles.

Overcoming obstacles also involves being equipped with the specific tools for addressing problems that get you stuck, such as

- overflowing email,
- distractions and interruptions,
- procrastination, and
- lack of motivation.

Personal effectiveness enables you to get unstuck because it addresses the three chief issues that get you stuck, thereby enabling you to

1. Learn what God wants you to do through the skill of personal leadership
2. Learn how to make those things happen through the skill of personal management
3. Keep going through obstacles

By learning the discipline of personal effectiveness, you will be more able to get unstuck when you need to. You will have the vision to know where you are going, the discipline to know how to get there and do it, and the passion and know-how to overcome the challenges along the way.

Behind Personal Effectiveness: Biblical Truth and Correct Principles

We can consider biblical truth as a component of personal effectiveness, but technically speaking, it is distinct because it goes behind personal effectiveness and enables it.

Personal leadership isn't about just going anywhere we want. It's about going in the *right* direction—and doing it in the right way (in line with God's commands and principles) and for the right reasons (out of love for God and others). The foundations show us the principles and truths of God's Word, which should in turn govern the development of our vision and how we spend our time.

Most time-management approaches focus only on strategies and tactics. They do not seek to ground those strategies and tactics or even vision in the most fundamental and ultimate reality of all: God's truth. But if we are to truly be unstuck, that's what we must do. Therefore, in the chapters that follow, we will start with God's truth.

RELATED DISCIPLINES: The Effectiveness Triad

Personal effectiveness also relates to two other core disciplines for getting things done: management and leadership.

Management

Management is about helping people unleash their potential. It focuses on the individual. It involves planning, staffing, coordinating, and so forth with the aim of speeding up the interaction between a person's talents and the organization's goals.[1] As renowned leadership expert John Kotter has put it, management is about coping with complexity—bringing order to things.[2]

Leadership

Leadership, on the other hand, is about coping with change. It is not about bringing order, but rather about casting a vision that changes things. It is about rallying people to a better future, as business consultant and speaker Marcus Buckingham has said so well.[3]

Note the term *rally*. A leader does not use control or push people but instead rallies people—motivates them to harness their resources to work together willingly and joyfully to bring about an envisioned future. Leadership is above all about tapping people's intrinsic motivation.

Personal Effectiveness

Of course, we cannot lead or manage others unless we can lead and manage ourselves. Likewise, the people we are leading and managing will not be very effective unless they can manage themselves as well. Hence, *personal* effectiveness is foundational.

The disciplines of leadership and management also shed light on another chief aspect of personal effectiveness: distinguishing between the roles of individual contributor, manager, and leader, for each requires different skills and approaches. The right approach to personal effectiveness includes knowing what your chief role is and tailoring your approach accordingly. We will talk about this more throughout the book.

In sum, these are the three skills we need to truly get things done, make ideas happen, and bring vision into reality: leadership, management, and personal effectiveness. We are focusing on the latter because it is foundational and so often overlooked. Christian views of management and leadership can also be built on this foundation.

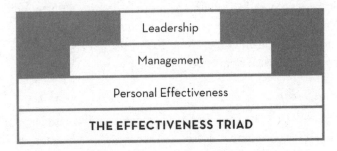

PERSONAL EFFECTIVENESS IN HISTORY

In chapter 4 of *What's Best Next*, I argue that personal effectiveness is biblical. Here I want to make the point that personal effectiveness is something we see throughout Christian history among the most effective Christians.

Consider William Wilberforce, the great evangelical social reformer who brought an end to the slave trade and then slavery in the British Empire. His two great objectives in life were the reformation of morals and the end of the slave trade. That is an example of the focusing power of life goals—an aspect of personal effectiveness.

Or consider Jonathan Edwards, widely regarded as one of the greatest intellectuals America has ever produced and one of the greatest theologians of all time, who created his seventy resolutions at the age of nineteen. These resolutions are an example of a mission statement—an aspect of personal effectiveness.[4]

Or consider John Calvin, the greater Reformer who is also widely regarded as one of the greatest theologians of the Christian church, who utilized feedback analysis in his pastoral ministry. Peter Drucker points out that this is one of the reasons Calvinism had such an impact in his time and after.

Today, consider John Piper, who is very disciplined with his time and for decades devoted every Saturday (and later Friday) to sermon prep and every Tuesday night to writing an article for the church newsletter. These are examples of scheduling and time management—aspects of personal effectiveness. (And the incredible results that added up over the years are visibly evident, as all of these sermons and articles are available on his website in a well-organized, easy-to-access way.[5])

Or consider Bill Hybels, who has spoken often of how he came to discover that he was working at too high a pace and needed more regular rhythms of rest—the productivity practice of renewal. He has recently written an excellent chapter in his book *Simplify* about keeping our schedules God-centered and in balance—an example of time management.[6]

A FORCE FOR GOOD

I've titled this chapter "Recovering Personal Effectiveness *as a Force for Good*." Why?

First, because personal effectiveness is something we do need to recover. The secular area has seen much growth in this discipline over the last few decades. But today's Christians have generally been slow to learn from the secular material and to adapt it and use it. As we've seen, however, Christians throughout history, and some today, have used personal effectiveness. So we need to recover it.

Second, we need to recover personal effectiveness for its true purpose—that is, as a force for good. It is not just about serving ourselves or gaining our own peace of mind, which is where so many secular approaches go. Just as with everything that God gives us in life, we are to ultimately use personal effectiveness to increase our ability to do good for others and serve them. Ironically, it is in this use that we will find the most fulfillment.

And so personal effectiveness is, at root, a tool for advancing God's purposes in the world. We are not to neglect it—it is a gift of God's grace for furthering the common good and advancing the gospel. In our current era of overload and yet extraordinary opportunity, this powerful tool is essential for doing work in a way that is balanced and doesn't get us stuck.

At the root of learning personal effectiveness is grasping the often-mentioned yet much misunderstood concept of *urgency and importance*. So that's next.

THE UNSTUCK CLINIC

Core Point

To abound in the work of the Lord, we need more than devotional fervency. We need the skill of getting things done. This is the discipline of personal effectiveness, and it provides the solution to the three main causes that get us stuck in our productivity.

Exercise

What is your experience with personal effectiveness? Has it been positive or negative? Write down your thoughts.

Further Resources

- David Allen, *Getting Things Done: The Art of Stress-Free Productivity*
- Stephen R. Covey, A. Roger Merrill, and Rebecca R. Merrill, *First Things First*
- Greg McKeown, *Essentialism: The Disciplined Pursuit of Less*

CHAPTER 5

UNDERSTANDING URGENCY AND IMPORTANCE (FOR REAL)

What it really means to act from priorities

What is important is seldom urgent and what is urgent is seldom important.

DWIGHT D. EISENHOWER

We hear certain concepts so often that we think we understand them more than we do. Such is the case with urgency and importance. Very rarely do people actually dive into the actual meaning of this concept to truly understand what it means.

Nevertheless, understanding urgency and importance is the essence of good time management, personal effectiveness, and getting unstuck because this understanding leads to the foundation we need in order to use personal leadership and personal management effectively in our lives.

Understanding urgency and importance will get us to the heart of personal effectiveness, and thus the ability to get unstuck—especially from busyness. Although I didn't have space to address it in *What's Best Next*, it is a crucial concept that underlies everything I wrote there, and which I will now address in detail.

YOU HAVE TO CHOOSE

First we need to recognize that we have to choose what we will do with our time. That is why time management and personal effectiveness are even necessary at all. If there were no limits—if we could do anything and everything we wanted, and even all the things we didn't want to do that we had to do, there would be no need for time management.

But we can't do everything. The root issue is not that we don't have enough time. If you had an extra hour every day—if each day was twenty-five hours long instead of twenty-four—would you feel less stressed and not pulled in as many directions?

I doubt it. A lot of us would waste that extra hour. Others might feel that they need an extra five hours. Some of us would start projects we think would only take an hour but would actually take five, thus leaving us with a desire for a twenty-nine-hour day the next day (that's me).

The fundamental issue, then, is not that we need more time (although I admit that is important and does play a part), but rather how we use our time. And that leads us to the central time-management concept: setting priorities. I came to see this a few years ago in a way I will never forget. I was feeling utterly overwhelmed. I was in the midst of my health problems, and my inbox was backed up by about four weeks (both physical and email). I simply did not have the energy I normally had, and nothing I did was helping. I was expressing this challenge to someone, and they said, "Well, would it help if you set priorities?"

I thought, *Well, I guess there is no other way.* That was very sensible advice from a "nonexpert" in time management—which I had been overlooking.

Since there is not enough time for everything, there is no escaping the need to set priorities. The question is: How are we going to choose?

WHAT IMPORTANCE VS. URGENCY ACTUALLY MEANS

Two factors influence the choices we make about how we spend our time: urgency and importance. Just because something is urgent doesn't mean that it is important. The urgent, in fact, often crowds out the important.

The key to effective time management is to avoid becoming dominated by the urgent. Instead, know what's important *and do that.*

Sounds simple enough. So why aren't we better at it? To answer that question, we need to delve deeper into the meanings and roles of urgency and importance.

Understanding Urgency

Urgent things demand our immediate action. A knock at the door, the buzz of a text message, or the pressure of a deadline are all examples of things that are urgent. All of these things represent urgency.

The central thing about urgency is this: *urgent things press upon us.* That is a key part of what draws us to do them. Because they come with pressure, there is a built-in urge to address and resolve urgent issues.

Or we may be inclined to deal with urgent things quickly because doing so can make us feel affirmed and validated. Many people get their sense of value from urgency because busyness is often seen as a symbol of importance. We think that if we are busy, we must be important, and that feels good.

Understanding Importance

Important things, on the other hand, are in line with our goals, life vision, and correct principles. They make the biggest difference and create a long-term impact.

Unlike urgent things, important things *do not press upon us.* That is a fundamental distinction between urgency and importance. Urgent things press upon us, pressuring us to act. Important things do not press upon us, and thus we easily put them off until later. As Stephen Covey notes, "When urgency is the *dominant factor* in our lives, importance isn't."[1]

And that's the problem. Urgency crowds out importance. The reason you aren't making more progress on what matters most to you is because urgency is crowding it out. You are *letting* urgency crowd it out.

We can see this more fully by taking a look at what is commonly called the four quadrants of time management.

THE FOUR QUADRANTS

	URGENT	NOT URGENT
IMPORTANT	**Quadrant 1** Important and urgent The quadrant of immediate needs and challenges	**Quadrant 2** Important but not urgent The quadrant of impact, growth, and increasing capacity
NOT IMPORTANT	**Quadrant 3** Urgent but not important The quadrant of deception	**Quadrant 4** Not important or urgent The quadrant of waste and deterioration

Quadrant 1: Urgent and Important

The things in quadrant 1 are both urgent and important. That is, they are in sync with your goals, *and* they are pressing upon you. Examples here include such things as a crying baby, a quarterly update to the board on Thursday morning, and your website being down.

Note that this quadrant is not bad in itself. If we ignore it, we will become buried alive—a very real form of being stuck. This is a quadrant where we produce, get things done, manage, and, as Covey words it so well, generally "bring our experience and judgment to bear in responding to many needs and challenges."[2] This quadrant matters.

We don't need to create a false dichotomy between urgency and importance. While it is essential that we recognize the difference, it is indeed possible for something to be both urgent and important. "Urgent" should not be automatically taken to mean "not important" (a mistake that I myself am easily prone to make).

The question is *why* you are in this quadrant. Are you here by choice, or are you here by default? You should be here because you are choosing to be, not because you are simply following the latest and loudest.

Quadrant 2: Important but Not Urgent

Quadrant 2 tells us that not everything that is urgent is important, and not everything that is important is urgent. Examples here are preparation, planning, anticipating problems, personal and organizational development, proactively thinking about how we can help others, and things like these.

When you are in this quadrant, you are doing activities of high impact and, in fact, increasing your capacity to produce. Things like taking time as a team to learn how to collaborate better may not feel like they have an immediate payoff, but over the long term, you will have less frustration, and more ideas from people will be unleashed—and executed better. The payoff in this category is very large but tends to happen over the long-term and is therefore harder to see and easier to forget.

The fascinating thing about this quadrant is that spending more time here will result in having to spend less time in quadrant 1. In other words, investing in quadrant 2 shrinks quadrant 1. So if you want to spend less time rushing around and feel less hurried and pressed and stressed, invest in quadrant 2.

On the other hand, if you ignore this quadrant, quadrant 1 will grow. You will have more stress and risk of burnout. By acting in quadrant 2, you can take care of things before they become urgent. This is key. Things often become "important and urgent" because they weren't taken care of when they were "important and not urgent." Quadrant 2 is really about getting the effects and results of quadrant 1 without the pain and stress that come from the added urgency.

The difficulty of quadrant 2, however, is this: this quadrant does not act upon us. It does not press upon us. Therefore, doing the important but not urgent takes personal leadership and character. *You* have to act. You cannot wait for or rely on others to nudge you. You are responsible.

Quadrant 3: Urgent but Not Important

Quadrant 3 is the "Quadrant of Deception," as Covey calls it. It is the phantom of quadrant 1. We *feel* we are getting important things done, but that is only an illusion because "the noise of urgency creates the illusion of importance."[3]

To be operating in this quadrant is to be hijacked by the priorities of others. The activities here are only important to someone else and do not align with your goals and priorities.

I received a phone call the other day from my health insurance company asking me to call them back to talk about some of the new aspects of their program. That might be important to them, but I didn't want to spend my time on that. I know how to stay healthy, and I don't need to let them add more things to my plate. They even tried to make me feel guilty by saying, "We've tried to call you several times." It doesn't matter. I'm still not calling back.

Microsoft Office emailed me several times and even called me twice wanting to explain how their new Office works. I don't need that, and I don't have time for it.

And one salesperson recently emailed me nine times and called me four times. He tried to use various forms of pressure to get me to set up a meeting with him. Now, it is not Christian to look down on that. He is an important person in the image of God. But it is important to realize, without judging him, that these are slightly shady attempts at pressuring me into giving away time that I don't have when I've already determined I don't need the services they have to offer.

More and more, certain apps are also trying to rope us in through urgency by the way they use notifications to get our attention.

Quadrant 4: Not Urgent and Not Important

Quadrant 4 is the quadrant of waste. The things here don't even have urgency going for them. When we feel deluged by the urgent, we often escape to this category for a sense of relief. Watching too much TV, mindlessly surfing the web and watching YouTube, and things like this are examples of things in this quadrant. The big problem is that these things don't provide the relief they promise. They actually make us feel worse. This is the quadrant of *deterioration*.

The Matrix Was Not Invented by Stephen Covey

Stephen Covey is perhaps best known for popularizing the urgency-importance matrix, but it didn't start with him. In fact, the matrix itself seems to have started with President Dwight Eisenhower, which is why it is sometimes called "The Eisenhower Matrix."

Yet the concepts go back further than that. For example, we even see echoes of them in the writings of the great eighteenth-century pastor and theologian Jonathan Edwards, who wrote in his journal "to allow everything its proportion of thought, *according to its urgency and importance.*"[4]

Edwards is best known for the theological impact he has made on the church as perhaps America's greatest intellectual. What is sometimes overlooked about Edwards—and which could help us quite a bit—is that he was also a master of managing his time.

And here we see that he explicitly sought to make time-management decisions (especially in the case of his studies, which is the context of the quote) on the basis of the two chief factors of urgency and importance.

Elsewhere he writes, "My time is so short, that I have not time to perfect myself in all my studies; wherefore resolved, to omit and put off *all but the most important* and needful studies."[5] Here we see once again that Edwards made his decisions on the basis of importance. This, in great part, is a key reason for his success and influence.

WHY WE OFTEN ACT ON THE BASIS OF URGENCY

If the key to personal effectiveness is to do what is important instead of what is merely urgent, then why don't we do it more? Why aren't we better at it?

There are at least five reasons.

The first reason why we don't always choose important over urgent is that we all too easily fall for the notion that because something is urgent, it must be important as well. Stephen Covey puts this best: "The noise of urgency creates the illusion of importance."[6] In other words, we determine that something is important because of its urgency rather than using more accurate criteria for determining importance. The solution here is to be on guard against this tendency and this illusion, and to know what the criteria are for determining whether something actually is important (see chapter 6).

Second, as I mentioned above, urgent things are often easier and more interesting. If you get a text message while you are working on a difficult PowerPoint presentation for an upcoming meeting, the text probably sparks your curiosity. You want to know who is texting you and what the text says. It makes for an enticing distraction.

Third, as we also saw above, sometimes we fall into the trap of getting our sense of importance from the urgent. We think that if we are busy, we must be important.

Fourth, society reinforces the primacy of the urgent. We often receive pressure from others to act on the basis of urgency. This false notion promotes the idea that "real work" consists of constantly responding to people, answering every email within an hour, and so forth. And we ourselves may use urgency to motivate other people because we don't know a better way. But guilt only works short term.

Fifth, technology—especially smartphones—is reinforcing responding to the urgent. The *choice architecture*, which is the way apps are designed to lead you to act, is all about "trying to tempt us to do things right now," as one person has put it.[7] The app designers don't care about what will affect your long-term productivity. They just want your attention and interaction right now.

And technology enables society to exert pressure all the more, because now if you aren't doing the urgent things, people can text you right away about it, making you feel guilty and behind, and perhaps goading you into action.

Now, remember, urgency does have its place. The issue is *what is your dominant perspective?* When urgency is dominant, then once the urgent things go away, instead of choosing to move back to important but not urgent items, you start to invent more urgent but not important items. You are driven by a quest for what is urgent rather than being driven by a desire to do what is important. You need to be able to say no to the social pressure, and learning the difference between urgency and importance enables you to do that.

THE PROBLEM WITH TRADITIONAL TIME MANAGEMENT

Traditional approaches to time-management rarely solve our time-management problems. They promise that if we can do things faster and more efficiently, if we can get more things done in less time, we will gain a sense of control and relaxed productivity. These approaches are fundamentally inadequate, and now we can see why: traditional time management approaches still rely too heavily on urgency.

Before practices for increasing our efficiency will work, we need an entire shift in perspective so that we are using this greater efficiency for the right things. Being more efficient at shuffling around the urgent will not help. We need to be more efficient at getting the right things done, not just the latest and loudest.

WHAT ACTING FROM PRIORITIES REALLY MEANS

As an example of how traditional time management is stuck in the urgency paradigm, consider something that is often recommended by it and at first looks like it has things right: prioritizing.

We are often exhorted to create a to-do list and then to prioritize that list. Put an *A* next to the top priorities, a *B* next to the medium ones, and a *C* next to the ones you will get to if you can; and then delegate those lowly *D*s and eliminate the poor *E*s.

Isn't this bringing us into the importance paradigm? It may look like it, because you are prioritizing, but it really isn't because all you are doing is prioritizing the urgent. Hence, you still have not necessarily broken free from the urgency paradigm when you are prioritizing your lists. To take the urgent things in front of you and assign priorities to them is still to be stuck in the urgency paradigm.

What you need to do is ask, "What *should be* on my list but isn't?" and "What *is* here but shouldn't be?" And you need to have a mind-set and criteria that enable you to make those decisions on the basis of importance. *That* is what it really means to act from priorities and on the basis of importance.

We can now boil this down: the reason we get stuck in our time management is because we act on the basis of urgency rather than importance. The question now is, how do we know what's important? That's next.

THE UNSTUCK CLINIC

Core Point

Acting from priorities does *not* mean you take what is pressing on you and in front of you on your list and prioritize it. If you do that, you may simply be prioritizing the urgent—and not doing anything important.

Acting on the basis of priorities means, instead, asking, "What is important?" Then you put those things on your list and prioritize those. Doing so requires having criteria for knowing what is important.

Exercise

What is your fundamental way of operating—urgency or importance? Describe a time you acted out of urgency alone. Describe a time you acted on the basis of importance.

Further Resources

- Stephen R. Covey, A. Roger Merrill, and Rebecca R. Merrill, "The Urgency Addiction," in *First Things First*
- Greg McKeown, "Choose: The Invincible Power of Choice" and "Trade-Off: Which Problem Do I Want?" in *Essentialism: The Disciplined Pursuit of Less*

CHAPTER 6

CHARACTER:
The Great Unsticking Force

The way to get unstuck at the deepest and fullest
level comes from changing your paradigm, which
has to do with character more than technique

There is no short-cut. But there is a path.
STEPHEN COVEY[1]

If the key to personal effectiveness and productivity is to act on the basis of importance, how do we know what's important? How do we know what the right priorities are? Is importance something we define, or is it objective?

This question is more sophisticated than we might at first think, for powerful forces are at work driving us toward urgency and *unimportant* things—which, therefore, get us stuck. We need to understand how these forces work if we are going to truly get unstuck.

THE PLACE OF PARADIGMS

A word that some claim has been way overused, but which I would argue has been even more misunderstood, is *paradigm*.

One time-management book gives a short review of Stephen Covey's *First Things First* at the end. Their chief critique is that it uses the word *paradigm* too much!

Paradigm came to be seen as a superficial buzzword by many people in the 1990s—much like *strategy*, *proactive*, and *synergy*. But as I argue in my What's Best Next post "In Defense of Buzzwords... Sort Of,"[2] the problem is not with the words; it's with the way certain people used them. The originators of the terms used them well. They defined what they meant and showed that these are indeed very powerful concepts. That is not something that should be disparaged; rather, it should be commended.

But then what happened, as often happens with powerful concepts, is that people started using them without knowing what they actually meant. Maybe they did this to look smart, or maybe they just weren't good at explaining themselves. Regardless of the reason, these terms then got a reputation of being meaningless buzzwords. Not because the concepts were wrong or bad or cliché, but because the words were being used divorced from their real meanings. And so many people threw the baby out with the bathwater.

These terms need to be recovered, because they embody rich, meaningful, and effective concepts that we all need. *Paradigm* is one such word.

What a Paradigm Is

In brief, a paradigm is the way you see the world. It is your understanding of what really matters, why we are here, and what is going on. The more common term for *paradigm* today is *worldview*.

Your paradigm is the rock-bottom convictions you have. They go to your root. Your paradigm includes more than just your cognitive beliefs about ultimate issues; it also encompasses your desires and loves. That is, your paradigm and worldview are not purely cognitive realities but are also emotional.

Your paradigm is the way you *see* things. It is the glasses through which you view the world and the assumptions you hold. Everything else you do stems from your paradigm. Your paradigm—the way you see the world—is behind not just your actions, but also your attitudes. Covey states this very well: "Our paradigms are the maps of our minds and hearts out of which our attitudes and behaviors and the results in our lives grow. . . . The way we see (our paradigm) leads to what we do (our attitudes and behaviors); and what we do leads to the results we get in our lives."[3]

Christian philosopher Ronald Nash says a worldview is "a conceptual scheme that contains our fundamental beliefs; it is also the means by which we interpret and judge reality." He goes on: "Worldviews function much like eyeglasses. The right eyeglasses can put the world into clearer focus, and the correct worldview can do something similar."[4] Nash summarizes well that there are five clusters of beliefs in any worldview: God, metaphysics, epistemology, ethics, and human nature. Our view of history could be added to this as well.

Metaphysics is our view of ultimate issues. Epistemology is our view of how we know what we know. The ethical component is not just about *what* is right and wrong; it's about *why* those things are right and wrong. Is there an ultimate standard? If so, where does it come from? Or is morality merely subjective? If there is a moral law, how do we know it? And anthropology is our beliefs about human nature.

The most powerful illustration of a paradigm shift I have ever encountered is the story Stephen Covey tells of a time when he was on the subway.[5] A dad and his young kids stepped on, and the kids immediately began misbehaving. They were bothering everyone else on the train, and the dad was doing nothing about it.

Covey and the other passengers started to get irritated. They couldn't believe the father was allowing this to happen. *How insensitive. Does he even care about the other people on the train? Does even care about his kids?*

But then the dad looked up and said something that literally transformed everything: "I'm so sorry about my kids. We just came from the hospital, where their mother just died. I guess they don't know how to respond. And neither do I."

That changed everything. Instead of questioning this father's sensitivity and ability to parent, Covey was immediately flooded with sympathy. Why? *Because his paradigm was changed.*

The story he was telling himself before was that this man was just inconsiderate. After all, that's how things appeared. From that way of seeing things came his irritation—his attitude. But that was the wrong story. When he got a different story—the right story— his attitude immediately changed.

That's the power of paradigms. And that's also the challenge of paradigms: they can be true—they can accurately reflect reality—or they can be false. Our paradigms are not reality itself; they are our *maps* of reality. And any map can be more or less accurate. The wrong maps will lead to wrong attitudes and wrong actions. It is therefore imperative that we get our paradigms right.

Why Addressing Paradigms Is Essential for Creating Change

Since our paradigms are the root of our actions and attitudes, then by definition, in order to change our actions, we can't simply address our actions themselves. We need to change something deeper—the source of our attitudes and actions. We must address and change our paradigm.

As Covey notes, "More essential than working on attitudes and behaviors is examining the paradigms out of which those attitudes and behaviors flow."[6] In other words, if we want to create significant change in the results, we can't just change attitudes and behaviors, methods or techniques; we have to change the basic paradigms out of which they grow. We have to change the way we *see* the world.

Hence, the solution to the gap between what we want to do and actually are doing is not found first in the right methods; for the very problem is embodied in the assumptions behind the methods themselves. The solution is in identifying the assumptions behind the methods and going to the root.

Addressing paradigms is remarkably effective. It is far more powerful than just making tactics and behaviors more efficient, because it goes to the roots. Addressing paradigms is *the key* to increasing your effectiveness in (ironically) the most efficient way. Covey explains this very well:

> How do we become more effective? I have found that if you want to make slow, incremental improvement, change your attitude or behavior. But if you want to improve in major ways—I mean dramatic, revolutionary, transforming ways—if you want to make quantum improvements, either as an individual or as an organization, change your frame of reference.
>
> Change how you see the world, how you think about people, how you view management and leadership. Change your *paradigm*, your scheme for understanding and explaining certain aspects of reality. The great breakthroughs are breaks with old ways of thinking. As the paradigm shifts, it opens up a whole new area of insight, knowledge, and understanding, resulting in a quantum difference in performance.[7]

Covey gives several examples that illustrate this: there was a paradigm shift in medicine when they discovered that infections are caused by bacteria; the Declaration of Independence expresses a paradigm shift from seeing government as an imposing overlord to a government that derives its powers from the consent of the governed; and during the Middle Ages there was a shift away from believing that wealth came from gold to realizing that it came from industry.

In our own lives, most of us have experienced the power of a paradigm change when our role changes. Focusing on our frame of reference is where the true power to change comes from. Covey says, "I submit that if we focus our attention on techniques, on specific practices, on 'to do' lists, on present pressures, we might make some small improvements. But if we want to move ahead in a major way, we need to shift our paradigm and see the situation in a totally new way."[8]

Approaches that ignore paradigms may help somewhat, but they fail to meet the deepest need because they aren't looking at the roots out of which the fruit in our lives is growing. They will not ultimately get us unstuck.

When we try to change the behavior or the method without changing the paradigm, the paradigm eventually overpowers the change. That's why so many attempts to "install" things, like the "management flavor of the month," in organizations are unsuccessful. For humans, change can't be installed; it has to be grown. Change then emerges organically out of the paradigms.

This is part of the reason some terms like *paradigm* and *empowerment* got a bad reputation and were slotted as mere buzzwords. Companies started trying to implement them not by going to the root, but superficially. They were looking for quick fixes, and the result was that they completely misused the concepts. The irony here is that these efforts were therefore doubly unproductive. By seeking to change merely through tactics rather than by addressing the roots of behavior, not only was the change undone, but there was a backlash causing even more harm.

Being unstuck is about fundamental change, not just short-term or superficial change. Fundamental change comes from addressing the issues of what you believe and what you love; that is, worldview—the roots out of which the fruit of our lives grows.

How Discipleship Happens

Understanding the place of paradigms also helps us understand how Christian growth and sanctification happen. Many have been pointing out more fully recently that Christianity is not about behavior modification. What do they mean by that?

First, they mean that Christianity is not just about our behavior at all. It is ultimately about a relationship with Christ. You can have "great" behavior, but you are missing everything if you do not know Christ and have fellowship with him (John 17:3; Phil. 3:7–11).

Second, they mean that Christianity is not about just external change, or changing from the outside in, but rather is about changing from the inside out. That is, it is about heart change. True and lasting change happens from the heart (Matt. 15:10–20; Rom. 12:1–2). And understanding paradigms helps us see more clearly how that happens. Change in our actions happens as change in our character happens, and change in our character happens as our paradigm changes—as our way of viewing and feeling changes.

Eric Gieger sums up the inside-out nature of discipleship well in *Transformational Discipleship*:

> Discipleship is transformation, not information overload or behavioral modification. When transformation occurs, there is an increasing hunger for more knowledge of Jesus and His Word, but the primary focus of acquiring knowledge must be the ongoing renewal of the heart. When transformation occurs, behavior will follow. But the focus must be the heart, or the behavior is self-manipulated and short-lived as opposed to flowing from the transformation offered by Christ.[9]

So transformed affections and beliefs lead to transformed people. How are affections changed? They are changed from an experience of God's grace in regeneration, and ongoing beholding the greatness of Christ: "And we all, with unveiled face, beholding the glory of the Lord, are being transformed into the same image from one degree of glory to another. For this comes from the Lord who is the Spirit" (2 Cor. 3:18).[10]

Time Management Must Address Worldview

And so, when it comes to our time management and the way we lead our lives, we need to address our worldview—our paradigms. What paradigm is governing the way you view your time management?

The urgency addiction we saw earlier is an example of a paradigm. Either urgency or importance is going to be your chief paradigm for how you make decisions.

HOW CHARACTER ENABLES YOU
TO MAKE GOOD DECISIONS

How do you know what is important? Importance is something even deeper than your own goals. Important things are things that align with correct principles and God's truth.

And that takes us to the heart of why character is essential to productivity, for principles bring us into the realm of character. There are two sources for knowing correct principles. First, the Scriptures: "Blessed are those whose way is blameless, who walk in the law of the LORD!" (Ps. 119:1). And second, we have the capacity to discern correct principles through our *conscience*, which is directly informed by our understanding of the Scriptures. We have an inner compass that enables us to detect what right principles are.

The way to put first things first is to *build this inner compass*—that is, our *character*—so that we are able to discern what right principles are and desire to follow them. Character enables us to see and understand correct principles so that we can base our lives and decisions on them. That is why character is central to true productivity.

We then can articulate our mission and values *flowing from those correct principles,* and our personal vision can become an accurate way of identifying what is important. *This* is at the heart of time management and why productivity is rooted first in character, not techniques, for it is character that enables us to discern what is important and *use the techniques well.*

CHANGE MUST BE GROWN, NOT INSTALLED

We can see from these things that we must understand that *change is grown, not installed.* It is grown because, as we saw above, there is something behind our attitudes and behaviors. True change focuses there rather than trying to rigidly install or force change from pure acts of will. This gives you power to actually make the change.

And since worldviews and mind-sets do not change overnight, change cannot just be dropped down from the sky. It is a process.

Thus, mistakes that come about as you do your best and stretch yourself but fail must be forgiven. For if change happens through a process, that process will include trial and error, and thus we must allow for mistakes. Change takes time, which means that efficiency must take a backseat to effectiveness. An efficiency mind-set will kill the crop. And it will kill the goose that lays the golden eggs, trying to get them all at once.

Many change efforts in organizations and among individuals fail because of efficiency mind-sets. We see efforts to "install" change (a hallmark of the personality ethic) in the business world when, as Covey summarizes it so well, executives seek to "buy" a new culture of improved productivity with morale boosters, smiling training, and external interventions, all the while ignoring the low-trust climate produced by such manipulations, as they are when divorced from character. When that doesn't work, they look for the next personality technique, not realizing (or refusing to admit) that it's the fundamental paradigm that's wrong. Such techniques are based on the willpower fallacy we saw in chapter 3.

Our attempts to install change rather than grow it is a huge reason we get stuck. If we want to change, we can't focus on immediate attitudes and behaviors. We have to focus on what is driving those things. We need to think like farmers, not factory foremen.

To get unstuck, we have to go after real fixes, not quick fixes. Real fixes address the roots and so are long-term and take more time at the start but less time down the road. They deal with character. Quick fixes address the symptoms and not the roots in an attempt to save time. They are quicker at the start, but they don't really address the problem, so it comes back—thus taking much more time down the road.

With these things understood, we now have the equipment we need to identify what "important" means so that we can truly make our decisions on the basis of importance.

THE ESSENCE OF CHARACTER IS HUMILITY

What is the heart of character? Humility. Humility is the "operating principle," and it has two components. First, humility means seeing yourself as nothing in comparison to God. John the Baptist said that he was not even worthy to untie Jesus's shoes (Luke 3:16). Paul said, "Neither he who plants nor he who waters is anything, but only God who gives the growth" (1 Cor. 3:7). And God said, "This is the one to whom I will look: he who is humble and contrite in spirit and trembles at my word" (Isa. 66:2).

The second component of humility is seeing others as more important than yourself. "In humility count others more significant than yourselves" (Phil. 2:3). In doing so, you will seek the good of others over your own good, as Paul then goes on to say: "Let each of you look not only to his own interests, but also to the interests of others." He bases this instruction in the gospel, saying, "Have this mind among yourselves, which is yours *in Christ Jesus*, who, though he was in the form of God, did not count equality with God a thing to be grasped" (Phil. 2:4–6, emphasis added).

And so humility seeks the good of others. John Dickson expresses this in the best way I've ever seen: Humility means that you *hold your power for the good of others*.[11] With humility, you begin to see everything you have as a stewardship to be used for God's purposes, not your own, and you seek to benefit and serve others with everything you have just as Christ does (Phil. 2:5–11; 2 Cor. 8:9–15). If you have influence, you use it first to advance others, not yourself. If you have authority, you use it to protect and serve, not make yourself feel important.

Thus the operating principle for our productivity is humility. And with that humility comes love. Love is humble, and humility includes love.

THE POWER OF HUMILITY IS FAITH

What is the power to have humility? Faith that God is working for you. Being centered on God takes faith and is the same as living by faith.

We see this relationship between faith and humility in Habakkuk 2:4: "Behold, his soul is *puffed up*; it is not upright within him, but the righteous shall live *by his faith*" (emphasis added). This is what Paul quotes in Romans when he argues that justification is by faith alone (Rom. 1:16–17).

In Scripture, there is a relationship between humility and faith. Since humility is about holding your power for the good of others, there is a relationship between humility and love. This truth, interestingly, sheds light on why justification is by faith alone—"so that no one may boast" (Eph. 2:9; see also Rom. 3:27–28). Paul is saying here that justification is by faith so that people may be humble. Or, to put it another way, that everyone may love.

So once again we see, as discussed in *What's Best Next*, that justification by faith apart from works is the root of love—that is, character—and thus truly effective living.

THE UNSTUCK CLINIC

Core Point

Getting unstuck is about fundamental change, not surface-level change. Fundamental change is the only change that truly lasts. To change fundamentally we have to change from the inside out, not outside in. This comes from addressing our paradigms—the way we see the world.

Exercise

Think of a time you were driven by urgency. Write it down and describe it. Then, think of a time you acted on the basis of importance. How did things go? What made it possible for you to do that?

Further Resources

- Michael Austin and Douglas Geivett, *Being Good: Christian Virtues for Everyday Life*
- Stephen Covey, "Inside Out," in *The 7 Habits of Highly Effective People*
- John Dickson, *Humilitas: A Lost Key to Life, Love, and Leadership*
- Andrew David Naselli and J. D. Crowley, *Conscience: What It Is, How to Train It, and Loving Those Who Differ*
- Matt Perman, "The Best Message on Humility I Have Ever Heard," What's Best Next, www.whatsbestnext.com/2011/08/the-best-message-on-humility-i-have-ever-heard/.
- John Piper, *Future Grace: The Purifying Power of the Promises of God*
- Francis Schaeffer, "The Lord's Work in the Lord's Way," in *No Little People*.

PART 2

PERSONAL LEADERSHIP

The Compass

Getting your life unstuck

Where there is no vision, the people perish.
PROVERBS 29:18 KJV

With the foundations in place, we are now ready for the second phase of getting unstuck: personal leadership. This is our compass—the way we know the right direction to head.

We have heard a lot about leadership in terms of leading other people. Hundreds of books are published on the topic every year, which I think is a good thing. (When people say, "There is already so much on this subject; why do we need more?" I want to reply, "Start reading the books, and you'll see that there's always more to learn.")

But not as much has been written about *leading ourselves*. For many this may even be a new concept. We can see why there is a need for leadership when it comes to accomplishing things with others, but why do we need to lead ourselves? What does that even mean?

THE DIFFERENCE BETWEEN LEADERSHIP AND MANAGEMENT

We can see the need for personal leadership (as well as what it means) when we see how leadership differs from management. Most of us tend to conflate the two concepts, resulting in a bit of confusion.

Management is a relatively familiar concept. It is about creating order and keeping things in that order. The stoplight at the intersection is a good example of management. It keeps traffic in order; it keeps people from running into each other. Or consider the discipline of time management. When you stay on task with your day, you are managing your time well.

Management is so essential to getting unstuck that we'll be talking about personal management in part 3 of this book. But what about when you need to *change* things? How do you do that? Management simply will not work, because change by definition involves some things being *out of order*—at least for a time. And so you need a fundamentally different skill to create change.

Beyond that, what about purpose? Even when we are bringing things into order and keeping them in order, we need to know the purpose of that order—the direction in which to point it.

And where do you get motivation? To go back to the traffic light example, what the traffic light cannot do is motivate people. It doesn't get them going. It helps keep them organized once they are moving, but it doesn't get them out in the street in the first place.

All of these things—change, purpose, and motivation—are the domain of *leadership*. They are what leadership does. Leadership is like gas in your car. It provides the fuel for action, which takes the form of passion and motivation. And it provides direction so that you know where to go and aren't just wandering aimlessly.

WHY PERSONAL LEADERSHIP MATTERS SO MUCH

In *What's Best Next*, I went into detail on the distinction between effectiveness (doing the right things) and efficiency (doing things quickly). That is an echo of the distinction between leadership and management. Leadership corresponds to effectiveness; management corresponds to efficiency.

Thus personal leadership is essential because it brings us into the realm of effectiveness. Personal management is not enough for the same reason that efficiency is not enough—doing things faster and more "in control" will not suffice if you are going the wrong direction.

Personal leadership is also essential because, like public leadership, it is the tool for making change.[1] In this case, the change is in ourselves. When you want to change things about yourself or your life, personal leadership is the tool. Leadership sets the direction for change and motivates you through it, while personal management is about implementing and executing the change.

One other reason worth noting why personal leadership matters so much is this: it is the necessary foundation for public leadership. We have to get this order right, and many leadership problems in society arise from getting it wrong. Stephen Covey says it best: "Private victory precedes public victory."[2] Personal leadership—being able to lead yourself with genuine integrity—is the private victory. We cannot lead others truly unless we can first lead ourselves authentically. Personal leadership comes before interpersonal and public leadership.

THE KEY TO GETTING UNSTUCK

How does using personal leadership to get ourselves unstuck fall short? Soon after I finished seminary and was working in my first full-time ministry position, I got a Franklin Planner and tried to develop my mission statement. But it was not as helpful as I thought it would be.

Only later did having a mission statement truly become helpful, when I understood more about what *God's vision* for us is as revealed in the Scriptures. Often we try to identify our mission mostly from reflection. That has its place. But the real power of vision comes when we understand more fully what God has revealed in the Scriptures about his purposes, values, and strategy. When these truths settle deep in your thinking, developing your personal vision begins to flow.

Moreover, I didn't understand why vision is so important and impactful. When I came to understand that, along with God's vision for our lives, vision started to come to life for me. We'll focus here on why vision is so powerful. For without grasping that, we will not know how to make effective use of it.

THE PROCESS OF PERSONAL LEADERSHIP FOR GETTING UNSTUCK

So that you can see the big picture before we get into the details, this is the process for personal leadership that we will look at in part 2:

- **Vision:** Understand the power of vision.[3]
- **Strategy:** Be missional and understand how your faith and work relate.
- **Mind-set:** See yourself as a professional.
- **Preparation:** Get the knowledge you need.

CHAPTER 7

UNDERSTAND THE POWER OF VISION

Why vision is the most powerful force for getting unstuck and why we need to make greater use of it if we are truly going to move toward God's purposes and do so together

The toil of a fool wearies him, for he does not know the way to the city.

ECCLESIASTES 10:15

Six years into his thirty-three-year ministry at Bethlehem Baptist Church, John Piper wrote in his journal on November 6, 1986:

The church is looking for a vision for the future—and I do not have it. The one vision that the staff zeroed in on during our retreat Monday and Tuesday of this week (namely, building a sanctuary) is so unattractive to me today that I do not see how I could provide the leadership and inspiration for it.

Does this mean that my time at Bethlehem is over? Does it mean that there is a radical alternative unforeseen? Does it mean that I am simply in the pits today and unable to feel the beauty and power and joy and fruitfulness of an expanded facility and ministry?

O Lord, have mercy on me. I am so discouraged. I am so blank. I feel like there are opponents on every hand, even

when I know that most of my people are for me. I am so blind
to the future of the church. . . . I must preach on Sunday, and
I can scarcely lift my head.[1]

John Piper, one of the most effective preachers in the history of
the modern church, was stuck.

STUCK FROM LACK OF VISION

Why was Piper stuck? Because of issues surrounding *vision*—one
of the most difficult yet important areas of leadership and personal
effectiveness.

Does Piper's experience mean that the entire enterprise of discovering a vision for a church (or your life) is misguided? Does it mean
that trying to develop a vision leads only to discouragement because it
is so hard to do? And is the concept of vision even necessary anyway?

Developing a vision is incredibly difficult, and it is made more
difficult by the ambiguity of terms surrounding the concept of
vision and the general lack of clarity most of us have about its meaning. Later in the book we will see how to overcome that fuzziness—
for it is possible.

More important right now, though, is the second issue: Is having a vision even necessary? And, for Christians, is it biblical?

We might think that John Piper wouldn't endorse the need for
vision, for he has been known to be skeptical of some concepts that
may seem to come from the business world. Maybe concepts like
"vision" are just tools of the business world and not relevant to the
church and individuals?

But notice that Piper did not go that direction. He did not
even hint at that direction. His issue was entirely one of uncertainty
about what the vision should be—not about whether there should
be a vision.

In fact, the primary reason that Piper was discouraged here
was precisely because he did not have a vision for the church. And,

beyond that, others in the church had tentatively arrived at a vision that he did not find inspiring or meaningful. Lack of a shared vision, which Piper was confident to be *God's* vision for the church, was the cause of Piper's great discouragement.

And so we see, from the negative side, the great importance of vision. Piper was stuck and discouraged because vision was lacking. He was so stuck and discouraged, in fact, that he almost quit—for that's what he titles the article where he recounts this journal entry.

Nevertheless, he did not quit. He went on to preach at Bethlehem for twenty-seven more years. More than that, Bethlehem went on to become one of the most well-known and influential churches in the nation. Piper's ministry touched a generation of millennials with a passion for God and a passion for missions[2] and expanded to reach millions online every month.

How did Piper get unstuck? How did God unleash such blessing through his ministry—and so consistently, year after year, so that today, even after retiring from his role at Bethlehem, he is writing and teaching more than ever before and his ministry continues to expand online?

Many components worked together to get Piper and his church unstuck. Perseverance was one of them. I am certainly not implying that Piper or the church was at fault or somehow flawed for not having clear vision at that time. We all go through a lack of clarity at times, and we need to know how to persevere even when our vision is not clear. We are not to let ourselves or our organizations languish without vision. That's not what Piper or his church did. The key component (after prayer) to how they got unstuck was that they persevered in developing a shared vision—and succeeded.

UNSTUCK THROUGH A COMPELLING SHARED VISION

Over a period of time, Piper and the other leaders developed a renewed vision for the church that gave the clarity, inspiration, and conviction they needed. When they received clarity on their mission, values, and ministry philosophy, they articulated these things in writing and wove them into the fabric of the church. Over the years, Piper has become one of the most effective vision casters in the entire North American church. Vision is central to his ministry and effectiveness, and vision can be central to your life, work, and ministry effectiveness as well.

In fact, developing a clear vision is essential to getting unstuck, staying unstuck, and being the people God has called us to be. It is not simply something nice to do or a good idea to try out "if we have time or are that sort of person." I will argue in this chapter that it is our *responsibility* to have a vision for our lives.

THE POWER OF VISION

There are two groups of people when it comes to the importance of vision. Some—and, in my experience, very few—don't think it matters much. The second group, on the other hand, are convinced of its importance and want to get on with the act of creating it.

If most people are in the second group, why spend any time at all on why vision matters? The reason is that you can't unlock the power of vision in your life unless you first understand why vision is so powerful and so vital. You must first understand why developing vision is not just a good thing to do but is your *responsibility*. When you grasp this concept, you gain a deeper commitment to living by your vision and a greater ability to live it out.

Perhaps the biggest truth about why vision matters is this: vision is essential for unlocking your full potential and achieving great things. It is, in fact, the most powerful tool for doing so. To understand this, we will look at examples of the power of vision in individuals, in times of suffering, and in teams. Then we will look at a few reasons why it is so powerful.

Vision and True Greatness

Don't be thrown off by the phrase "achieving *great* things" here. You might think, *I don't want to make a lot of money, I'm not looking to build a large organization, and I'm not trying to be famous.* That's just fine, because that is not what I mean by "great."

As we saw in part 1, those things, while not bad in themselves, are aspects of secondary greatness. They are aspects of outward success and not essential to having a meaningful life. What really matters is primary greatness—goodness of character and making an impact to extend this goodness in the lives of those you encounter.

Vision is essential for true greatness, properly understood, because vision is the definition of what true greatness is. What Jim Collins has said about companies and greatness is also true of individuals: "Vision isn't necessary to make money; you can certainly create a profitable business without it. There are plenty of people who have made a lot of money, yet had no compelling vision. But if you want to do *more* than just make a lot of money—if you want to build an enduring, great company—then you need a vision."[3]

Collins's point for organizations also holds true for individuals: if you want to do more than simply make money in your life or be well liked; if you want to live a life that makes the kind of difference God wants you to make; then you need to have a vision. It is ironic that if you simply want to do what our culture often defines as success—namely, make money—vision is not necessary, but if you want to do something more than that, it is essential.

Vision not only leads to the right kind of accomplishment in life; it also tends to lead to *high* accomplishment. By this I don't mean that the endeavors in your life have to be vast. If that's not your vision, then that's probably not going to be a good way to go. What I do mean is that clear vision leads to performing at your potential, which is indeed a good thing and something you are designed to do.

In fact, vision has been shown to be incredibly powerful in

every aspect of life. Experience backs this fact, and it has been veri-
fied by studies. Consider the following.

The Power of Vision in Individuals

Peter Senge, author of *The Fifth Discipline,* notes that "people
with a high level of personal mastery share several basic characteristics. They have a special sense of purpose that lies behind their
visions and goals. For such a person, a vision is a calling rather than
simply a good idea."[4]

Likewise, Stephen Covey notes, "One of my favorite essays is
'The Common Denominator of Success,' written by E. M. Gray.
He spent his life searching for the one denominator that all
successful people share. He found it wasn't hard work, good luck, or
astute human relations, though those were all important. The one
factor that seemed to transcend all the rest [was] . . . putting first
things first."[5]

Putting first things first requires a vision. As Covey notes,
"Discipline derives from *disciple*—disciple to a philosophy, disciple
to a set of principles, disciple to a set of values, disciple to an
overriding purpose, to a superordinate goal or a person who rep-
resents that goal."[6] In other words, you cannot put first things first
unless you know what "first things" are. And it's your vision that
defines them.

The Power of Vision in Suffering

Perhaps the greatest illustration of the power of vision in individuals' lives is that of Viktor Frankl, the Austrian psychologist who
survived the Nazi death camps of World War II. During his time in
the concentration camps, he was sustained by his vision of reunit-
ing with his wife and lecturing after the war on the psychological
lessons learned from the concentration camps. He also observed
how others endured, intrigued by the question of why anyone at
all survived when most did not. Stephen Covey summarizes his
findings very well:

[Frankl] looked at several factors—health, vitality, family structure, intelligence, survival skills. Finally, he concluded that none of these factors was primarily responsible. The single most significant factor, he realized, was a sense of future vision—the impelling conviction of those who were to survive that they had a mission to perform, some important work left to do.

Survivors of POW camps in Vietnam and elsewhere have reported similar experiences: a compelling, future-oriented vision is the primary force that kept many of them alive.[7]

Frankl summarized his experiences—and his approach to psychology that resulted from it—in his classic book *Man's Search for Meaning*. In the foreword to the 1992 edition, Harold Kushner writes, "[Frankl] describes poignantly those prisoners who gave up on life, who had lost all hope for a future and were inevitably the first to die. They died less from lack of food or medicine than from lack of hope, lack of something to live for."[8]

He then summarizes Frankl's central conclusion from his observations and research, and it is about the centrality of vision: "Life is not primarily a quest for pleasure, as Freud believed, or a quest for power, as Alfred Adler taught, but a quest for meaning. The greatest task for any person is to find meaning in his or her life."[9] Vision answers that quest for meaning.

Frankl's example and that of other prisoner of war survivors shows that vision is so powerful that it motivates and sustains even through the greatest suffering. Research reveals that part of the reason vision sustains is that it provides an internal locus of control that cannot be swept away by external hardships. Mihaly Csikszentmihalyi writes in his classic book *Flow* that research into the writings of survivors of extreme conditions, such as Viktor Frankl and Bruno Bettelheim, has led some to the conclusion that the most important trait of survivors is a "nonself-conscious individualism," or a strongly directed purpose that is not self-seeking. People who have that quality are bent on doing their best in all circumstances, yet they are not concerned primarily with advancing their own interests. Because they are intrinsically motivated in their actions, they are not easily disturbed by external threats. With enough psychic energy free to observe and analyze their surroundings objectively, they have a better chance of discovering in them new opportunities for action. If we were to consider one trait a key element of the autotelic personality, this might be it.[10]

In other words, vision is an affirmation of the one thing that no circumstances or concentration camp torturer can ever take away: a person's ability to *choose* how to respond to a situation. Then, in addition to that, while preserving an internal locus of control and freedom, it also provides external focus, which is essential to not having too tight of a grip.

If you do not have an external focus, that is, if you are narcissistic, you become isolated within yourself. Certainly the vision of some people is themselves. But that is not the type of vision I am affirming here. The kind of vision God advocates for us is by definition outward focused and others oriented, and so inclines you to center your attention on good things beyond yourself.

The Power of Vision in Teams

Teams with a vision also perform better. Abraham Maslow is well known as one of the most significant psychologists of the last century. His research into high-performing teams found that the most striking characteristic of these teams was shared vision and purpose.[11]

In his excellent book *Start with Why*, Simon Sinek shows that vision is why the Wright brothers succeeding in being the first to build an airplane that could fly. It is a very interesting story, for there was another person who set out to build an airplane at the same time, and he was much better funded.

His name was Samuel Pierpont Langley, and he was seemingly "armed with every ingredient for success."[12] Langley was a professor at Harvard and senior officer at the Smithsonian. He was given a grant of $50,000 from the War Department (which is many million in today's dollars) and assembled a team of some of the best talent of the day. Further, the press followed his every move as the nation closely followed his story.

He had all the ingredients that conventional wisdom would say bring success. But Langley was not the first to pilot an airplane and, in fact, gave up his aim to do it altogether when the Wright brothers beat him to it.

The Wright brothers did not have the equipping and support that Langley had. Quite the contrary. There were no government grants for their endeavor or other forms of external funding; they funded it out of their own earnings from their bicycle shop. No one on their team was regarded as being among the great minds of the day; in fact, no one on their team even had a college education.

Yet it was the less-equipped, less-noticed Wright brothers who were the first to take flight in human history—not the better-funded, more prominent Samuel Pierpont Langley. Why? Sinek tells the story in his book, but here is his conclusion:

> It wasn't luck. Both the Wright brothers and Langley were highly motivated. Both had a strong work ethic. Both had keen scientific minds. They were pursuing exactly the same goal, but only the Wright brothers were able to inspire those around them and truly lead their team to develop a technology that would change the world. Only the Wright brothers started with Why.[13]

In other words, the Wright brothers succeeded because they had vision. In Sinek's words, they "started with Why." Some might say, "Langley had a vision also—to be the first to pilot an airplane." But such a view misunderstands the concept of vision. As we will see, vision is not just about the "what." It is even more about the "why." In other words, "why" is an essential component of vision, and Langley overlooked it.

Sinek himself experienced the power of vision in his own life. He was at a point in his life when he was making a good living, working with great clients, and doing his work well. He writes that "by all superficial measurements, I should have been happy." But he wasn't. He wasn't fulfilled by his work, and he said, "I found myself in a very dark place."

That's when Sinek discovered the power of vision, or what in his book he calls "starting with WHY." He writes, "The discovery of WHY completely changed my view of the world and discovering my own WHY restored my passion to a degree multiple times greater than at any other time in my life."[14]

Vision Is Recognized across Disciplines, Including Psychology

Finally, I find it significant that the central role of vision in living a meaningful life is formally acknowledged and accepted in philosophy and modern psychology. In other words, there is multidisciplinary recognition of the power of vision—not just from self-development, but also from the studies of suffering, business, philosophy, and psychology.

In noting the place of vision in psychology, Mihaly Csikszentmihalyi first notes its place in philosophy: "Philosophers like Heidegger, Sartre, and Merleau-Ponty have recognized this task of modern man by calling it the *project*, which is their term for the goal-directed actions that provide shape and meaning to an individual's life." Then he makes the connection to his field, psychology: "Psychologists have used terms like *propriate strivings* or *life themes*. In each case, these concepts identify a set of goals linked to an ultimate goal that gives significance to whatever a person does."[15]

In his own research, Csikszentmihalyi notes that "people who find their lives meaningful usually have a goal that is challenging enough to take up all their energies, a goal that can give significance to their lives. We may refer to this process as achieving *purpose*."[16] Having a central goal is important, he argues, for achieving unity and harmony of consciousness. He points out that "as long as enjoyment follows piecemeal from activities not linked to one another in a meaningful way, one is still vulnerable to the vagaries of chaos."[17] But "if a person sets out to achieve a difficult enough goal, from which all other goals logically follow, and if he or she invests all energy in developing skills to reach that goal, then actions and feelings will be in harmony, and the separate parts of life will fit together—and each activity will 'make sense' in the present, as well as in view of the past and of the future. In such a way, it is possible to give meaning to one's entire life."[18]

And, once again, lest we think having a guiding goal is simply a luxury for some, Csikszentmihalyi points out that having such a goal has always been recognized by society as part of being a mature adult. He notes, "Someone who knows his desires and works with purpose to achieve them is a person whose feelings, thoughts, and actions are congruent with one another, and is therefore a person who has achieved inner harmony. In the 1960s this process was called 'getting your head together,' but in practically every other historical period a similar concept has been used to describe this necessary step toward living a good life."[19]

Developing an overall vision for your life, then, is simply part of being an adult. Perhaps the failure of so many to deeply think through their vision these days is a reflection of the wider societal trend toward perpetual adolescence. That is an impoverished existence. Csikszentmihalyi then notes the personal benefit of having a clear vision: "Inner congruence ultimately leads to that inner strength and serenity we admire in people who seem to have come to terms with themselves."[20]

WHY VISION IS SO POWERFUL

Vision enables us to operate from the importance paradigm rather than the urgency paradigm in three ways. First, in part 1 we argued that crucial to getting unstuck and being truly productive is to shift from the urgency paradigm to the importance paradigm. But how do you make this shift? How do you know what's important? You need to have criteria. Your vision is that criteria. It is your picture and definition of what is truly important and where you are going, and therefore it is essential to operating from the importance paradigm.

In other words, we saw that productivity is not just organizing and executing around priorities; it is organizing and executing around *the right* priorities. That is personal effectiveness in a nutshell. Your vision is what enables you to clearly determine what the right priorities are. It gives you concrete criteria for knowing what is important, and thus moment-by-moment importance-based direction.

As Covey notes, "[Vision] empowers us to put first things first, compasses ahead of clocks, people ahead of schedules and things. Creating and integrating an empowering personal mission statement is one of the most important Quadrant II investments we can make."[21]

Second, vision also gets us beyond reactive living. Without vision, it is all too easy to live reactively instead of proactively. We let crises, firefighting, and unconsidered opportunities guide and direct us rather than maintaining a deliberate approach to life.

Related to this, Andy Stanley notes how vision provides the power of focus: "A clear vision has the power to bring what's most important to the surface of your schedule and lifestyle. A clear vision makes it easy to weed out of your life those things that stand in the way of achieving what matters most. Vision empowers you to move purposefully in a predetermined direction. Once you have clarified your vision, or visions, many decisions are already made. Without vision, good things will hinder you from achieving the best things."[22]

Third, vision enables us to get beyond the control perspective to the release perspective. As we saw, we often think that the way to get things done and to change is to impose a tight regimen on ourselves. But that's the control perspective, which is based on extrinsic motivation and therefore lacks the power to truly motivate us. Covey writes that vision enables intrinsic motivation and thus the release perspective that pulls us toward our goals rather than pushes us:

> Without the passion of vision, "discipline" is regimentation and restraint—control yourself, grit your teeth, white-knuckle your way through life. The basic paradigm is that without some form of tight control, we'll mess up. We don't have trust in ourselves that, left to our own internal motivation, we would moment by moment make effective choices.
>
> But the passion of vision releases the power that connects "discipline" with its root word, "disciple." We become followers of our own internal imperatives, voluntarily subordinating the less important to that deep burning "yes!" Instead of "control," we're focused on "release."
>
> The key to motivation is motive. It's the *why*. It's the deeper "yes!" burning inside that makes it easier to say no to the less important.[23]

Vision gets us into the release perspective because it draws us rather than pushes us. It draws us because it captures our imagination and taps into higher purpose, which gives it the potential to engage our hearts. As Andy Stanley writes, "Once our hearts have felt the energy that comes with a well-cast vision, we gain a sense of destiny." Hence, "vision serves as intrinsic motivation." We move in the direction of the vision because we want to, not because we are told to. "Instead of pushing and cajoling us into action, a vision draws and even enchants us."[24]

Vision Is the Fundamental Driver of Human Action

"Vision," according to Stephen Covey, "is the fundamental force that drives everything else in our lives."[25] Elsewhere he echoes this: "More than any other factor, vision affects the choices we make and the way we spend our time."[26]

Essential to the motivating force of vision is that it needs to be outward focused, on contribution and others rather than on yourself. Daniel Pink notes from his research on purpose that "the most deeply motivated people—not to mention those who are most productive and satisfied—hitch their desires to a cause larger than themselves."[27] People with a sense of vision are more enthusiastic and fulfilled. They are more energetic, courageous, and persevering. Andy Stanley notes that "vision-driven people are motivated people. Find me a man or woman who lacks motivation and I'll show you someone with little or no vision."[28]

Vision Evokes Emotion

One of the reasons vision ignites passion is that it evokes emotion. Because it paints a picture of the future, it taps into the imagination and emotional side of human nature. Andy Stanley notes, "A clear, focused vision actually allows us to experience ahead of time the emotions associated with our anticipated future." Hence, "the clearer the vision, the stronger the emotion." Emotions, in turn, "reinforce our commitment to the vision."[29]

Because of the motivation and clarity vision gives, it enables you to overcome many obstacles—including internal ones. Vision gives you the passion that enables you to "transcend fear, doubt, discouragement, and many other things that keep us from accomplishment and contribution."[30] Senge also points out the place of vision in creating courage: "Shared visions compel courage so naturally that people don't even realize the extent of their courage. Courage is simply doing whatever is needed in pursuit of the vision"—despite the obstacles and fear.[31]

Vision Provides Fulfillment

Vision not only provides motivation; it also provides meaning and fulfillment. We saw this in Dan Pink's quote above, as well as in Csikszentmihalyi's observation that "people who find their lives meaningful usually have a goal that is challenging enough to take up all their energies, a goal that can give significance to their lives." Andy Stanley captures this idea well: "A vision gives you a reason to get up in the morning. If you don't show up, something important won't be accomplished. Suddenly, you matter."[32]

As a result, a good vision that syncs with people's own values "forms the basis of extraordinary human effort."[33] Jim Collins summarizes this, capturing perhaps the most fundamental reason vision is so powerful:

> Human beings respond to values, ideals, dreams, and exhilarating challenges. It's our nature. We will go to phenomenal lengths in an effort to live up to the ideals of our organization, peer group, or society if we share those ideals and consider them worthy. Managers who build their organizations based on a set of worthy values, sound beliefs, and a compelling mission are laying the groundwork for extraordinary human effort.
>
> Most people want to do more than bring home a paycheck. They want work they can believe in and that has meaning. This may not be true of all people, but it's certainly true of the people most likely to be solid contributors to a great company. Tap into the basic human desire for meaningful work and the traditional management problem of "how to motivate employees" largely evaporates. People will be self-motivated when doing work they believe in.[34]

One of the key reasons vision motivates is because it often encapsulates high ideals and convictions. Another reason it is so motivating is because it provides direction, which is the next point.

Vision Gives Direction

Vision is how you know where you are going! Thus, vision provides a context to your decision making and an overall direction to your life. Speaking about companies (but the same concepts transfer to our personal lives), Collins rightly says:

> *The importance of [vision] cannot be overemphasized.* A shared vision is like having a compass and distant destination in the mountains. If you give a group of people a compass and destination point and then turn them loose in the mountains to reach that destination, they will probably figure out a way to get there.
>
> They may encounter obstacles, detours, bad turns, and side canyons along the way. However, with the general directions of the compass, a clear end-goal, and the belief that they are working towards a worthy destination, they will probably reach the target.[35]

God Is a God of Vision

The need for a vision for our lives is rooted in the nature of God, for God is a God of vision. He is always casting pictures of the future—of where we are headed and are to be headed. And he is a God who calls and sends—which is a type of vision.

GOD CASTS VISION

We see God casting vision everywhere, and vision is especially concentrated in the Prophets. The book of Isaiah is full of pictures of the future and high ideals that God puts before us. The Minor Prophets, such as Haggai, Nahum, and Micah, are filled with pictures of where God is taking his people. And in the New Testament we see Jesus giving a vision to the apostles, to Paul, and to the entire church.

GOD SENDS

God is also a sending God. Sending has to do with purpose, and therefore vision. God sent Joseph into Egypt to deliver his people from famine (Gen. 45:5; 50:20; Ps. 105:17–19); he sent Moses to deliver Israel from Egypt (Acts 7:32–34); he sent Isaiah (Isa. 6:8), Jeremiah (Jer. 1:5–9), and the prophets (Jer. 7:25–28); he sent Jesus (Gal. 4:4); he sent Paul on his mission to the Gentiles (Acts 26:16–18); he sent the disciples (Matt. 28:18–20; John 20:21); and he sends all of us (John 17:18). God is a sending God, and that means he is a God of mission and vision.

SUMMARIZING HOW VISION HELPS YOU GET UNSTUCK

Now we can see that you simply can't get unstuck if you can't create vision. Developing a vision for your life is fundamental in helping you get unstuck, for it provides four things:

1. **Direction.** A vision defines where you want to go, and if you have no destination, then you are by definition stuck.
2. **Power.** A vision provides the power to get to your destination because it generates passion, motivation, and commitment. Motivation is the power you need to get going and keep going. So direction and power are both necessary— direction without motivation might make the destination clear, but it won't get you going down the path. Likewise, sometimes you just need more power to get out of the mud.
3. **Focus.** Having a vision helps you stay focused, avoiding detours to nowhere because you can see more clearly what truly needs to be done and what doesn't. A vision gives you a mental model of how you expect things to proceed, and as Charles Duhigg writes in *Smarter Faster Better,* when you have such a mental model then "when distractions inevitably arise, it's easier to decide, in the moment, whether they deserve [your] focus or can be ignored."[36]
4. **Unity.** A vision enables you to work together with others, because shared vision unifies action.

And further, vision provides all of these things from the fundamental level. That is, refining your vision *is* fundamental change because vision goes to the roots rather than simply being superficial, surface-level behavior modification. Vision goes to the roots of our actions by getting to our core beliefs and affections, and so changes us from the bottom up. And so it gets us unstuck at the fundamental, and therefore truly lasting, level.

Going into detail on *how* to create your vision is beyond the scope of this book. However, I have listed some resources that are helpful for this in "The Unstuck Clinic" below.

THE UNSTUCK CLINIC

Core Point

Vision is essential to providing the motivation and direction to get unstuck. It ignites passion, connects to purpose and meaning, creates motivation, gives direction so that the energy of motivation goes to the right place, and enables you to prioritize and cut things out along the way so that you avoid detours to nowhere.

Exercise

Reflect on a time in your life when you've experienced the power of vision.

What is your vision for your life? Jot down a few initial ideas in preparation for the next chapter.

Further Resources

- Jim Collins and William Lazier, "Vision," in *Beyond Entrepreneurship: Turning Your Business into an Enduring Great Company*

- J. I. Packer, *A Quest for Godliness: The Puritan Vision of the Christian Life*
- John Piper and Justin Taylor, *A God-Entranced Vision of All Things: Living the Vision of Jonathan Edwards*
- Andy Stanley, *Visioneering: Your Guide for Discovering and Maintaining Personal Vision*

RELATED IN *WHAT'S BEST NEXT*

- Chapter 11, "What's Your Mission? How Not to Waste Your Life"
- Chapter 12, "Finding Your Life Calling"

CHAPTER 8

BE MISSIONAL

Understand How Your Faith and Work Relate

From having a mission to being missional:
how Christianity and culture relate,
and the central role of our work

*Skeptics need more than an argument in order to believe;
they need to observe intelligent, admirable fellow human
beings and see that a big part of what makes them this way is
their faith.*

TIM KELLER[1]

As Christians, we have an extraordinary mission. It is motivating, all-encompassing, and meaningful. It is to participate with God in his work to renew all things, working as agents of his love in all areas of life.

Yet we are stuck in our mission in many ways because we have not fully understood how our faith is to relate to the culture. Central to getting unstuck here is getting clearer on that. That is, we need a *strategy*. That strategy is being missional.

Much has been written on this topic, but let me summarize a few core points to help us get unstuck and then point to some resources (such as Tim Keller's excellent book *Center Church: Doing Balanced, Gospel-Centered Ministry in Your City*).

SHOULD WE SEEK TO CHANGE THE WORLD?

First, we need to ask: Should we seek to change the world at all?

Being productive as a Christian is ultimately about doing good for others, and we should seek to do good for others and society in the greatest possible sense—changing the structures of society so that it is organized in a way that supports the doing of good and advancement of God's purposes more naturally and fully instead of opposing his purposes.

The extent to which we can transform culture in this strong sense is debatable. But we can all agree that we are called to transform the culture at the very least in the sense of making a positive difference. Through our *collective* efforts, we want to see a difference made for the good of others on a large scale in society. That is "culture change." Whether we can do that to a high degree or just a *better degree* than we are doing now can be debated; the issue is simply that we do need to work together to improve our society.

WHY WE NEED TO BE MISSIONAL

To change the world, we need a strategy that is appropriate, good, and in line with our values as Christians. Being *missional* is that strategy, and it is vital for two reasons.

First, it is how we impact and renew the culture. By doing our work in a gospel-centered way, we create culture and impact culture in a way that benefits others and thus brings renewal.

Second, being missional is crucial for people to come to faith. Years ago, attending church was commonplace, and we could assume that most people were hearing the gospel message. Now that is not the case, and we need to make greater efforts to go to the people, which is at the heart of being missional. And we need to do it through our ordinary vocations and in a way that winsomely and accurately reflects God's character.

Keller puts it well: "Skeptics need more than an argument in order to believe; they need to observe intelligent, admirable fellow human beings and see that a big part of what makes them this way is their faith."[2]

WHAT DOES IT MEAN TO BE MISSIONAL?

Now, what does it mean to be missional? For our call is not only to be evangelistic but missional as well.

Outwardly Focused

To be missional means being the kind of outwardly focused Christian that is necessary now that our society has become post-Christian.[3] It means going *into the culture* to reach people, not making ourselves distinct through Christian trinkets and tactless presentations of the gospel but through love serving others. We are to be a contrast to mainstream society, but in the right way. We are to be a counterculture for the common good, always looking for opportunities to tactfully and appropriately bring up the gospel.

Contextualizing

Being missional includes being intentional about reaching the culture. That is, you study the culture to identify how to serve it best and how to *communicate* best, much like an overseas missionary would do in a new mission field. You adapt to the culture in all ways that Scripture allows, while remaining fully faithful to the unchanging truth of God's Word. You *contextualize* the gospel through word and deed so that it can be best understood by the culture without *compromising* the gospel. This is exactly what Paul did:

> For though I am free from all, I have made myself a servant to all, that I might win more of them. To the Jews I became

as a Jew, in order to win Jews. To those under the law I became as one under the law (though not being myself under the law) that I might win those under the law. To those outside the law I became as one outside the law (not being outside the law of God but under the law of Christ) that I might win those outside the law. To the weak I became weak, that I might win the weak. I have become all things to all people, that by all means I might save some. I do it all for the sake of the gospel, that I may share with them in its blessings. (1 Cor. 9:19–23)

Holistic

Being missional is a comprehensive approach to life. We do everything we do as a conscious participation with God to fulfill his purposes in the world, as Christopher Wright says in *The Mission of God's People.*[4] As we saw earlier, this can lead to the temptation to think that only evangelism matters. But since God is renewing all of creation and making new heavens and a new earth, a holistic doctrine of work is key to being missional. Thus, being missional means thinking deeply about how to use our work and vocation to advance the common good. So we have to know better how to be public about our faith—in tactful, winsome ways that are not high pressure or off-putting.

You Don't *Have to Work in a Church*

Being missional means that you don't have to be a professional church worker to fully follow Christ. You certainly can do that. But you can follow Christ fully in any job or life circumstance, because work matters in itself *and* is a platform for advancing the gospel when done in love and with appropriate attention to evangelistic opportunities.[5]

Everything we do—secular work *as well as* church work—thus becomes infused with a special dynamism and significance—which is, in fact, the doctrine of vocation!

WORKING ACCORDING TO CHRISTIAN VALUES IS KEY FOR CHANGING THE WORLD

Our work is central to changing the world and renewing the culture. This is something the church lost over the last one hundred years but is regaining. Hugh Whelchel writes, "The most overlooked reason for the failure of the church to influence the culture is the loss of the biblical doctrine of work."[6] Our professional callings are inextricably linked with our impact on the culture, for they are the chief way we interact with the culture and create culture.

But it's not just any kind of work that changes the world. It is *gospel-centered work* that changes the world. Going even beyond excellence, gospel-centered work is done as worship to God and out of love for others. It is done with a generosity of spirit that truly puts others first by our thinking hard about how to serve their needs and then doing that—rather than cutting corners. So living according to Christian values such as love and generosity *in the workplace* is central to gospel advancement and changing the world.[7]

HOW DOES OUR WORK CHANGE THE WORLD?

Our work changes the world in at least two ways. First, it is through our work that we change the structures of society, and it is by changing the structures of society that we change the world (as James Davison Hunter argues in *To Change the World*).[8]

Simply doing your work accomplishes this change. And managers and leaders who have the authority to set policy can make change to a very influential degree. They can influence the structures of their company and organization in people-centered ways. This doesn't mean imposing Christianity, but rather designing policies around the value of people—which business research is now showing many organizations have overlooked, but which actually leads to the greatest effectiveness.[9] Simon Sinek, for example, writes,

Studies show that over 80 percent of Americans do not have their dream job. If more knew how to build organizations that inspire, we could live in a world in which that statistic was the reverse—a world in which over 80 percent of people loved their jobs. People who love going to work are more productive and more creative. They go home happier and have happier families. They treat their colleagues and clients and customers better. Inspired employees make for stronger companies and stronger economies.[10]

So if you have a place in shaping the policies of your organization, make them reflect generosity and the value of people. Turn your organization into one that does not hinder people from doing their best work and fully advancing the mission, but fully enables them to do it. Part of being missional is *building organizations* where people flourish.[11]

Second, our work changes the world because through our work we are able to join with networks of leaders from all over, which is central to how culture actually changes. James Davison Hunter makes this argument in *To Change the World*. He also points out that the reason why Christians are not having an impact on the culture that is proportional to their numbers is because we are mostly absent from the centers of power where culture is forged. He writes,

> Cultures are shaped when networks of leaders, representing the different social institutions of a culture, work together towards a common goal. Again and again we see that the impetus, energy and direction for changing the world were found where cultural, economic and often political resources overlapped; where networks of elites, who generated these various resources, came together in common purpose.

And so why aren't Christians influencing culture more? Hunter continues,

Because they have been absent from the areas in which the greatest influence in the culture is exerted. The cultural producing institutions of historical Christianity are largely marginalized in the economy of culture formation in North America. Its cultural capital is greatest where leverage in the larger culture is weakest.[12]

We can be more present in those areas if we reembrace the biblical doctrine of work. It isn't chiefly evangelism, or politics, or social reform movements that change the world, but people working in their vocations. Thus we need to be in the centers of cultural production, the cities.

And so, as Tim Keller and James Hunter write, "Christians cannot simply rest satisfied with individual conversions or separated enclaves when they discern the central plot-line of the Bible."[13] Since the whole world broke, and God is renewing the whole world, we do have a role to play in transforming culture. "God's purpose is not only saved individuals, but also a new world based on justice, peace, and love, rather than power, strife, and selfishness." And our work—done according to real Christian values in a gospel-centered way—is part of how that happens.

Our work is part of "God's ongoing work to bring everything to a higher state of goodness," says T. M. Moore. And so, "God intends your work to contribute to the restoration of the creation, and the people in it, to raising life on this blue planet to higher states of beauty, goodness, and truth, reflecting the glory of God in our midst. We will only fully appreciate the value and potential of our work when we see it in that light."[14]

The bottom line is that we must recognize the broad concept of our mission as Christians not only to do evangelism but also to serve the common good and create culture. Ironically, this broader concept of our mission actually serves the cause of evangelism better. John Stott sums it up best:

If we accept this broader concept of mission as Christian service in the world comprising both evangelism and social action—a concept which is laid upon us by the model of our savior's mission in the world—then Christians could under God make a far greater impact on society, an impact commensurate with our numerical strength and with the radical demands of the commission of Christ.[15]

THE UNSTUCK CLINIC

Core Point

We are called to impact the culture as Christians. If we are to do so, we must learn to be missional—how to understand and relate tactfully with the culture without compromising the gospel.

Exercise

In what ways does your work influence culture?

Does the way you interact with coworkers create a good reflection of the gospel?

What character traits of Christ can you reflect more fully in your work and community?

Further Resources

- Tim Keller, *Center Church: Doing Balanced, Gospel-Centered Ministry in Your City*
- Tim Keller, "A New Kind of Urban Christian" in *Christianity Today*, http://www.christianitytoday.com/ct/2006/may/1.36.html.
- Gabe Lyons, "Influencing Culture," *Made to Flourish*, February 23, 2010, www.madetoflourish.org/resources/influencing-culture/.

CHAPTER 9

SEE YOURSELF AS A PROFESSIONAL (... SORT OF)

Gaining the skill to keep getting consistent
great results, over and over—with an
ethic of generosity and service

---

*Being a professional is doing the things you love to do, on the days
you don't feel like doing them.*
JULIUS ERVING

Getting unstuck is not just about *getting* unstuck. It's about *staying* unstuck as well. You consistently have to get things done, done well, and with continual improvement. That's what it means to be a professional. And being a professional is essential to being unstuck.

WHAT BEING A PROFESSIONAL MEANS

Consider things you do for fun or as a hobby. You do those things when you feel like it. If you don't feel like going boating, for example, you aren't going to do it.

With your work, it has to be different. Certainly, you should enjoy your work. But you can't just do your work when you feel like it. You have to do it even when you don't feel like it—and still perform well.

That's what it means to be a professional: you show up every day and deliver regardless of how you feel. As Steven Pressfield has put it so well: "A professional is someone who can keep working at a high level of effort and ethics, no matter what is going on—for good or ill—around him or inside him."[1] As a professional, you show up every day. You play hurt.

More than this, you don't just do your work even when you don't feel like it; you consistently deliver results. You can be relied on to deliver consistent, excellent results. Delivering that great project is an awesome thing. But to truly be unstuck means that you are able to keep doing that over and over again.

It's the difference between a musician who is a one-hit wonder and one who has an established, successful career. Your goal is not to do one great project and then fizzle out. Your goal is to deliver consistent results over time again and again. Being a professional is about creating a career out of your ability. You produce a shelf of books with your name on them or a portfolio of awesome website designs or great code or consistent revenue growth in your organization.

Such consistency seems like it should be easy. If you can do something once, you can do it again—right? I thought it would be easy, but for some reason (to be discussed shortly), it's often not.

WHAT FIGHTS AGAINST YOUR PROFESSIONALISM?

Being a professional can be hard for three main reasons.

Lack of Preparation

One reason that being a professional is hard is that we just don't have the skills. Sometimes we have the desire to do something and maybe a bit of natural ability, but when we step out and try to do it, we realize it takes much more skill beyond our natural ability.

For example, one of the very first speaking engagements I had (in college) went great. It was a huge hit. I spoke on the historical evidence for the resurrection of Christ, and my message got through to the audience. The organizer loved it so much she invited me to speak at her camp that summer.

When I was getting ready for the message at the camp a few months later, I thought to myself, *Well, I can't say the same things I did in the previous message; I'd better find something new.* Now, this was a classic mistake. For although I had an entirely different audience, I felt I had to say something very different. But, of course, the different things I had to say meant leaving out the points I had made in the previous message that had made the big impact. The message did not go well.

What was my lack of skill here? Not necessarily in delivery, nor even in the understanding of the subject. Part of it was my lack of preparation for that message (I didn't spend a lot of time preparing—I thought I could wing it).

My lack of skill stemmed primarily from a deeper lack of preparation—not understanding the *skill of speaking* itself. I made a tactical mistake of thinking I had to say something new and different every time I spoke, not realizing that this new audience would benefit if I said the same thing as before. Further, I should have realized that a lot of times people want to hear the same thing. You don't go to a concert and expect your favorite artist to avoid playing your favorite song.

We will talk about preparation in chapter 10.

No Guiding Theme

You will notice that most of the best authors or recording artists have a certain theme that centers their work. With John Piper, it's Christian hedonism and the glory of God. With John Maxwell, it's leadership. With Bill Hybels, it's winsomely pointing unbelievers to Christ. With Tim Keller, it's gospel-centeredness. These men say new things, but things coming from the same center.

Rather than making things overly simple, this strategy actually creates a depth that leads people to keep wanting to hear more. Because the central theme makes sense of things, what speakers say becomes more helpful, and the listeners know what to expect.

Resistance

Resistance is the third and strongest thing that can make professionalism hard. Steven Pressfield focuses on resistance in his work on being a professional in *The War of Art*. He defines it as "that self-created and self-perpetuated, invisible, impersonal, indefatigable force whose sole aim is to prevent us from doing our work, from becoming our best selves, and from rising to the next level of competence, integrity, and generosity."[2]

Resistance rears its head every time you want to do something important. It takes the form of writer's block, procrastination, diversion from your task, or inability to execute. It doesn't come from laziness or bad intentions. That's why it's so tricky—and powerful. Pressfield argues that it ultimately comes from fear. It is almost part of ourselves, working against us, perhaps out of fear of success—because success brings change.

It's hard to know exactly what causes resistance. Is it really fear of success? I don't know for sure. What I do know is that everyone who seeks to create encounters it in one way or another.

HOW DO YOU DEVELOP THE CAPACITY TO CONSISTENTLY PRODUCE?

How do you fight resistance? For a full treatment, I recommend Pressfield's classic *The War of Art*. I love that title—he captures right away that doing great work is a battle.

While there is much we can do, here is a simple process that Pressfield suggests, which I think is perhaps the most effective and promising approach.

He recommends this:

- Stage one: being able to work for a single hour
- Stage two: being able to do it again
- Stage three: being able to finish

You just repeat these steps over and over again, forcing yourself if necessary. Yes, use tactics and strategies, including the ones I recommend throughout this book! But success all comes down to these three steps.

THE BAD SENSE OF PROFESSIONAL

Now, some who see the title of this chapter might take pause. Being a professional, of course, is generally considered a good thing. But authors like John Piper have shown that it can also be a bad thing—especially in ministry. In fact, he wrote an entire book on pastoral ministry called *Brothers, We Are Not Professionals*.

Is what I'm saying contrary to Piper's message? Would what I'm saying here kill the ministry if pastors took it seriously?

What we need to see is that there are two senses of the word *professional*—a good sense and a bad sense. The good sense is what we've just seen: you show up every day and you deliver regardless of how you feel.

Piper would certainly agree with that definition of professional. He embodies it almost more than anyone else! He delivers, day after day, what he is called to do. For thirty-three years he preached every weekend; now he is teaching on desiringGod.org through Bible study labs, articles, and messages. He consistently delivers excellent content. What Piper is critiquing is the bad sense of the term *professional*. This is the "professionalism" that is associated with a detachment, an inauthenticity, and a lack of interaction, conversation, and real community. These things characterize persons who don't get emotionally involved in their work because they are "professionals" and their work is just "about business." They omit emotions and true caring from their work. They are like the HR consultant I once worked with who never smiled because he wanted to be "professional" and keep the right power distance.

That is not what I mean by being a professional! Further, the best business thinkers today also reject being a "professional" in this sense. People like Seth Godin and Tim Sanders argue that being emotionally engaged and caring about our work and the people we do the work for is at the heart of doing great work and the driver of true excellence. Even more, it's what people want from us. They don't want emotional detachment. That fails to treat ourselves, and others, as fully human. It's a segmented, truncated view of humanity.

In *A Sense of Mission*, Andrew Campbell and Laura Nash well summarize the common view of detached professionalism, pointing out that some question the benefit of creating passionate employees and managers. They write, "It can be argued that business needs calm, rational, clearheaded managers who can be dispassionate and caring about their companies. Managers who fall in love with their business are dangerous. Moreover, in larger organizations these passionate managers can create divisiveness and cultural conflict that hinder smooth operating."[3]

But their research disproves this view. In contrast to this common approach, they point out the many deficiencies of this type of detached professionalism: "In this book we are going to argue that the opposite is true. Most organizations, we believe, have become depersonalized to the point where energy levels are low, cynicism is high, and work fails to fulfill or excite. Our observation is that committed employees perform many times more efficiently than apathetic ones do, and this is even more true for teams."[4]

As many leadership thinkers have noted, an energized team doesn't just perform a little bit better, but exponentially better—ten or even fifty times better. And recent research is showing even more the importance of *emotional* intelligence and *social* intelligence in the workplace, not just hard skills.[5]

And so I would argue that "professionalism" in this sense—the sense that Piper is talking about and critiquing—is not only killing the ministry; it is killing the business world.

Rejecting this detached type of "professionalism" gets us unstuck from wrong ways of thinking about work and helps us see that being human in our work is not a drawback but an asset. We are to be our whole selves everywhere. The best workers, if you think of it, are actually the most human. Tim Sanders lays out the business case for this argument in his classic book *Love Is the Killer App*. He describes "love as the point of differentiation in business."[6]

The old, bad form of professionalism even taught a rigid distinction between personal and professional lives. "Don't develop friends on the job; if you need friends join a bowling club," it counseled. But we spend more time working than doing anything else. How miserable it would be not to see work as an arena where we can develop friendships! In fact, some of the best friendships can be built in the workplace because you have a common cause. And as much research has shown, friendships in the workplace actually increase performance.[7]

THE ETHIC OF A TRUE PROFESSIONAL

We are seeing something here that helps us round out our definition of *professional*. A professional is not only someone who delivers great results over and over again; a professional is also someone *who has a certain ethic*, and this ethic includes emotional intelligence. Being a professional means working with consistency *and* having a certain ethic—an ethic of emotional involvement and generosity, and being *human* in your work.

Here are five components that are part of a professional ethic in the fullest sense.

Passion

Passion is the element of emotional involvement in your work. You *care* about your work and the people you are doing it for. Your work becomes, as Seth Godin puts it, "emotional labor."

John Piper summarizes this concept well in his interview "Ten Principles for Personal Productivity":

Kill half-heartedness. Do what you do with all your heart. Be done with half-heartedness. Oh, so many people limp through life doing what they do with a half heart, with half of their energy. If it is worth doing, it is worth doing with your whole soul. Ecclesiastes 9:10 says, "Whatever your hand finds to do, do it with your might." Jonathan Edwards's resolution probably had more impact on me in the last 30 years than anything else he said—in his resolutions, at least—when he said, "Resolved, to live with all my might, while I do live" (resolution #6). Those words took hold of me a long time ago. I thought: Oh, yes Lord.[8]

Some people downplay the importance of enjoying our work, but it matters! It can't be the only consideration, but it is an important one. I have heard it over and over again from effective people that one of their keys to success is enjoying their work, because without that they wouldn't have the fuel to persist. The value of enjoying our work is also backed by research, from the Gallup organization's research on strengths[9] to Jerry Porras and his coauthors' research for the book *Success Built to Last* on what leads to holistic success. They have an entire chapter on why it's dangerous not to love your work. This is not a pie-in-the-sky notion but a necessity for effectiveness. You will do better work when you enjoy it *most of the time*.

Joyfully Doing Hard Things

Many hard tasks are motivating and enjoyable, and even the ones that aren't enjoyable have a place. To say we should enjoy our work does not mean that the *only* things we do in our work will be things we enjoy. We are more effective, Marcus Buckingham points out, when we are in our strengths (doing things that energize us and at which we excel) *most of the time* during our day.[10] But of course there will be times we are not, and that's okay and even essential. The key is to keep tasks in balance. Piper captures this well: "Joyfully embrace hard tasks. Be willing to do many things in life cheerfully that at first you don't want to do. They don't come naturally to you. There is no worthwhile role in life that does not require you to do things you don't at first feel like doing or that only let you do what comes naturally. So be cheerful in doing the parts of your life that you do not at first prefer to do."[11]

Remarkability

The era of average stuff is over. Being remarkable means providing goods and services that stand out—that are *worth remarking on, that get people excited. Being remarkable* is good for business too because it gets people talking, which is the most effective form of marketing and is free.

A lot of times when people think of Christian work, they think only of ethics. Rock-solid ethics are of course central, and a part of most professional codes as well. They should never be compromised. But ethics are not the sum of what God requires. He calls us to go beyond moral work to *righteous* work—work that inspires and delights like his work does. More than functional, it is beautiful, and people connect emotionally with it.

Christian work requires passion and a sense of beauty and love, for ethics alone can be selfish and even used to the detriment of others—such as when people mindlessly enforce rules that actually harm people rather than thinking things through and finding a better way. I have seen people who are ethical in their work but don't lift a finger to help others. Such behavior is not generous and not the full ethic God requires.

Why is the flourishing of the righteous a cause for rejoicing (Prov. 11:10)? It's not just because they are ethical; it's because they are *good*. They don't just avoid breaking certain codes (as important as that is); they bring their humanity to work and do things that truly benefit and delight people.

Recognizing the Centrality of Good Design

Essential to being remarkable is recognizing the centrality of good design. Good design is not just product packaging, but everything the customer experiences from start to finish. It means the promotion is beautiful, the product or service is beautiful, and the way of acquiring it is beautiful. And design extends even beyond products and services to *systems*. The systems, policies, and principles of an organization are to be beautiful and to embody good design as well.

Good design is fundamental because God created us as whole people, as emotional as well as functional. Good design connects especially with the emotional side of people and creates an emotional connection with the brand. Hence, it is a component of effectiveness as well as the right thing to do. And "executing good design is everybody's job, not just the designer's."[12]

Generosity

Generosity is the new model of working. Generous people are uplifting and encouraging to others. They are also always sharing— with coworkers and with their customers. With their coworkers they share their knowledge, network, and compassion, seeking to help others succeed just as much as they are seeking to succeed themselves.

And with customers, they avoid having an adversarial mind-set, or even a merely transactional one, and seek not just to earn revenue from them but to truly serve them and build them up. This involves putting the needs of customers ahead of their own. So often when there is a conflict between the desires of corporate leadership and the needs of the customer, the company wins. This is one reason some websites are hard to use. Making a website more user friendly takes a bit more time and requires seeing from the customer's viewpoint. Therefore many organizations take shortcuts. But a generous ethic says, "The purpose of a business is to serve the customer, so I am willing to make things harder for myself in order to make things easier for my customers. I will take the extra time to make this website [or other product] easier to use so that my customers can have a more pleasant experience."

This principle of generosity applies even in sports. Football coach Bill Belichick points out that in sports, generosity is what makes great players great: "I think great players help other players play better, and I think that's what makes them great players. . . . There are a lot of players that go out there and play very well, and they add a lot to your team. There are certain players that help their teammates play better. Those guys are special, because it's not just what they do—it's the uplifting of the players around them."[13]

Generosity is not just good for others; it is also good for you. People want to do business with those who are generous. As many have pointed out, generosity creates a powerful personal brand. Keith Ferrazzi says it well: "Remember, it's easier to get ahead in the world when those below you are happy to help you get ahead, rather than hoping for your downfall."[14]

In sum, "loving your neighbor as yourself" is the way to success in work.

INSTITUTING PRO-PEOPLE POLICIES

Finally, it's not just people and employees and managers who should be generous and human. Companies should be too! This means instituting pro-people policies. It means having *human* systems rather than bureaucratic systems—systems that encourage doing good rather than creating red tape.

For example, some churches require that homeless people asking for assistance fill out forms. Why? To ensure that the person has a real need and that the church is stewarding their resources well. But what does that say about the homeless person's need? That it can wait. But this is not like waiting in line for a new iPhone. Homeless people have essential needs. Nevertheless, they are made to wait while the forms are processed.

If we go to the Apple Store to buy an iPhone, except in an extreme circumstance, it's going to be there because they care about selling it to us. And a phone is just a convenience. Why, then, are we

okay with making the homeless wait until the benevolence commit-
tee can meet? What if Apple sold iPhones that way? We'd say they
are not customer oriented. So is the church people oriented when
they make the homeless wait for help?

Sometimes policies that seem reasonable because they appear to
steward the resources of the organization well do so at the expense
of compassion and genuine humanity. This is just one example, and
perhaps an extreme one at that. The point is that organizations
need to think about the impact their policies will have on employees and others, and seek to make it a beneficial impact that will
encourage and uplift and motivate, not just make sure it meets the
organization's own needs. And, interestingly, often that which best
serves the employees and customers also benefits the organization
most. Thinking win-win, rather than win-"I don't care" or win-lose,
is usually an advantage to both parties.

THE UNSTUCK CLINIC

Core Point

Reject professionalism in the bad sense of detachment
and distance; embrace it in the good sense of doing great
work even when you don't feel like it, bringing an ethic of
generosity and humanity to your work.

Exercise

Have you ever experienced resistance? How have you
dealt with it? What has worked—and what hasn't? Write
your thoughts down.

Further Resources

- Adam Grant, *Give and Take: Why Helping Others Drives Our Success*

- Steven Pressfield, *The War of Art: Break through the Blocks and Win Your Inner Creative Battles*
- Tim Sanders, "Exercise Your Gratitude Muscle," in *Today We Are Rich: Harnessing the Power of Total Confidence*
- Emma Seppälä, "Understand the Kindness Edge: Why Compassion Serves You Better Than Self-Interest," in *The Happiness Track: How to Apply the Science of Happiness to Accelerate Your Success*
- Dallas Willard and Gary Black, "Professionals," in *The Divine Conspiracy Continued: Fulfilling God's Kingdom on Earth*

CHAPTER 10

PREPARATION

Get the Knowledge You Need

Why preparation is so essential and new evidence from neuroscience on why it works

---

Desire without knowledge is not good, and whoever makes haste with his feet misses his way.

PROVERBS 19:2

I've seen a lot of bloggers say things like "You already know all that you need to know—you just have to get going." Is that true?

Their point is that we should not get caught up in trying to be perfectly prepared and in making everything perfect—and that is good. But we are taking that too far if we assume that we always already know what we need to know, for sometimes we don't. And if we don't take the time to prepare and get the knowledge we need, we will not succeed. In fact, even if we know how to manage our time well, we will still not be effective unless we also know how to do the content skills of our work well.

This is the other side of the coin. I have emphasized how content skills are not by themselves enough, since you also have to have the underlying skill of personal effectiveness to enable you to use those content skills well. It is also the case, however, that without the content skills, your time management is not going to be effective either.

And so we must prepare and get the knowledge we need. This is especially true today since the economy keeps demanding new skills of us. We need to be able to learn new skills and prepare quickly so that we aren't spending all our time preparing. I experienced this when I first started writing books. I knew how to manage my time and had written hundreds of articles and blog posts. Writing came quickly to me. But when I sat down to write my first book, I got stuck. The words would not come.

What was the problem? Writing books, it turned out, was very different from writing articles. A book is not just a long article; it is something entirely different. I did not yet have the skill of writing books, as opposed to articles and blog posts, mastered. Thus my time-management skills were not of much help to me.

Sometimes I would spend the large chunks of time I had blocked off just staring at the screen, trying to figure out what to say! Other times I would take the advice to "just write anything" and end up writing so much that it was almost too much to manage. And, unfortunately, most of the chapters I wrote following that advice were not needed in the final book. As I began to grow in my skill of writing books, I started to be able to do it faster and more efficiently. It took time, but it did start to come.

Developing the skill to do the tasks of your work is an essential, yet often overlooked, key to getting unstuck. Part of getting unstuck, in other words, is *developing the capacity to achieve*.

WHY DID RUDY GIULIANI LEAD
SO WELL AFTER SEPTEMBER 11?

The most effective leaders have discovered the crucial role preparation plays in getting unstuck.

Rudy Giuliani, one of the most effective mayors of New York City in recent decades, who brought crime levels down and is admired for his leadership after 9/11, writes in his book *Leadership*: "Preparation . . . [is] the single most important key to success, no matter what the field."[1] He continues: "Leaders may possess brilliance, extraordinary vision, fate, even luck. Those help; but no one, no matter how gifted, can perform without careful preparation, thoughtful experiment, and determined follow-through."[2]

Giuliani speaks of the crucial role preparation played in enabling him to lead effectively after September 11. He had actually been working on his book on leadership in the months preceding 9/11, so all of the leadership lessons he needed were fresh in his mind. He writes, "By September 11, I had been working on the book for months. It had become almost a seminar for me, a self-imposed program on how to run an organization. It was as if God had provided an opportunity to design a course in leadership just when I needed it most. By the time of the horrible events of September 11, because of all that I'd been working on, the elements were fresh in my mind, which gave me confidence." Then he adds, "Every single principle that follows [in the book] was summoned within hours of the attack on the World Trade Center."[3]

Preparation is what sets apart those who want to succeed from those who actually do. The great basketball coach Bobby Knight noted, "Everyone has the will to win, but it's only those with the will to prepare that do win."[4]

Likewise, Tim Sanders says, "The best prepared will always win. To be the best prepared, you need to do some things that aren't necessarily fun or easy."[5]

WHY WE NEED TO PREPARE: Four Reasons

Preparation Allows Tasks to Require Less Effort

Earlier we learned about the skill-will matrix, which showed us that success is not simply a function of desire but also ability. Proverbs 19:2 teaches the same thing: "Desire without knowledge is not good, and whoever makes haste with his feet misses his way." Not to prepare—not to get the knowledge you need—is hasty, and simply having desire without ability will not allow you to succeed.

Preparation is the building up of your abilities. It helps you understand a situation better and develop your skills so they are ready for action. You will be able to envision more effective approaches and as a result use less energy. As Ecclesiastes 10:10 says, "If the iron is blunt, and one does not sharpen the edge, he must use more strength, but wisdom [skill!] helps one to succeed." Higher skill for a task means the task will take less effort.

Preparation connects with the principle we saw earlier of the need to value production *as well as production capacity*. Preparation increases your ability to produce.

Preparation Enables You to Adapt and Be Resilient

Tim Sanders writes that great preparation makes you "resilient when faced with adversity and proactive when shown opportunity."[6] You are resilient because you are ready for many different possibilities.

Planning is one type of preparation. Some people have said planning is not worth it because nothing goes according to plan. But that idea misses the point of planning. The main goal is not the plan itself, as though it has to be perfectly followed (it can't be, since circumstances always change). The main value is what planning does for your mind—it prepares you. As Dwight Eisenhower once said, "In preparing for battle I have always found that plans are useless, but planning is indispensable."

Preparation Is Part of Continual Learning

Leaders are always learning. As leadership expert John Kotter has observed, "The most notable trait of great leaders is their quest for learning."[7] Churchill embodied this trait, with one of his biographers noting that "Churchill was relentless in his drive for mastery of affairs."[8] Willie Pietersen, one of the best authors on strategy, writes, "You should never stop learning. Unfortunately, many promising managers derail their careers when they stop striving for self-improvement, either because they think they've learned all there is to know or because they fail to translate their learning into meaningful leadership development."[9]

This is especially true today because the environment keeps changing. We need to learn our jobs really well, and then *keep learning* because "information flows in too many directions, knowledge is fleeting, and power can be perilous."[10] The ability to learn is now just as critical—often more critical—as what you know.

This truth holds for organizations also. Knowledge "is the underlying lifeblood of business in the twenty-first century."[11] The Dutch business executive Arie de Geus said, "The ability to learn faster than your competitors may be the only sustainable competitive advantage."

Success Brings New Challenges

Not only does the environment constantly bring new challenges, but success itself brings new challenges. In other words, as you succeed, success brings its own new potentials for getting stuck. So you need to always keep learning and always keep preparing. As David Allen says, "Just when you learn how to enhance your productivity and decision-making at one level, you'll graduate to the next accepted batch of responsibilities and creative goals, whose new challenges will defy the ability of any simply formula."[12]

WHY PREPARATION WORKS

Understanding not just that we need to prepare but also *why* preparation works is crucial, for knowing why it works actually helps us prepare better—as well as motivates us to do it. The primary thing I mean by preparation right now (though we will see more aspects of it soon) is becoming *really good* at your job—achieving mastery at what you do through experience, practice, and accumulating knowledge.

Here's why this is so powerful: when you become really good at something, more aspects of it move to autopilot. And that is valuable because actions on autopilot save you mental energy. For "tasks done on autopilot don't use up our stockpile of energy like tasks that have to be consciously completed."[13] Your mental energy is freed up to focus on greater challenges—thus enabling greater expertise. In other words, when you are really good at your work, more is ingrained in the hard drive of your mind rather than in your very limited and energy-consuming short-term memory. That's why you can do more and do it better.

Daniel Goleman describes this very well in his excellent book *Focus: The Hidden Driver of Excellence*, showing how the brain science works. In short, we have a top system, which requires a lot of energy and is for less familiar things requiring more conscious focus, and a bottom system, which requires less energy and works a lot like autopilot.

> The bottom/top systems distribute mental tasks between them so we can make minimal effort and get optimal results. As familiarity makes a routine easier, it gets passed off from the top to the bottom. The way we experience this neural transfer is that we need pay less attention—and finally none—as it becomes automatic.
>
> The peak of automaticity can be seen when expertise pays off in effortless attention to high demand, whether a master-level chess match, a NASCAR race, or rendering an oil painting. If we haven't practiced enough, all of these will take deliberate focus. But if we have mastered the requisite skills to a level that meets the demand, they will take no extra cognitive effort—freeing our attention for the extras seen only among those at top levels.[14]

In other words, as you practice and prepare, less of the routine and standard aspects of your tasks will take deliberate focus. This allows you to give deliberate focus to the things that really set you apart and create excellence—which is the mark of high performers.[15] "The more you can relax and trust in bottom up moves, the more you free your mind to be nimble."[16]

Martin Seligman explains this concept well in *Flourish*: "Any complex mental task . . . has fast automatic components and slower voluntary components that take much more effort. . . . The more components of a task you have on automatic, the more time you have left over to do the heavy lifting."[17] This is crucial because "what distinguishes . . . a great surgeon or a great pilot from the rest of us mortals is how much they have on automatic. When the bulk of what an expert does is on automatic, people say she has 'great intuitions.'"[18]

Hence, learning a skill really well enables you to go faster . . . so that you can then go slower. Going faster means you have more time to give to the harder parts—the parts that require your executive functioning. And it is going slow that "allows executive function to take over."[19] On the other hand, "overloading attention shrinks mental control." Learning a skill really well helps prevent the skill from overloading your attention.[20]

In sum, with practice and preparation, what at first requires lots of energy and attention needs to become automatic. Learning your field really, really well enables that. Your mind is freed up and quicker to focus on the extras that really make a difference.

Now we can also understand better why preparation increases our agility. Giuliani noted, "I would prepare for everything I could think of so that I'd be prepared for the thing I hadn't thought of." Why is that? Because by being prepared, when new circumstances arise that you haven't anticipated, your brain has the working memory available to attend to those issues.

WHEN SHOULD YOU PREPARE?

The short answer to "When should you prepare?" is "Before you need to!" But to be more specific, there are two times to prepare.

Before the Task

The most effective preparation is done in advance of the need. Before Rudy Giuliani became mayor of New York City, he did vast amounts of reading and brought together the best experts to essentially give himself a class in all aspects of running a city well. That is an example of very thorough advance preparation.

You don't have to go to that extent, but here are a few examples of prior preparation:

- *Before a meeting.* Define the purpose of the meeting and create the agenda! That is a very easy way to prepare. Even if you aren't running the meeting, review the agenda in advance (if it's distributed) and jot down some initial contributions you feel you can make.
- *Before taking on new responsibilities.* When you are given new responsibilities in your job (or life—for example, starting a family), find a couple of the best books on the subject and read them, or talk to others who have been effective with those responsibilities or roles.
- *When a major challenge or opportunity comes up.* When something unexpected—whether a problem or opportunity—comes up, don't just rush in. Take some time to reflect and do some learning.

Simultaneously with the Task

Of course we can't prepare for or anticipate everything in advance. By preparing for more things in advance, though, we will be more able to devote our mental resources to doing the preparation that we need to do "as we go" in certain areas as well.

Simultaneous preparation is preparation that you have to do while attending to a task. A new project might be given to you, and you haven't done anything like it before, and it starts right away. There isn't time to do much prior preparation. You have to learn as you go, analogous to a "design-build" approach in construction. Include in the time you plan for doing the tasks some time to learn as you go. This can be effective and also can help you avoid the trap of getting stuck in continual prior preparation—just preparing, preparing, and preparing, and never doing.

Simultaneous preparation is also an aspect of ongoing adapting. Willie Pietersen brings this out well in his excellent book *Strategic Learning*. He makes learning and situation analysis a phase at the start of the strategy process. But then he also makes it a step at the end, thus creating a cycle of learning that continues. You develop strategy, do it, observe and *learn*, then refine the strategy. Thus, learning (preparing!) becomes a continual process, integrating into how you do things.

The strategic learning process is a process of continuously learning from your environment and your own actions, then adjusting your strategies in light of those insights, and thus navigating through the current needs while at the same time building capacity and readiness for the next challenges.

CREATING THE TIME FOR PREPARATION

How do you create the time to prepare? Two things here.

Don't Sacrifice Preparation for Efficiency

First, decide not to skip the time to prepare! The temptation to do so can be strong. Justin Menkes expands on this in *Executive Intelligence*: "Because we know speed is of the essence, too often we immediately start moving without first taking the time to think about what we're trying to accomplish. There are hundreds of stories about this. Everyone is trying to act quickly, but too often they run out to solve a problem without fully understanding what they are trying to solve."[21] Remember: go slow to go fast. Preparing at the start may initially take a bit more time but will ultimately speed things up because more will be on autopilot for you.

Shape Your Job to Include Preparation

Second, the best way to create time for preparation is to shape your job to include time for it. This may at first seem extravagant, but it is not at all—it is essential, given what we have seen on the benefits and necessity of preparation.

To think that including time to prepare in your actual work responsibilities is not "real work" is to fall for the fallacy of valuing only production, not also *production capacity*. You don't have to overdo it by committing massive amounts of time to preparation. Craft your job to include what time you can for preparation.

HOW TO PREPARE

When it's time to prepare, how do you do it? Here are a few principles for how to prepare.

Prepare Deeply: Learn the Fundamentals

You cannot just do surface-level preparation. Many people *think* they are preparing, but they are only skimming the surface. For example, you can't just do tactical preparation (what Tim Sanders calls "gathering resources, organizing them, and practicing my craft."[22]); you have to do *fundamental* preparation. You need to know the fundamental concepts of your subject area—the *principles* that make the practices work—so that you can adapt the practices when circumstances change.

You need to know why the area you are preparing for matters, which will enable you to remain motivated and truly connect things; and you need to know the *history* of the area, so that you can see the effects that different approaches have had over time and not repeat mistakes.

Such preparation will require a lot of hard work. Tim Sanders writes, "To be deeply prepared, you'll need to delve into your challenge, often tapping into a different part of yourself than you are used to. Deep preparation is strenuous and taxing. It will push you outside your comfort zone. To the outsider who's happy just to get by in life, it will look like overkill. Only the obsessive would go that far. That is why most people end up choosing to prepare at the surface level."[23]

Practice (and Know What Practice Actually Is)

It has been well said that "mastery takes focus and deliberate effort."[24] That's what practice is: focus and *deliberate* effort.

Many people misunderstand the meaning of practice. They think it just means doing something a lot. But that is not practice—that is mere repetition! Mere repetition does not make you better.

Practice doesn't mean just doing something a lot. It means working *deliberately* to improve. That is, as you practice you *observe your actions* and make course corrections. On the other hand, if you are just doing something a lot, you could be reinforcing bad habits.[25]

Practice is what makes it possible to improvise and respond to the unexpected. Remember that to improve at anything, including personal leadership and execution, you need to *push yourself.* This is how you develop capacity at the physical level, and it is also true in the mental, emotional, and spiritual dimensions.

And so it needs to be a key component of how you build your capacity through preparation. Tim Sanders notes, "To truly get smart, you'll have to strain yourself on many levels. You'll read more than you ever thought you would. You'll have to think purposefully about what you've read and digest it into nuggets of insight. You'll need to put yourself out there, discussing these nuggets with colleagues—and being willing to debate the issues. Often you'll have to employ creative powers, associating unrelated facts or examples to give new insights."[26] As you are practicing, include obstacles and challenges in the process so that you are preparing for reality.

Create Mental Models

By preparing and practicing, you are creating a mental model of the skill and area. This is not just study. It's *study with intent to apply.* You are preparing for the sake of turning knowledge into action. Mental models enable you to interpret the world as you go about your work and life. They enable you to understand why things are the way they are, and therefore how to change them. And they enable you to make predictions and test them. You will continually refine your mental models.

In *Smarter Faster Better: The Transformative Power of Real Productivity*, Charles Duhigg has an excellent discussion of mental models and how they enable pilots to fly with skill and avoid crashes in challenging situations.[27]

Duhigg says that mental models help with information overload, organizing our knowledge to make it more efficient. They help us "by providing a scaffold for the torrent of information that constantly surrounds us."[28]

How do you create and use mental models? Duhigg points out that we create and use mental models by constantly developing theories on why things are happening the way they are and testing those theories. We constantly tell ourselves stories about why things are happening the way they are. As we do this, our mental spotlight is ready to shine right away when we encounter a problem, and we will be able to pay attention to what matters without getting overwhelmed and distracted by the constant flow of information.[29]

Using our knowledge and talking with others also helps us understand it more deeply, remember it, and refine our models: "Find other people to hear your theories and challenge them," Duhigg advises.[30] As you do this, you'll see that this is not just brute knowledge you are developing. Mental models are about making connections. That's what learning itself is—making connections between ideas, not just knowing them.

In sum, "to become genuinely productive, we must take control of our attention; we must build mental models that put us firmly in charge."[31] Research shows that "people who know how to manage their attention and who habitually build robust mental models tend to earn more money and get better grades."[32]

And anyone can learn to habitually construct mental models:

> By developing a habit of telling ourselves stories about what's going on around us, we learn to sharpen where our attention goes....

Narrate your life, as you are living it, and you'll encode those experiences deeper in your brain. If you need to improve your focus and learn to avoid distractions, take a moment to visualize, with as much detail as possible, what you are about to do. It is easier to know what's ahead when there's a well-rounded script inside your head.[33]

Gaining Knowledge by Reading

One of the best ways to gain knowledge is by reading. Here is a summary of how to use reading to prepare.

Your Aim

This is key: Your aim in reading is not first to gather details or to just plain read. Your aim is to find the central, governing idea of the subject. Without this, you will not be able to get a sense of the whole, and the specific parts and aspects of the subject will not gel together in your mind effectively.

Most people do not realize that there is a single governing idea behind most concepts. You have to grasp this idea, because without it, you will not understand the area. Many experts in various fields have vast knowledge but do not truly understand their area—that is, they do not have wisdom—because they are missing the core idea (or have the wrong one).

The Process

Here is a summary of the process. First, find the best books on a subject. You can start to find the best books by asking people who are familiar with the subject. Then review what they've pointed you to on Amazon, reading the endorsements and some customer reviews, and usually the top two or three books will emerge. Note that books should be chosen over magazines and blog posts. Books bring depth; news and articles tend to bring awareness, which is helpful, but doesn't generally take you to the roots.

Second, read the books, looking for the big ideas and the overall framework. Underline while you are reading.

Third, after reading a book, go back over it and take some key notes. This is crucial, as you need multiple exposures.

Fourth, as you read additional books, relate the concepts to each other. Real learning takes place when you relate ideas rather than simply having them in your head.

Fifth, integrate the notes. This is the synthesis process. It helps you to relate ideas even more fully.

Sixth, review the notes and put the concepts to use. For example, when I was given leadership of the web department at Desiring God, I followed the above process to learn usability—our core philosophy for the website design. After I had integrated my notes, I started using them. That is, I used the principles of usability and information architecture I had learned to develop the site blueprints. This really cemented the concepts in my mind.

Seventh, as you are learning, connect things to your experience—especially by using the ORID process. Learning is not just the objective information. There are actually *four steps* to learning—not one. The four steps spell ORID:

1. **Objective.** This is learning the facts. It is essential, but it is not everything there is to learning. To think that it is reduces learning to mere information transfer. But that's not what learning is. Learning is understanding the concepts, being changed by them, and being able to use them. This implies much more than just knowing the facts, which leads to the next steps.

2. **Reflective.** Adults learn especially by connecting knowledge to their experience. That's what the reflective step is. Take the objective information and think about a time you've experienced it in your life. That really starts to anchor the concept. For example, when I was learning usability principles and thought about inferior websites I had encountered that violated the principles, that was the "reflective" step.

3. **Interpretive.** As you reflect, look for patterns and develop insights into why things have the effect they do. This helps you understand even more deeply, as you can now interpret the knowledge and make predictions. For example, when I was learning usability, I came to understand that most sites that are easy to use have a clear global navigation. Why is that? Because a good global navigation gives you the big picture of the site. It creates an easy framework for you. Understanding not just the *what* but the *why* enables you to much more fully grasp the concept.

4. **Decisional.** This is where you take the patterns you've learned from the objective knowledge and make decisions about what you will do differently now, and implement them. This is the central component of learning—it is the concept linking to and changing behavior. For example, after we learned why global navigation is so essential for a usable website, we created the global navigation for our site based on the principles we had learned. We were doing things differently because of what we learned and applying it, and this enabled us to see it fully in action and truly be changed by the learning.

The importance of connecting learning to experience should not be overlooked. Interestingly, since learning usability principles worked so well for me by taking the notes and integrating them, a few years later I sought to do this with leadership as well. I read almost twenty books on leadership, took notes, and integrated them. I expected the same thing to happen.

But it didn't. I certainly learned some things, but it wasn't clicking like usability was. Why not? It was too much, and I didn't have enough background knowledge from *experience* yet (the *R* in the ORID). I was simply seeking to connect the facts *to one another*, not to *my own experience.* I wasn't thinking of times, for example, when I had utilized a certain leadership style, and good (or bad!) results had followed. I was just thinking about leadership style in general. This negligence prevented the deep learning I needed to do and made the subject stick less. This finally began to turn when I began connecting what I was learning to experience.

Interestingly, as we in fact just saw, this connection to experience was essential for me in learning usability as well. I reflected on bad websites that violated the principles, did the interpretive step to understand why, and made decisions to do things differently. I followed the full ORID. For some reason, with my initial leadership study, I focused only on the *O*. That was a big mistake that cost me time and lots of energy.

Eighth, use your knowledge through doing and speaking. We've already talked about the importance of doing. Another thing that helps is talking about what you are learning. Talk about applying knowledge makes it stick; rote memorization and repetition do not.

This is one reason, perhaps, that it was much harder for me to learn time management than theology. Although I've read much more on time management, I understand theology far better than time management. Why hasn't time management connected and stuck as much?

Part of the reason is the work of the Spirit and my gifting. But another is that as I was learning theology, I always sought to make use of new knowledge right away and to talk about it with my friends. I would write articles, for example. Instead of just taking notes over a book (which I typically did with the time-management books), I would write an article articulating my own thinking and conclusions on the subject, informed by the books. Doing that enabled me to truly grasp things in a way that stuck.

Of course, reading is great, and so is talking about things, but we will not make connections until we take time to *reflect* and *draw conclusions*.

WHAT TO LEARN: For the Workplace

Develop a Philosophy for Your Position

One of the most important types of preparation you can do is develop a philosophy for your position. This serves as a strategy and set of guiding principles to anchor your actions in a consistent, effective framework.

So take some time to develop a specific philosophy for your role. You can do this by reading some of the best thinkers on a subject and then drawing conclusions based on your own experience. For example, if you are in internet and marketing, read some of Seth Godin's writings. If you are in human resources, read Laszlo Bock's *Work Rules! Insights from Inside Google That Will Transform How You Live and Lead*. If you are a freelancer, read Daniel Pink's *Free Agent Nation: The Future of Working for Yourself*. If you are a manager, read Marcus Buckingham's *First, Break All the Rules: What the World's Greatest Managers Do Differently*. If you are a top executive, read Jim Collins's *Built to Last: Successful Habits of Visionary Companies*.

Prepare in Areas That Aren't Your Main View

As a leader, you need to have firsthand knowledge of as much as possible. Rudy Giuliani writes, "Sometimes, you have to know the material as well as the experts who work for you. That's the only way to develop an independent view and not be held captive by the people around you, who may want to spin in one direction or the other."[34] By getting firsthand knowledge, you will be more able to identify spin and protect yourself from it.

Know Your Company's Business Model

Knowing how your company makes money is crucial so that you can work in alignment with what brings in revenue rather than against it. You want to be a revenue-positive employee, not a revenue-negative employee.

So know what a business model is (it's what your company does over and over to make money), exactly what your company's business model is, and how your job contributes to it. Especially do those things in your job that make the biggest contribution to the business model and eliminate the things that don't (without guilt—but also without making the mistake of superficial efficiency).

Know How Your Organization Works

You can do your own job more effectively if you have an understanding of the total organization—how it all works together. Understand the parts of a business and the specific departments in your own business or nonprofit. Talk to people in each area to learn what they do, and read a book or two on how business works, such as Steven A. Silbiger's *The Ten Day MBA: A Step-by-Step Guide to Mastering the Skills Taught in America's Top Business Schools*.

Be Aware of Your Environment

Keep an eye on changes in trends and keep innovating so you can adapt and do new things.

Hone Your Professional Skills

Improve your reading, writing, public speaking, and the specific content skills of your job.

Adapt to Specific Challenges That Arise

When there is a challenge, learn as much as you can about it as soon as you can.

WHAT TO LEARN

There is also much to learn about! Here are just a few things to highlight.

Understand the Christian Faith

If you are going to be unstuck and effective in carrying out God's purpose, you need to understand the Christian faith very well. All Christians are called to understand the Bible and theology well.

First of all, you must know the difference between religion and having a relationship with Jesus. Christianity is first of all a relationship with Christ, not a set of rules or behavior modification. One of the best and most enjoyable recent discussions of this is Jefferson Bethke's book *Jesus > Religion*.[35]

Second, you must understand the great doctrines of the faith so that you can articulate them. The best book here is Wayne Grudem's *Systematic Theology*. Also important is understanding apologetics—how to defend the faith. The best book here is William Lane Craig's *Reasonable Faith: Christian Truth and Apologetics*.[36]

You also need to understand cultural engagement so you can point the world to Christ without turning them off through spiritual weirdness, lack of tact, and lack of social intelligence. As Paul says, we are to "walk in wisdom toward outsiders" (Col. 4:5). One of the best resources here is Tim Keller's *Center Church: Doing Balanced, Gospel-Centered Ministry in Your City*.[37] It is not just for pastors but for all Christians!

Understand Economics

Understanding economics is also important, as many seemingly well-intentioned policies actually hurt more than they help! This is because many politicians overlook basic economic principles in formulating their positions. We have a responsibility to be informed citizens, and understanding economics helps us discern good policies from bad—which is important for the flourishing of our communities and nation. The best book on economics is Thomas Sowell's *Basic Economics: A Common Sense Guide to the Economy*.[38]

Know How to Love Your Spouse and Kids

If you have a family, you can serve your spouse and kids by learning more fully what your spouse needs and what it means to be an effective parent! Some of this comes naturally to us, but some doesn't. So there is a place to do much learning. One of the best and most accessible books on marriage is Shaunti Feldhahn's *The Surprising Secrets of Highly Happy Marriages: The Little Things That Make a Big Difference*. One of the best books on parenting is *Grace-Based Parenting: Set Your Family Free* by Tim Kimmel.[39]

ORGANIZATIONS: Train Your People!

Finally, a word to managers and organizations: train your people! This is part of preparation as an institution. Jim Collins nails it: "Train people at all levels, not just managers. Keep in mind that training isn't a perk; it's a tremendous business advantage."[40]

What do you need to train your people in? Customer service employees need product knowledge of course. But they also need (along with all employees) emotional and social intelligence (not just technical skills). We all need to know how to relate to people well. This includes skills like empathic listening, not being judgmental or critical, and being affirming.

Do not miss this. Project management training now points out that most projects fail not due to lack of technical skills, but due to insufficient *people skills*. Training people in authentic and good social and emotional intelligence is essential for effectiveness in the workplace.

Various training methods may include reading, audio messages, videos, apprenticeship programs "where seasoned, successful employees educate new people,"[41] outside training courses, and courses that you develop inside the organization.

What about smaller companies? They need training in people skills too. In fact, they need it most: "Many smaller companies complain that they don't have the resources to do training. We ask them: how can you possibly expect to develop into a great company without it?"[42]

TOOLS FOR LEARNING MORE QUICKLY

Here are three quick tools for learning more quickly.

Rapid Learning

Liz Wiseman talks about rapid learning in her excellent book *Rookie Smarts*. She recommends that you see how fast you can ascend the learning curve. You don't have to become an expert in everything—but you can get halfway, and that can make a huge difference. "Don't just learn enough to be dangerous. Learn enough to stay out of danger. Learn enough to know the right questions to ask. Then find the right people to ask and let the true experts answer them."

Becoming an expert can be an arduous, lengthy process. But "one can quickly learn the basics and the latest developments through deliberate inquiry." To do this, "interview experts and ask them to teach you the essentials of their field or their expertise."[43]

Speed Leading

The speed leader implements what I call simultaneous preparation. Instead of preparing and acting, they act, learn from the consequences, and adapt based on those. Acting first and in small ways can generate important insight for traversing unknown territory.

Speed Reading (Sort Of)

I've never been able to make speed-reading work, but you can use the underlying concepts to read faster. One key concept is not to look back and reread but force yourself to keep going forward by using your finger as a pacer. This also helps you speed up. Eventually you can try to read chunks of words at a time.

WHAT TO DO WITH YOUR PREPARATION

What can you do with your preparation? Use it, of course! And instill preparedness in others. Once again, this connects to doing good and always building others up. As Giuliani notes, "Creating reasons for those who work for you to establish their own culture of preparedness is part of being a good leader."[44]

THE UNSTUCK CLINIC

Core Point

Preparation is central to effectiveness because it puts routine elements of a task on autopilot so that you can give your focus to the higher-level challenges involved.

Exercise

For what activities in your work and life are you especially prepared?

How frequently and well are you using this preparation? For what do you need to do deeper preparation?

Further Resources

- Rudy Giuliani, "Prepare Relentlessly" and "Study. Read. Learn Independently." in *Leadership*
- Tim Sanders, "Knowledge," in *Love Is the Killer App: How to Win Business and Influence Friends*
- Tim Sanders, "Prepare Yourself," in *Today We Are Rich: Harnessing the Power of Total Confidence*

PART 3

PERSONAL MANAGEMENT

The Clock

Getting Your Time Unstuck

The ability to be successful, relaxed, and in control during these fertile but turbulent times demands new ways of thinking and working. . . . There is a great need for new methods, technologies, and work habits to help us get on top of our world.
DAVID ALLEN[1]

How we spend our days is, of course, how we spend our lives.
ANNIE DILLARD[2]

Y ou are probably wondering how you can translate your vision and strategy into your daily life.

Envisioning and strategizing is not enough. You have to *organize* in a way that aligns with and supports your goals. And you need to know how to do it at the macro level in the day-to-day, with specific tasks and workflow.

And so you need a process—one that is adaptive and allows you to respond to new opportunities and changing circumstances. If it doesn't, you will miss key opportunities or stay on a road that environmental changes show will not pan out (by analogy, the road may have been flooded or be undergoing construction work). Your approach must stay true to your vision and values or you will drive off course and accomplish nothing. Further, your mission matters and must be accomplished. The world and the kingdom of God will miss out if you fail to follow through on your mission.

We must, as Jim Collins often says about great organizations, preserve the core (mission and values) and *stimulate progress* by being willing to adapt everything else as we move along, finding the best path to our goal.

Following is the process for personal management. I will outline the whole process here, and in the chapters that follow, I will cover the core components in detail.

THE PROCESS OF MANAGING YOURSELF

Analyze and Consolidate Time

When it comes to managing yourself, your plan does not actually come first. Instead, you first need to know how you are actually spending your time, what time wasters you can get rid of, and how much time you have left to work with. Then you will be in position to create a good plan. Hence, the first step is to *assess and analyze* the way you are currently spending your time. We will look at this in chapter 11, "Start with Your Time, Not with Your Tasks."

Determine the Chief Areas of Your Job

With the amount of time you have to work with clear and consolidated into large chunks, you can then determine the *major areas* of your job where you need to be spending your time. After that, in the next step, identify the key activities you need to be doing in those time periods.

The steps here include the following:

- determining your core strategy concept and value proposition
- identifying the chief categories of your job. This is crucial because "you cannot successfully manage your time if you don't know *how* you should be spending it. The biggest problem new managers [and most people] face is understanding their goals and priorities. They are not really sure what they should be doing."[3] The result is spending your time working on the wrong things, being driven by the urgent, or being pulled by others to accomplish their agendas. There will usually be four to seven main areas.

Chief categories include the following:

- growth tasks—things like innovation, product development, process improvement, and personal development
- leading and managing people—things like developing vision and strategy, communicating the vision and strategy, planning and facilitating meetings, motivating people, and holding reviews. If you are a leader or manager, these are the main activities of your job.

- ongoing daily operational activities. If you are an individual contributor, these are the main areas of your job. They might include designing buildings if you are an architect, writing code if you are a programmer, or designing website interfaces if you are a graphic designer.
- administrative tasks—things like compiling expense reports, setting up meetings, and arranging travel
- determining how much time each category of your job needs

Create a Time Plan

Now, within each results area of your job, determine which specific activities you need to do in them. Then use these determinations to create a time plan, a simple chart listing the chief categories of your job, how much time each gets, and what the key activities are in them. Compare this chart to your actual time allocation from your time audit, and make adjustments as necessary. (Note: You may need to add staff or obtain additional resources to get your job done.)

The last step here is to put the priority activities you've identified into your schedule. Your aim is to allocate your time to the activities that will generate the biggest return toward your goals.

Create Your Task Management System

Your personal management system as a whole consists not just of a literal task management system, but of *processes and methods* as well as *structures and systems*. Since I have dealt with creating a task management system in *What's Best Next*, we are not going to focus here on the specific structures of the task management system, such as to-do lists. Nevertheless, understanding what the components of a full task management system are is helpful. The key components are these:

1. Your mission statement
2. Your role plans
3. Your project and action lists

4. Your calendar
5. Your contacts, files, journals, and other supporting systems
6. Your methods and practices for keeping your system going: daily workflow, weekly planning, execution in the moment, and longer-term planning.

Note that your personal management system is more than a calendar. Many tasks and projects don't have a good spot in a calendar. Nor do your mission statement, vision, and goals.

A quick word on software. Unfortunately, no single app will organize all the elements of your management system. You may, for example, keep your mission statement in a document, your role plans in an outliner program (I recommend OmniOutliner—and I keep my mission statement there also), your project and action lists in a task management program like OmniFocus, your schedule in a calendar program, and your procedural checklists in Evernote.

Execute: Make Decisions Consistent with Your Priorities

As you implement your management system, work to keep your tasks in their time boundaries by "controlling to plan." That is, identify ways you may be letting your work expand beyond scope, and identify shortcuts to get it done faster.

These principles from Robert Pozen's *Extreme Productivity* especially help with controlling to plan.

- "Focus on the final product. In tackling high-priority projects, quickly formulate tentative conclusions to guide your work."
- "Don't sweat the small stuff. Deal with low-priority items in a way that allows you to spend as little time on them as possible."[4]

One of the aims of a good approach to personal management is to enable you to get into the "zone" easily. The zone is the state in which you are able to do your best work in the most efficient way.

It is when you are operating at your highest capacity. Your mind is clear, and you are fully engaged, doing proactive and productive things. You are not stressed, and you are wholly absorbed in the activity. You feel in control, and time seems to disappear. You are making clear progress toward outcomes that matter to you, and you feel it.

You can adjust certain characteristics of the work itself to help you get into this state, and you can control certain features of your environment to keep them from interfering. Working in the zone is increasingly necessary to energize you and protect you from burning out as your environment becomes more demanding. As Allen says, this is more and more "a required condition for high-performance professionals who wish to maintain balance and a consistent positive output in their work."[5] We will look at how to get into the zone in chapters 13 and 14 on "deep work."

When we get out of the zone too much and for too long, we begin to feel less in control, more stressed, less focused, and *stuck*. Being stuck is both a feeling and result of not being in the zone. It is to be doing your work in a way that is not energizing and fulfilling; you feel less in control and more frazzled.

And being out of the zone leads to being stuck further because being in the zone is the engine by which you move and progress. When you are out of the zone, you can be like a car that is spinning its wheels, stuck in the snow or mud. But when you are in the zone, you are like a truck that has sufficient traction and horsepower to *move*—despite the snow and despite the mud. Being "in the zone" is our power for moving from here to there and thus is essential to getting unstuck and not being stuck.

The objective is to be able to devote your full attention to the task you are doing, being completely absorbed in it, and yet also to have this ability under your control so that it doesn't just happen by chance or, alternatively, so that you don't have to constantly try to get into this state only to fail.

The Aim: Flourishing

The aim of working in the zone is flourishing—for yourself, for the world, and for the kingdom of God. By flourishing for yourself, I mean not only that you are getting the right things done, which includes having appropriate proportion between your four fundamental needs and the five main areas of your life, but that you are also doing the work in a way that is relaxed and energizing, not hurried and exasperating.

David Allen, perhaps without intending to connect his words to the concept of human flourishing, captures this concept well in the goal of his GTD (Getting Things Done) approach: "There *is* a way to get a grip on it all, stay relaxed, and get meaningful things done with minimal effort, across the whole spectrum of your life and work. You *can* experience what the martial artists call a 'mind like water' and top athletes refer to as the 'zone,' within the complex world in which you're engaged."[6]

TRANSITIONING FROM PERSONAL LEADERSHIP TO PERSONAL MANAGEMENT IS LIKE SHIFTING GEARS

Transitioning from personal leadership to personal management is like shifting gears. Multiple gears are needed to get unstuck.

Consider being stuck in the mud. You start out in the highest power gear—first. That's vision. It will get you out of the mud. It's inspiring, providing power (it provides the most power of any step) and direction so that you don't fly out of the mud and into the trees.

But once you are out of the mud, you can't stay in first gear. You have to shift in order to keep going. And that's essential to getting unstuck, because if you are out of the mud but then can't get to where you want to go, you're just stuck in a different sense.

Second gear is personal management. It provides less power but more control. Third gear is the laser—enabling you to break blocks. And though we aren't talking about them in this book, the fourth gear is leadership (getting others involved to do bigger things) and management (bringing a measure of control and stability to those things—essentially analogous to the process of personal leadership and personal management).

This is the approach you must use to get your life unstuck, and then you repeat it to get specific obstacles unstuck. You ask: *Where am I? Where do I want to go? What's the problem and reason for the gap? What's the path?*

CHAPTER 11

START WITH YOUR TIME, NOT WITH YOUR TASKS

You need to start in the opposite place you might think

Work expands to fill whatever time is allotted to it. To be productive, therefore, you must manage your time, not your work.
JIM COLLINS[1]

Peter Drucker starts off the second chapter of his classic book *The Effective Executive: The Definitive Guide to Getting the Right Things Done* with a big surprise: "Most discussions of the executive's task start with the advice to plan one's work. This sounds eminently plausible. The only thing wrong with it is that it rarely works. The plans always remain on paper, always remain good intentions. They seldom turn into achievement."[2] That is, *the plans get stuck*.

A plan is precisely the thing we would intuitively come up with to make sure the most important things get done. So why does starting with a plan result in getting stuck? Why don't the plans get done?

Because, counterintuitively, we need to reverse the order. Instead of starting with our plans and then arranging our time to sync with our plans, we need to set the table with our time so that we can then put our plans into it.

In other words, we have to make room for our plans. You would think you could just use your plan to overrule what you might otherwise do with your time, but in practice that does not work.

163

Other things—the prior things, the urgent things—will crowd out your planned work and be almost impossible to overcome. Drucker sums up the process that actually works: "Effective executives, in my observation, do not start with their tasks. They start with their time. And they do not start out with planning. They start by finding out where their time actually goes. Then they attempt to manage their time and to cut back unproductive demands on their time. Finally they consolidate their 'discretionary' time into the largest possible continuing units."[3]

So we have a three-step process here:

1. Record your time and identify where it is actually going.
2. Cut out the unproductive demands on your time (this is what Drucker calls "time management"; we typically use the phrase more broadly).
3. Consolidate the remaining time.

I can testify that Drucker's process here works, because I have tried literally everything possible to avoid it. This is because by nature I have very little interest in the first step: tracking my time (I think I probably speak for most people in this). Who wants to write down what they are doing every five minutes? And yet I've found that I've never achieved the results I'm capable of, in a smooth and nonoverwhelming way, without following Drucker's approach and starting with my time rather than tasks. So, unfortunately, if you truly want to maximize your effectiveness, this is something you must do. I am truly sorry!

WHY START WITH YOUR TIME?

Tasks Are Unlimited

The biggest reason we have to start with our time is because that's where the limitation is. The supply of time never goes up; you can't make more of it. Tasks, on the other hand, are infinite—there can always be more. So if you start with your tasks, there can be no end. But if you start with your *time*, you can contain your tasks to the most essential and not constantly be overwhelmed and behind.[4] The next two points help us understand this idea better.

Time Is the New Scarcity

Drucker points out that the limits of any process are set by the scarcest resource. Let's say you want to take a trip to the Himalayas and hike up to the base of Mount Everest. This expedition will cost $4,000 and take ten days. Further, it requires excellent physical condition.

Let's say you have $10,000 in the bank that you are able to spend on this trip and that you meet the physical conditions required. But due to work commitments, you only have seven days available. Can you make the expedition?

It doesn't matter that you have far more money than is needed to pay for the trip; the time you have available is insufficient and is the limiting factor. You will need to find a different expedition that requires less time or you won't be able to go at all. Even having all the money in the world would not change this. The scarcest resource sets the limits.

With performance and accomplishment, we need three resource inputs: time, money, and people. Which one is the scarcest?

Most people think it's money. This explains why so many managers and organizations are focused on cost cutting, even at the expense of their employees' well-being. They have a misguided understanding of what is scarcest, and it skews their decision making.

Money is not the scarcest resource. As Drucker pointed out years ago (and it has only increased since then), "Of the other major resources, money is actually quite plentiful. And when it comes to people, while it is hard to find enough good people, you can hire and train more people." But you cannot get more time. You cannot rent more of it, hire more of it, or in any other way obtain more of it. Time is the scarcest resource—not people and not money.

And therefore "nothing else, perhaps, distinguishes effective executives as much as their tender loving care of time."[5]

This is true especially today (about twenty years after Drucker last revised *The Effective Executive*). We are bombarded with requests for our attention and with complicated situations that demand our time. Yet most people continue to think that money is the scarcest resource and that we ought to focus our efforts on saving money.

As mentioned above, this thinking results in unhelpful and detrimental decisions. Since time is scarcer than money, we should focus our efforts on saving time over money. We should be willing to spend money to save time because we can get more money, but we can't get more time. This simple change in orientation would make many organizations much better places to work and reduce stress and increase well-being (and therefore productivity) for their employees.[6]

Time Is Inelastic, Perishable, Irreplaceable, and Necessary

At this point in his discussion, Drucker has the best summary of the characteristics of time that I have ever seen. Many people try to make these points, as they are the precise reason that we need to care about time management at all, but Drucker makes them in the most concise and compelling fashion of all. He points out the following reasons why we need time management, listing these characteristics of time:

- **Inelastic.** "No matter how high the demand, the supply [of time] will never go up."
- **Perishable.** You cannot store time. What you don't use can't be put in the fridge or the bank, but goes away forever. "Time is, therefore, always in exceedingly short supply."
- **Irreplaceable.** You can often substitute one resource for another. If we run out of almond milk, I can put regular milk in my coffee. A manufacturer can, within limits, use copper instead of aluminum. "But there is no substitute for time."

- **Necessary.** Not everything requires money or even people to do. But "everything requires time. It is the one truly universal condition. All work takes place in time and uses up time."[7]

As Jonathan Edwards said so well in his sermon on procrastination, "Time is exceedingly precious."[8] Yet, as Drucker points out, "Most people take for granted this unique, irreplaceable, and necessary resource."[9]

Don't be one of those people. You cannot accomplish what you are called to do without good stewardship of your time. If you waste your time, you will waste your life. Or, to put it conversely, if you are on board with John Piper's call to "not waste your life,"[10] then you need to learn time management so you don't waste your time.

And that point brings us to the three-step process for managing our time so that we can then make the most of our time for the sake of the God-centered priorities we define.

TRACK YOUR TIME

While it can seem burdensome, the good news about tracking your time is that you don't need to do it constantly. Once a year for a week should be enough.[11] But once is not enough, because you will likely drift back into old habits. Constant effort at managing time is required to keep from drifting.

I suggest starting right now. Decide to track your time from this moment for the next week. To do so, you can go high tech or low tech. If you want to go low tech, carry a journal with you and record it in the journal. If you want to go mid tech, use a Word document or Excel spreadsheet. And if you want to go high tech, use an app such as Hours or Hours Tracker.

How do you do this well?

The first rule of tracking your time is not to rely on your memory, as it will not be accurate. Psychological experiments have shown that our time sense is not very reliable. We tend to grossly underrate it or overrate it. Drucker points out that in his experience with executives, he has seen this over and over again: "I sometimes ask executives who pride themselves on their memory to put down their guess as to how they spend their own time. Then I lock these guesses away for a few weeks or months. In the meantime, the executives run an actual time record on themselves. There is never much resemblance between the way these men thought they used their time and their actual records."[12]

So don't rely on your memory. Instead, in your journal, every fifteen minutes stop to write down how you've been spending your time. Do your time log in real time.

ELIMINATE TIME WASTERS

Once you have your time log completed, you will likely feel a bit of a shock as it becomes obvious that you clearly don't have enough time to do everything you want, and that much of your time could be allocated to better uses. So the next thing to do is to identify activities that are wasting time or are not necessary for your mission and role. But how do you identify them?

Personal Time Wasters

The DEAD tool we learned in *What's Best Next* is helpful here. Remember that there are four ways to reduce your tasks:

1. *Delegate.* Assign tasks to others or invite them to help.
2. *Eliminate.* Get rid of tasks that don't need to be done at all.
3. *Automate.* Get computers doing whatever you can.
4. *Defer.* Schedule tasks that don't need to be done now for later.

You can use these four categories as a grid for finding tasks to remove.

Though it's second in the acronym, I suggest starting with finding the tasks you can eliminate altogether. To do this, look at all the activities in your record and ask yourself, *What would happen if this activity were not done at all?*[13] If the answer is *nothing*, then eliminate it. Most likely a lot of things are taking a toll on your time and energy that will not be missed, and thus can unlock a fresh well of new time.

The potential here is probably greater than you realize. Drucker notes: "I have yet to see an executive, regardless of rank or station, who could not consign something like a quarter of the demands on his time to the wastepaper basket without anybody's noticing their disappearance."[14]

Another set of tasks you can delete is ones that not only would not be missed if they weren't done, but that actively waste other people's time. That's right, you are probably doing some things that are not only wasting your time but other people's time as well. This is a much overlooked category of time that we need to find and free up. You likely won't be able to identify these things on your own, which means you need to ask your coworkers what things you are doing that take away their time and do not contribute to their effectiveness. This takes boldness, but "to ask this question, and to ask it without being afraid of the truth, is a mark of the effective executive."[15]

Note, however, that some of these items will be false positives. Sometimes you have to do your work a certain way, and yet another person will suggest that it is unhelpful to them. For example, for various reasons I need to have about eight different categories in my calendar. This is because certain people need access to certain events and not others, and the categories make that possible. Once, I had a temporary assistant who had been assigned to me say, "The way you do your calendars doesn't work for me." Aside from the fact that the top priority in this case was what worked for *everybody*, not just (or chiefly) her, there simply was no other way to do it. Her desire that I take a different approach to save her time would have cost everyone else even more time.

Next I suggest moving to the first *D*, "delegate," and asking yourself which activities could be done by others. The aim here is not to be lazy or push your real work onto others, but to free up the time so you can actually do your own work—the work only you can do.

Delegation can be incredibly empowering. It can be tempting to resist delegation at first, out of fear that the tasks won't be performed right or of missing out on some things you might enjoy doing. The best way to overcome this temptation is to delegate anyway, starting small if you must, so you can get a taste of it. You will find that it frees up enormous amounts of time and that, ironically, many of the tasks actually get done *better* than when you were doing them. Most people rise to the challenge and do great work, and they bring a unique creativity and style that will likely bring great benefit to you.

Time-Wasting Management Defects

Some time wasters result not from your own actions but simply from bad management in your organization or team.

Lack of foresight. One such example is the "recurrent crisis," which shows that foresight has not been given to anticipate routine problems and correct them.

Overstaffing. Another time waster can sometimes, ironically, be adding staff. Large organizations and large teams are typically a good thing—great insight is often unlocked from the dynamics of large teams. Nonetheless, in some instances, especially if work on something seems to be going slowly, we may think, *Oh, we need to add more people to speed this up.* If this has to do with an ongoing operation, that is likely the case.

But if it is with a project, it might not be the case. Recent project management studies have shown that adding more people to a project sometimes *slows down the project* because the new people need time to get up to speed, the existing people need to take time away from what they are doing to get the new people up to speed, and the increased communication can divert time and attention. So, in some circumstances at least, adding staff can be another organizational time thief. But again, beware of concluding this too quickly for operational activities, as I think most organizations these days err on the side of being too lean.[16]

Bad meetings (resulting from bad organization). The most commonly discussed and felt organizational time waster is bad and excessive *meetings*. There is no avoiding meetings, and many of us resonate with the idea that meetings are a necessary evil, and that work would be a whole lot better if we just didn't have to go to meetings.

But I agree with Patrick Lencioni that this is *not* a good mindset. Meetings are a critical forum through which those who lead and manage organizations get their work done. For an executive to say, "I'd like my job more if I didn't have to go to any meetings," is like a surgeon saying, "I'd like my job more if I didn't have to operate on people," or a professional baseball player saying, "I'd love my job if I didn't have to play in these games."[17]

In fact, if we hate meetings, it is unlikely that we are able to "[make] good decisions and successfully lead our organizations." For a major purpose of meetings is to "extract the collective wisdom from a team"—which is essential for making good decisions, staying on the same page, and acting as a real team. "There is no substitute for a good meeting—a dynamic, passionate, and focused engagement—when it comes to extracting the collective wisdom from a team."[18]

Further, meetings deal with compelling issues. They are "where presidential cabinets discuss whether to go to war; where governors and their aids debate the merits of raising and lowering taxes; where CEOs and their staffs decide to launch a brand, introduce a product, or close a factory."[19]

Meetings done well are crucial and invigorating. Nonetheless, it is still the case that there are too many meetings (and too many of them are bad meetings). These overly abundant meetings, in turn, generate additional work beyond the time in them, including follow-up emails, assigned tasks, and ironically, more meetings.

A solution to this is to make meetings better, first of all by making sure all meetings are purposeful. You should never have a meeting without defining the purpose and, in most cases, the agenda. But making meetings better is a solution for another place.

How do you know when you are having too many meetings? Look at your time log, and see how much time you spent in meetings. If it is more than about a fourth of your time, you likely have too many meetings, and they are the result of deficient organization and management practices. Drucker gives us a good principle here: "As a rule, meetings should never be allowed to become the main demand on an executive's time. Too many meetings always bespeak poor structure of jobs and the wrong organizational components. Too many meetings signify that work that should be in one job or in one component is spread over several jobs or several components."[20]

Malfunctioning information. The last organizational time waster I'll mention is information—too much information and information that is not presented in a usable form. It is worth spending extra time to make whatever you are creating *easy to use* for others—whether it's a report, presentation, email, or website. Speak in language your audience will be able to understand. Define any terms only experts would know, and know the form people need your information in.

Do Not Be Afraid to Prune Activities

Even with seeing the activities you can eliminate and delegate, it can be tempting to keep doing them anyway out of fear that you might cut back too much or eliminate something that you really should keep doing. This is a very understandable concern, and I tend to err on the side of caution here. Nonetheless, I am trying to change my default opinion because I believe Drucker is ultimately right in his observation that if you do cut back too much, that mistake "can be speedily corrected. If one prunes too harshly, one usually finds out fast enough."[21]

There are ways to delegate that are more and less empowering, and there is a process for delegating that ensures clarity of expectations and builds up the other person. To learn about these principles and practices for effective delegation, see *What's Best Next*, chapter 17, "The Art of Making Time."

CONSOLIDATE YOUR TIME

Once you have pruned the time wasters, you can see how much time you have that is under your control and available for your top priorities—the "big tasks that will really make a contribution."[22] How much time will this be? It's helpful to know what is normal, because otherwise you can easily have expectations that are too high and be continually frustrated.

A general rule is that the higher you are in an organization, the less time you will have under your control. You will have to give more time to keeping the organization running, focusing internally, than being able to focus your efforts outside, where the results are, making the organization move ahead. Drucker points out that among senior executives, it is rare to have more than 25 percent of their time truly and fully at their disposal, which equals about ten to fifteen hours per week.

This statistic shows how important it is to consolidate your time. Important matters take large and continuous chunks of time, and "small driblets are no time at all." Yet here is a word of hope: "Even one-quarter of the working day [about two hours!], if consolidated in large time units, is usually enough to get the important things done. But even three-quarters of the working day are useless if they are only available as fifteen minutes here or there."[23]

How do you consolidate your time effectively and give your full attention and focus to your work during that time? In chapters 13 and 14 on deep work, we will learn the principle of "working fully when you are working, and resting fully when you are resting." But first we need to learn how to define our priorities so that we can know what is most important to work on in this concentrated time.

┌─────────────── THE UNSTUCK CLINIC ───────────────┐

Core Point

Since work expands to fill the time available, the key is to start with your time, not your tasks.

Exercise

Write out an action list for tomorrow. First determine how much time you have available to do tasks. Then make estimates for how long each task you would like to do will take. Finally, refine your list to include only the tasks that are important and fit the time you have.

Further Resources

- Jim Collins and William Lazier, "Leadership Style," in *Beyond Entrepreneurship: Turning Your Business into an Enduring Great Company*
- Peter Drucker, "Know Thy Time," in *The Effective Executive: The Definitive Guide to Getting the Right Things Done*

Related in **What's Best Next**

- Chapter 17, "The Art of Making Time"
- Chapter 18, "Harnessing the Time Killers"

└──┘

SET YOUR PRIORITIES:
Make Importance Truly Work

How to avoid getting stuck in the trap of
being busy but not productive: exclusion
as the secret of effectiveness

---

*[You need to have] a clear sense of where you're going as a company,
and then work towards that in a prioritized way.*
SUNDAR PICHAI, CEO OF GOOGLE[1]

We saw in the last chapter that many plans for our time fail because we start with trying to plan our tasks rather than first organizing our time. But now that we have eliminated time wasters and consolidated our time into the largest possible chunks, it's time to plan our work and determine what goes into the time we've freed up. Although we may be tempted to try to put everything we want to do into that time, we will soon see that because we have limited time, everything simply will not fit. So we need to choose. We can do only some of the tasks that we want to do. That, then, brings us to the concept of *priorities*. We need to make priority decisions among all the tasks available to us, then slot those priorities into the time we have consolidated. That is the key to time management. And that means we need to know what our priorities are, how to set them, and what it looks like to truly slot them into our time.

WHAT ARE PRIORITIES?

Your priorities are not everything you have to do. They are not the same as your responsibilities. They are your *chief* responsibilities. More specifically, in Peter Drucker's words, a priority is one of the very few major areas "where superior performance will produce outstanding results."[2] Something is not a priority if it is not a task, project, or responsibility that will result in high contribution. Why would you focus your efforts on low-value tasks? A priority is a *high-value task* and therefore something that takes precedence over other tasks.

Priorities are *the key* to effectiveness. Time-management experts consistently make this point. Peter Drucker famously wrote: "If there is any 'secret' of effectiveness, it is concentration. Effective executives do first things first and they do one thing at a time."[3] And Greg McKeown's recent book *Essentialism: The Disciplined Pursuit of Less* is all about living according to priorities rather than trying to do everything.[4]

If you think about it, it makes sense that priorities are central to effectiveness. If you have a choice between a low-value task and a high-value task, choosing the high-value task will make you more effective by definition, for it's the thing that will bring about greater and more meaningful results. If you practice prioritizing day after day, over time you will have developed an ongoing pattern of effectiveness.

Nonetheless—and this is a huge reason we get stuck—most of us don't truly set priorities. For years I didn't—at least not consistently in an ongoing, disciplined way. And the reason I didn't set priorities was because I didn't understand why doing so was truly necessary. I think that's the same reason most people don't set priorities. We therefore need to look at why setting priorities is not simply a nice idea but is absolutely essential to effectiveness and getting unstuck from the trap of constantly being busy but unproductive. Of doing an awful lot of things, feeling spread way too thin, and yet getting nowhere. That's a really bad type of being stuck! And setting priorities is the answer.

WHY ARE PRIORITIES THE KEY TO EFFECTIVENESS?

So, why is setting priorities unavoidable for those who want to be unstuck and effective?

The reason I initially didn't think priorities were necessary is simple: I thought I could do the high-value tasks and the low-value tasks as well. I didn't see a high-value choice and low-value choice; I didn't think there was a need to choose at all. But the lower-value tasks weren't just sitting there harmlessly; they stole from my *ability to do higher-value tasks.*

So *that's* why we need to set priorities. It's not simply that tasks are not of equal value; it's that there are limits on what you can do, and to spend time on lower-value tasks is not to spend that time on higher-value tasks. And therefore, by definition, you will be less effective. Conversely, if you choose to spend your time on higher-value tasks *instead of* lower-value tasks, then you are on to something.

More specifically, Peter Drucker gives two fundamental reasons why we have to prioritize. Let's take a look at his quote again: "If there is any 'secret' of effectiveness, it is concentration. Effective executives do first things first and they do one thing at a time."

Look at how he defines concentration: *doing one thing at a time*, and making sure that the one thing you do is a "first thing." There is the concept of prioritizing: doing a very important thing (a "first thing") and doing that one thing only, "one thing at a time."

By saying effective people "do one thing at a time," Drucker isn't chiefly speaking against multitasking during the day, such as checking text messages while writing a report (though he would have much to say against that). Rather, he's speaking of high-level priorities, of how many large projects and responsibilities you have going on at once. He's saying that you have to do only one of those at a time.

Why?

The first reason is because of the nature of work itself. Drucker writes that "there are always more important contributions to make than there is time available to make them."[5] In other words, no matter how well you can manage your time, you will always have more to do than you can accomplish. You will *always* have a time deficit. So you have to focus—concentrate, exclude, prioritize.

The second reason for doing one thing at a time is because of human nature: we simply do not have the capacity to focus on more than two things at once. Some people do better work with two tasks in parallel because doing two projects provides a change of pace. But "few people," Drucker notes, "can perform with excellence three major tasks simultaneously."[6] Drucker points out that the only known exception to this is Mozart. The other great composers, such as Bach, Handel, and others, composed only one major work at a time. They began the next only when they had finished their current one or had stopped work on it for a time.

If you try to do three or more large tasks at once, you will never have the minimum time quantity for any of them because important work requires continuous chunks of time. Having the same amount of time totaled up through smaller chunks does not work because there are some things that cannot happen unless at least two hours are given to them at once. Focusing on everything scatters your powers, and so you get less done even though you are trying to do more.

WHAT THE LATEST RESEARCH SHOWS

The latest research confirms what we have seen. I really enjoy Charles Duhigg's *Smarter Faster Better: The Secrets of Being Productive in Life and Business* because he looks deeply at what science shows us about productivity. In his chapter on focus, he discusses a study of the most productive people at a midsized recruiting firm.

One of the things that stood out in the study was that the most productive workers worked on far fewer projects than the others. This is surprising because you would expect them to be working on more projects at once (thus making them more productive—doing more faster). Instead, the most productive workers tended to have only five projects at once, whereas the others tended to have ten or twelve at once. Nonetheless, the employees with more projects at once "had a lower profit rate than the superstars, who were more careful about how they invested their time."[7]

Further, the most productive workers weren't choosing easy projects—projects that only leveraged existing skills and that they could do really fast. Instead, they chose projects that demanded that they learn new abilities and develop new networks.

"That's why the superstars worked on only five projects at a time: Meeting new people and learning new skills takes a lot of additional hours."[8] In other words, they choose fewer projects so that they could do them better. And this showed up in the company's bottom line. By prioritizing, they made a bigger impact.

THE CONSEQUENCES OF NOT SETTING PRIORITIES

And so we have seen why, without setting priorities, you ultimately get stuck. You get stuck because you become busy but not productive. You are busy because you are doing so many things. But you aren't productive because you are "making a millimeter of progress in a million directions,"[9] and you are majoring on minor things.

Instead, you should get more done by doing *fewer things of higher impact* than by doing *more things of lower value.* And so you need to "stop doing some things and start spending more time on the few activities that can really make a difference in your life."[10] As McKeown says so well, "Only once you give yourself permission to stop trying to do it all, to stop saying yes to everyone, can you make your highest contribution toward the things that really matter."[11]

HOW YOU REALLY STICK TO THIS:
Beyond Priorities to *Posteriorities*

Because of the centrality of priorities, we might think that once we set priorities, that is enough. Unfortunately, that is not the case!

Our priority decisions will be challenged. The environment (and sometimes our own tendencies) will constantly try to pull us away from our priorities. This means that "the job, however, is not to set priorities. That is easy. Everybody can do it. The reason why so few executives concentrate is the difficulty of setting 'posteriorities'— that is, deciding what tasks not to tackle—and of sticking to the decision."[12]

And so setting priorities must be complemented with the flip side of the coin, and the real challenge: setting posteriorities. That is how you stay with your priority decisions—you say no to things outside of them instead of doing a little of everything. That is why we can see that the core principle of effectiveness is, in a sense, exclusion. For it is by excluding things that you are able to stick with your priority decisions.

And then, within your priority decisions, you fully commit and give them all the resources they need to thrive. You don't skimp once you have taken something on as a priority. Exclusion is as important as selection; indeed, they imply each other. For to focus on the one main thing means that you do not do the things that are outside of its scope.

Why do most people not set posteriorities? First, it is risky because what you postpone often ends up being abandoned altogether. Second, it is unpleasant because "every posteriority is somebody else's top priority." And so we often try to hedge by "trying to do 'just a little bit' of everything else as well." This makes everyone happy, but "nothing whatever gets done."[13]

THE RESULT OF RADICAL EXCLUSION

What is the result of concentration? You will get more done, and faster. As Drucker notes, "Concentration is necessary precisely because the executive faces so many tasks clamoring to be done. For doing one thing at a time means doing it fast. The more one can concentrate time, effort, and resources, the greater the number and diversity of tasks one can actually perform."[14] On the other hand, you can't be successful when you splinter your resources among too many initiatives.

And so excluding doesn't result in getting less done. By doing the first thing all the way to completion, and then moving on to the next first thing, you build a large chain of progress that accomplishes far more of the things you want to do than if you tried to do them all at once.

HOW TO DETERMINE YOUR PRIORITIES

Now, how do we determine our priorities? There are a few principles and a process you can use. But first, an important question.

How Many Priorities?

To choose our priorities, we need to know how many to choose. And we have already seen the answer above. Drucker's observation has proven true in my experience: most of us can only effectively do at most two large things at once.

Choosing one major responsibility area of your job and one major goal at a time is what it means to concentrate at the level of priorities. This may sound very risky—and even unrealistic!—at first. However, note that this does not mean that these two things are the only things you are doing. Remember how in chapter 11 we sought to identify fifteen hours a week for top-priority tasks. That's about the amount of time we consolidated because that's the amount we can realistically expect to have full control over in our jobs.

So it is in fifteen hours a week that you work exclusively on your two top priorities. With the rest of your time, you will be doing other things—many things—so other things will get done. In Duhigg's example, the effective people tended to have five projects. They were still limited (they weren't trying to do fifteen like the others), but having five projects certainly does sound like having more than two priorities. They were able to do five projects, however, because they were doing their two top priorities in the specified fifteen hours of "priority time."

So, in sum, I am assuming that you aren't able to put all forty (or however many) hours of your workweek under your control, but that about twenty-five hours a week are devoted to other things. Then you devote the fifteen hours a week that are under your control to one or two large priorities.

Principles for Choosing Priorities

Your priorities are the things through which you can make the greatest contribution. Thus, to determine your priorities means to determine where your highest points of contribution are. Along with your strengths, there are some principles that can help you identify your priorities. No one has surpassed the principles Drucker articulated for choosing priorities.

1. Pick the future against the past.
2. Focus on opportunity rather than problem.
3. Choose your own direction—rather than climb on the bandwagon.
4. Aim high, for something that will make a difference rather than something that is "safe" and easy to do. [15]

The Process for Determining Priorities
EXPLORE

The key to making good priority decisions is to first "explore and evaluate a broad set of options before committing to any." Because you are going to "commit and 'go big' on only the vital few ideas or activities," you need to explore more options than most people do (who do not prioritize) so that you will be able to pick the right one.[16]

In *Essentialism* McKeown outlines five things that assist this step of exploration: allowing space to think, taking time to observe, making time to play, getting enough sleep, and then applying highly selective criteria.[17] While many people might see these things as low priorities or luxuries, they are actually essential because they enable your capacity to make good choices. We saw earlier that central to true productivity is valuing the development of *productive capacity* as well as direct results themselves, and that's what these activities do.

As McKeown says, "Essentialists spend as much time as possible exploring, listening, debating, questioning, and thinking. But their exploration is not an end in itself. The purpose of the exploration is to discern the vital few from the trivial many."[18]

This is something, of course, that needs to have taken place over a period of time, before you get to this point.

IDENTIFY THE CATEGORIES OF YOUR JOB

For each of your roles, you can identify the main responsibilities.[19] You need to do that to have a full picture. Then you need to determine the most important responsibilities and slot them into your calendar in the time you've consolidated.

RECALL YOUR GOALS

Your priorities need to derive from and reflect your goals, so make sure to review your goals. (Note: you may also find that you have too many goals!)

SELECT TWO PRIORITIES

Now it's time to select. You have the big picture; now apply radical selection and determine the top two large things that will make the biggest difference.

EXCLUDE EVERYTHING ELSE.

Then let the other stuff go. One way to help identify these things and feel good about letting them go is to ask, "If we didn't already do this, would we go into this *now*?"

One of the big reasons we don't get moving on our priorities is because we are overloaded with what Drucker calls "the tasks of yesterday."[20] Many of these programs and activities have outlived their useful life and have ceased to be productive. And so one of the biggest time wasters are old tasks you keep doing just because you are already doing them.

WHAT TO DO WITH YOUR PRIORITIES

To translate your priorities into action, you need to record them in a place that enables you to see them, and to see them in the context of the big picture. To do this, I recommend creating a time leverage chart.

Creating a Time Leverage Chart

A time leverage chart has four simple columns. From left to right, they include the following:

1. The five to seven responsibility areas of your job and top current goal
2. A brief statement of what success looks like in that area
3. The percentage of your time required to reach your goal, stated also in terms of hours
4. The key activities for making your goal happen

Responsibilities	Success	Time (hrs.)	Activities
• • • • •			• • • • •

For readers of *What's Best Next*, this is similar to the role map I outlined in chapter 13, but it extends the concept further because it contains time estimates that allow you to see the responsibilities and tasks for your work in relation to their time commitments.

Put your two priorities—I recommend one responsibility area and then your current goal for the second—in bold.

Now it's time to allocate your time to them. You want to allocate 40 percent of your time to them. For our purposes here, I will assume a forty-hour workweek. This means sixteen hours.

Does this mean that twenty-four hours go to the other categories? If so, it seems that this can easily undo your priority focus. Instead, while the workweek is forty hours, allocate only thirty hours' worth to leave room for flexibility. That means allocating fourteen hours between the other categories.

Now you have a picture of your two priorities in the context of the whole, with a specific time allocation.

Creating a Time Map

A time leverage chart is helpful, but it is not enough. You also need to translate your priorities into your schedule—actually allocate your time to them.

Doing this utilizes and builds on the concept of a time map, which I discuss in chapter 14 of *What's Best Next*, "Setting Up Your Week." Specifically, having your priorities defined allows you to have a more specific, targeted, and accurate time map. Slot your priorities into specific time slots on your time map. This forces you to carve out the time for your priorities rather than leaving them simply at the level of good intentions. I recommend a three-hour uninterrupted block each day for your priorities. Note two things about that.

First, I recommend spending time on your priorities each day. One time I did this by putting one of my priorities into my time map for once a week—every Monday night. (I tried to do this priority in just three to four hours a week.) I found that this was detrimental because every week I needed extra time to clear the cobwebs and remember where I was. This project was also a lot more vulnerable to being skipped since it only had one slot a week.

By having your priorities in your schedule *each day*, it isn't as big of a deal if one block has to be skipped, and you won't have to spend as much time remembering where you were and getting ramped back up since it will have only been since the previous day that you last worked on it.

Progressing with Your Priorities

In the way I am defining them here, your priorities are big projects that you are completing. And so your priorities will be continually changing as each project is completed. You progress with your priorities by doing one (in this case, two) at a time. Focus on the priority until it's done, and then do the next. Then the next. That's how you get that thing done *and* a lot of other things done as well. Each time you complete a priority, instead of simply going to the next one you've been wanting to get to, reevaluate, because circumstances change.

Progressing in this manner should help to allay the fear that concentrating on one thing will mean that the other things won't get done at all. Sometimes that happens, but in general, focusing on one thing at a time is the only way to get many things done. Concentrating enables you to do more and do it better.

Two Examples

We will conclude with two examples to crystalize this concept.

When Harry S. Truman took over as president, he realized that his top priority had to be foreign affairs, so he organized his day around this priority. The start of his day consisted of tutorials on foreign policy from his secretary of state and secretary of defense. What was the result? He became one of the most effective US presidents in foreign affairs we have ever seen.

Truman's practice is an example of what I mean by acting on the basis of priorities—organizing your time around your top one or two responsibilities or initiatives and making them the cornerstone of your calendar.

Peter Drucker tells the story of the CEO of a pharmaceutical company who accomplished more than any CEO he had ever known. The company was small and in one country when this man became CEO; eleven years later when he retired, it was a worldwide leader. To get it to that point, this man didn't try to do everything at once. Instead, he worked in three priority phases: research direction for the first years to make the company strong, then building the company internationally, and then working out what their strategy should be in light of the fast-happening changes in the healthcare industry.

Drucker writes, "It is unusual for any one chief executive to do one task of such magnitude during his entire tenure. Yet this man did three—in addition to building a strong, well-staffed, worldwide organization. He did this by single-minded concentration on one task at a time."[21]

This is an example of what I mean by setting priorities and doing them one at a time. By lending your entire focus to one or two priorities at a time, working on them until they are completed, and then moving on to the next, you accomplish many things— often very important and difficult things that you could not have accomplished otherwise. Things that count, make a difference, and move the world forward.

THE UNSTUCK CLINIC

Core Point

It is not enough to decide what you *will* do. To truly make those things happen, you need to decide what you *won't* do.

Exercise

Create a "stop doing" list.

Further Resources

- Stephen R. Covey, A. Roger Merrill, and Rebecca R. Merrill, "The Clock and the Compass," in *First Things First*
- Peter Drucker, "First Things First," in *The Effective Executive: The Definitive Guide to Getting the Right Things Done*
- Greg McKeown, *Essentialism: The Disciplined Pursuit of Less*

CHAPTER 13

DEEP WORK, PART 1

The New Superpower of Knowledge Work

Introducing the new superpower
of the knowledge economy

While the link between attention and excellence remains hidden most of the time, it ripples through almost everything we seek to accomplish.

DANIEL GOLEMAN[1]

Peter Drucker said, "If there is one 'secret' of effectiveness, it is concentration."[2] Concentration means focus. As we've seen, we first need to focus our *time* because the most important work requires large, continuous stretches of time. Then we need to focus our *tasks* because not everything is going to fit into our time. Now we are going to see how we need to focus our *attention* so we can work with the highest possible intensity on the tasks we've selected to do in the time we have.

In other words, we don't just manage our time to maximize the amount of time spent on important tasks; we maximize the amount of time we can spend on important tasks *in a state of high focus*. Protecting our time is not enough; we also have to protect the mental focus to get things done, for we don't just have limited time; we have limited brainpower. Because our cognitive capacity has limits, we need to make the most of our limited capacity by focusing it on the task at hand in a state of high concentration. This is called "deep work," and it is the new superpower for the knowledge era. It is the opposite of being stuck because it is doing work in a state of *flow*.

The state of flow, however, can be hard to get into. Sometimes it seems random and subject to unpredictable inspiration, delivering inconsistent results. But it doesn't have to be that way—you can bring the power of flow more under your control so that you can utilize it almost on command.

This chapter is about how to get into the flow and bring it under your control so that you can utilize it as a regular approach to your work. It is about taking the time you've consolidated and maximizing your focus during that time so that you get better results in less time.

Deep work is not only a superpower for getting more high-quality work done in less time; it will also make you stand out because most people can't engage in deep work. Unfortunately, there are also obstacles to engaging in deep work because the behaviors required to do deep work don't usually produce short-term rewards. To resist these obstacles, we need to understand in more detail what deep work really is, why it matters so much, and how to do it. And we need to understand just how different it is from how most people work.

HOW DO MOST PEOPLE WORK?

Many people confuse being busy with being productive. They think someone is productive if they are doing a lot of tasks, especially if they respond quickly to requests. Conversely, if someone is *not* responding quickly and tends to do fewer tasks, they are thought of as less productive.

While I affirm the benefit of quick responses and accomplishing a lot, this way of thinking easily gets taken to the extreme. In some organizations, looking busy is nearly as important as getting great results. People walk fast, check their email while waiting for the elevator, and work late because they need to be *seen* as productive, and being seen as productive is as important to their job security as actually being productive.

Further, now that we are constantly technologically connected, we have requests coming to us at all times and in all places, and more of them. We can easily come to think we are productive if we are responding in a timely manner to all of these texts and emails and phone calls because it *feels* productive—we are getting immediate feedback and results, it seems—and *looks* productive.

But what if the behaviors involved in constant connectivity and looking productive actually undermine real productivity? If you feel worn out by this way of working, I have good news: you don't have to do it this way. And if you enjoy this way of working, I concede that not every aspect of it is bad, but I commend to you a more productive way that involves reversing your mind-set from "reactive work first" to "deep work first."

UNDERSTANDING THE PRODUCTIVITY EQUATION

How does productivity happen? We can illustrate it through a simple equation that I first encountered in Cal Newport's excellent book for college students, *How to be a Straight A Student*, and which he expounded on more fully in his more recent book *Deep Work*.

The productivity equation is this:

high quality work produced = time spent × intensity of focus

The Power of Focused Attention

We see here that a relationship exists between the time we spend and how focused we are. Most of us recognize this intuitively, and contemporary research is confirming it. For example, Daniel Goleman writes in *Focus: The Hidden Driver of Excellence*:

> In very recent years the science of attention has blossomed far beyond vigilance. That science tells us that these skills determine how well we perform any task. If they are stunted, we do poorly; if muscular, we can excel. Our very nimbleness

in life depends on this subtle faculty. While the link between attention and excellence remains hidden most of the time, it ripples through almost everything we seek to accomplish.[3]

If you work with a low degree of focus, you will have to work a much longer time to get the same results. Conversely, if you work with a high degree of focus, you can do the same amount of work in much less time. Hence, if you want to get your projects and tasks done more quickly and with greater quality, then you need to work with greater focus. If desired, you can use the extra time you've freed up to get more done, or do other things that enhance the quality of your work and quality of life.

The Flow State

To do things with greater focus is to do them in the flow state. The results of working in the flow state are not small. As the classic work on flow and getting into the zone says: "A person who experiences flow in an activity will end up with a product that others will find more valuable."[4]

Flow is the opposite of being stuck. It is being totally absorbed in a task with everything moving as it should be. You feel alert, strong, and at the peak of your abilities, and the task feels almost effortless. Your sense of time disappears. You are working deeply and efficiently, and your work is highly fulfilling. You are in a state of full concentration and deep enjoyment.

Flow stands in contrast to frazzle, which is a great description of what being stuck often feels like. Workers in a state of frazzle experience "constant stress [that] overloads their nervous system with floods of cortisol and adrenaline. Their attention fixates on their worries, not their job. This emotional exhaustion can lead to burnout."[5]

Flow is the "optimal brain state for getting work done well." It is marked by great "neural harmony—a rich, well-timed interconnection among diverse brain areas." In the state of flow the brain is "precisely attuned to the demands of the moment." Consequently, "when our brains are in this zone we are more likely to perform at our personal best whatever our pursuit."[6]

More than this, flow is not simply a tool for getting more and better work done. It is an essential component of a fulfilling life. For when you are in a state of flow, the activity is its own reward. According to Csikszentmihalyi's research, "The highest, most satisfying experiences in people's lives were when they were in flow."[7] If we are going to live truly flourishing lives and not be stuck, then it is important not just for results, but for its own sake, that we experience flow in our work—since work is where we spend the bulk of our time. Yet, only 20 percent of people get in the zone at least once a day.[8]

HOW DO YOU GET IN THE ZONE?

The flow state does not have to be left to chance. You can have control over it and *make use of it every day*. How do you get into the zone, or a state of flow? There are two chief conditions for getting into the zone.

A Challenge That Is Just Right for Your Skills

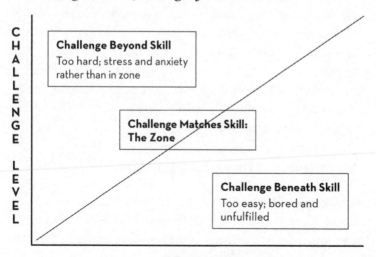

The core idea is that the state of flow happens when we are involved in challenges that are neither too difficult nor too simple. It is "a just-manageable demand on our skills."[9]

When a task is too difficult, you get anxious. When it is too easy, you get bored. But when the task is a just-right challenge, just slightly beyond your ability so that it is a stretch but not too much of a stretch, the result is full focus and a state of flow.

Clear Goals with Immediate Feedback

As Dan Pink writes, "In flow, goals are clear. You have to reach the top of the mountain, hit the ball across the net, or mold the clay just right. Feedback is immediate. The mountaintop gets closer or farther, the ball sails in or out of bounds, the pot you're throwing comes out smooth or uneven."[10] If the goal is not clear, you have confusion and not flow; likewise, if you can't see progress happening, the sense of momentum that is such a part of flow does not materialize.

Flow is common in sports because the goals are clear and players see results as they go. But the flow state isn't limited to sports; the highest performers in every area of life experience it. To move toward a state of flow in your work, define clearly what the specific goals are for the task you are doing—what success looks like. And set up the task in such a way that you can see your progress as it happens. In particular, this means observing what is working and isn't working in how you do the task, and making decisions to take actions that you think will improve things. See what effect those have, and keep progressing in this way.

IS GETTING IN THE ZONE ENOUGH?

Getting in the zone is crucial for high performance. But it is not enough because, as Daniel Pink points out, the zone is about right now, whereas mastery requires sustained effort over time. And the effort required to gain mastery is not always going to be carried out in the zone. Grit—willingness to endure through hard tasks, fueled by passion—is essential to mastery.

We see both of these aspects in Scripture. First Corinthians 15:58 is the key verse of this book and, interestingly, actually alludes to getting in the zone. Paul tells us to "be steadfast, immovable, always *abounding* in the work of the Lord" (emphasis added). We see being in the zone in the word "abounding," which includes being energized, flourishing, being wholehearted, and even in some measure being in the zone. It is to be engaged, doing what we do from the heart and with full attention, not simply because we have to (cf. Eph. 6:6). This is a crucial part of what it means to be unstuck—to be motivated, engaged, and making progress with joy on the right goals.

God wants us to experience this "abounding," yet note that Paul describes what we do as "labor," for he continues: "knowing that in the Lord your labor is not in vain." As one commentator points out, Paul's use of this word calls attention to the fact that some of the things we do will be burdensome. They will be difficult, highly challenging, even arduous, and likely not carried out in the zone.

So while the Scriptures affirm the importance of what modern research has classified as flow, just like that same research, they also recognize that not all of our work will be carried out in that state. Yet what the Scriptures do affirm without reservation is being wholehearted in our work, giving it our full effort.

And that brings us back to the issue of *focus*—that is, full attention. Focus often brings us into the zone but is also possible when we are not in the zone. It leads us to the broader concept of how to make the most of the time we've consolidated to work on our priority tasks by harnessing the power of our full attention. This is a concept Cal Newport has labeled "deep work," and it is rapidly becoming an essential operational style.

DEEP WORK

Deep work is the practice of focusing "without distraction on a cognitively demanding task."[11] Or, as Newport puts it in a bit more detail, deep work is when you perform professional activities "in a state of distraction-free concentration that push your cognitive capacities to their limit."[12]

Deep work, in other words, is right in line with what we have seen about the importance of consolidating your time. Instead of working in a way that allows for constant interruptions and engages our attention at a partial level, we focus *entirely and without distraction* on the work that we are doing for an extended period of time.

We work fully while we are working, rather than engaging in pseudo-work where we are dividing our attention between the task at hand and interruptions that come our way or distractions such as social media. We give uninterrupted, entirely focused concentration to cognitively demanding tasks. Deep work is highly valuable because "these efforts create new value, improve your skill, and are hard to replicate."[13]

Deep work includes *deliberately harnessing the benefits of flow* in your work life by making it a regular practice, yet you also continue your focus and concentration even when you are not in a state of flow.

The opposite of deep work is shallow work: "noncognitively demanding, logistical-style tasks, often performed while distracted. These efforts tend to not create much new value in the world and are easy to replicate."[14] The unfortunate thing is that many of us operate in a state of shallow work most of the time, and our environment is ever more pressuring us in this direction.

Deep work is the way to apply the productivity equation most effectively to your work. It means giving total focus to your work so that you can therefore get more done in less time, rather than working in a less focused way that therefore takes more time.

How do you get into the state of deep work? We have already seen a bit about how to get into the zone. The other thing we need to know is how to fit deep work into your schedule. That's the next chapter.

THE UNSTUCK CLINIC

Core Point

High quality work produced = time spent × intensity of focus.

So to get more done in less time, increase your focus by using deep work.

Exercise

Reflect on these questions:

1. When is the last time you recall engaging in deep work?
2. How did you feel?
3. What are some ways you could create more time for deep work in your schedule?

Further Resources

- David Allen, "GTD and Cognitive Science," in *Getting Things Done: The Art of Stress-Free Productivity* (2015 ed.)
- Mihaly Csikszentmihalyi, *Flow: The Psychology of Optimal Experience*
- Daniel Goleman, *Focus: The Hidden Driver of Excellence*
- Cal Newport, *Deep Work: Rules for Focused Success in a Distracted World*
- Daniel H. Pink, "Mastery," in *Drive: The Surprising Truth about What Motivates Us*

CHAPTER 14

DEEP WORK, PART 2

Put Deep Work into Your Schedule and Overcome Distractions

How brain science helps us get in
the zone and keep our focus

---

*The ability to concentrate intensely is a skill that must
be trained.*

CAL NEWPORT[1]

al Newport asks, "Once you accept that deep work is valuable,
isn't it enough to just start doing more of it?"[2]

The answer is no. The reason is that the environment *and our
own tendencies* fight against doing more deep work. Consequently,
just starting to do it won't work. You have to put strategies and
mechanisms in place to make it a habit you stick with. You need
to train yourself for deep work and build your capacity to do it.
Newport writes, "Just as a basketball player making a free throw
on a rival team's court has to train his body to perform despite the
screaming crowd, creative minds must learn to train their attention
and marshal their creative energies under the most chaotic circumstances."[3] The good news is that it is possible to train yourself to be
better at deep work. Here are three strategies that will enable you to
build your capacity for deep work.

STRATEGY #1: Put Deep Work into Your Schedule

You must protect time for deep work. If you don't put deep work into your schedule, it won't happen.

But there isn't just one way to do this. Newport says, "You need your own philosophy for integrating deep work into your professional life."[4] There are four main approaches you can take to deep work, and you need to pick the one that is best suited to your preferences and your environment. (Those who fear that deep work might mean working alone on individual tasks all day will find the third and fourth approaches liberating and refreshing!)

Monk

The monk approach is the simplest—and is also the rarest, the most radical, and the hardest to do. It is not for everyone. In this approach you almost exclusively do deep work. You aren't totally cutting yourself off from the world, but activities other than deep work are batched into perhaps one day a month. This is for people whose professional success comes from doing just one thing exceptionally well, such as writing novels. Someone with this philosophy might say, "All of my time and attention are spoken for—several times over. Please do not ask for them."

Bimodal

For those who cannot handle the monk approach, the bimodal approach allows you to integrate deep work with more ordinary activities through an approach that is analogous to taking retreats.

You don't have to literally take a retreat. What you do is have a period of time, say a week or month, engaged in interactive, give-and-take activities. Then you transition to a period of time, say a week or month, where you focus exclusively on deep work activities. In other words, you set aside clearly defined stretches for deep pursuits, and then the rest of the time you are open to everything else.

This is the approach taken by Swiss psychiatrist and psychoanalyst Carl Jung, who ran a busy practice seeing patients. He would often retreat to his cabin in the woods to focus on writing. This approach works well for those who have to (and want to) have open time to respond to what comes their way, without letting that eliminate their ability to engage in deep work. As Newport summarizes this approach in relation to Jung, he says, "[Jung] needed his clinical practice to pay the bills and the Zurich coffeehouse scene to stimulate his thinking." His life in Zurich was much like "the hyperconnected digital-age knowledge worker."[5] But his retreats to write and refine his thinking enabled him to produce the articles and books needed to establish his analytical psychology school of thought and become one of the most influential thinkers of the twentieth century.

You can do the bimodal approach at several levels. On a smaller scale, you might devote two days a week to open activities and three days a week to deep work. Or on a larger scale, you might devote a season of several months to deep work (which can work well if you are an academic). Newport points out that, in this approach, the shortest period of time needed to "reach maximum cognitive intensity—the state in which real breakthroughs occur" is one full day.[6]

Many people might be concerned about becoming inaccessible even for just a day. But in an experiment by Leslie Perlow with management consultants, it was found that though the consultants thought the clients would be very frustrated if they disconnected for a full day, it turned out that this did not matter to the client. Newport makes a good inference that Perlow's research, along with his examples like Jung and, in more recent times, Adam Grant, show that "people will usually respect your right to become inaccessible if these periods are well defined and well-advertised, and outside these stretches, you're once again easy to find."[7]

Rhythmic

In the rhythmic approach, instead of planning seasons for deep work, you make deep work a part of your routine every day.

This way you don't have to think about when you will go deep in a bimodal retreat or set of days.

Newport gives the example of Brian Chappell, a PhD student who also works full-time. He would start every day at 5:30 a.m. working on his dissertation until 7:30 a.m. Then he would go about the rest of his day with his dissertation obligations completed. He described this as "both astronomically productive and guilt free."[8]

In this approach you don't necessarily get the most intense levels of deep thinking that come from day-long concentration sessions, but it does fit the reality of human nature very well. Newport writes, "By supporting deep work with rock-solid routines that make sure a little bit gets done on a regular basis, the rhythmic scheduler will often log a larger total number of deep hours per year."[9]

Jonathan Edwards used a variation of this approach. Technically, he seemed to have utilized something close to a monk approach, working in his study most days and doing pastoral visits only in cases of extreme need. But within this approach, he divided up the way he used his deep work time among his various demands. One of his earliest biographers says that his method of distributing his time was central to his effectiveness:

> [Because of Edwards's] uniform of regularity and self-denial, and the force of habit, the powers of his mind were always at his command, and would do their prescribed task in the time appointed. This enabled him to assign the preparation of his sermons, each week, to given days, and specific subjects of investigation to other given days; . . . It was rare, indeed, that he failed of accomplishing every part of his weekly task, or that he was pressed for time in the accomplishment.
>
> So exact was the distribution of his time and so perfect the command of his mental powers, that in addition to his preparation of two discourses in each week, his stated and occasional lectures, and his customary pastoral duties, he continued regularly his "Notes on the Scriptures," his

"Miscellanies," his "Types of the Messiah," and a work which
he soon commenced, entitled, "Prophecies of the Messiah in
the Old Testament, and their Fulfillment."[10]

The rhythmic approach works especially well because, by
making deep work a daily habit, it becomes almost automatic. This
is especially great for the self-employed and others who have to
almost entirely run their own schedules, as it makes it easier to stick
to your intentions. It also works well for those in jobs (most jobs,
unfortunately—but not all!) that "don't allow you to disappear for
days at a time when the need to go deep arises," in Newport's words.[11]

Journalistic

The journalistic approach does not involve extended seasons
like the monk or bimodal approaches, and neither does it utilize
the simplicity of making deep work a daily routine. Instead, on this
approach you just fit deep work into your day wherever you see the
opportunity.

This is the approach that Walter Isaacson used to write his
first book, *The Wise Men: Six Friends and the World They Made*.
Newport's uncle happened to share a summer beach rental with
Isaacson when he was writing this book, and noted that "anytime
he could find some free time, he would switch into a deep work
mode and hammer away at his book."[12]

The name for this approach comes from the fact that journal-
ists are "trained to shift into a writing mode on a moment's notice,
as is required by the deadline-driven nature of their profession."[13]

Newport notes that "this approach is not for the deep work nov-
ice.... The ability to rapidly switch your mind from shallow to deep
mode doesn't come naturally. Without practice, such switches can
seriously deplete your finite willpower reserves."[14] For this approach
to work, you need to have your professional skills firmly in place.

This is also the approach that Newport himself uses. He says,
"I face each week as it arrives and do my best to squeeze out as much

depth as possible." This doesn't mean deciding in the moment when he will work deep. Rather, at the beginning of the week he maps out when he plans to work deeply, and refines that at the beginning of each day.

STRATEGY #2: Protect Your Energy for Deep Work

Determining your schedule for deep work gets you started but will not be enough. Tony Schwartz is right that having time in your schedule for something is by no means a guarantee that you will bring sufficient energy to it.[15] That's why it's not enough to manage your time; even more significantly, you have to manage your energy. Three things here are especially important.

Do Creative Work First and Reactive Work Second

Reactive work responds to others; creative work originates new ideas and thoughts for projects. If you take the monk or bimodal approach to deep work, then the "creative work first" principle is already going to be in place automatically. But if you take the journalistic or rhythmic approach, doing creative work first and reactive work second is something you need to be intentional about.

When you start your day, you may be tempted to "clear the decks" before getting into a state of deep work. Mark McGuinness explains this very well in *Manage Your Day-to-Day*: "No one likes the feeling that other people are waiting—impatiently—for a response. At the beginning of the day, faced with an overflowing inbox, an array of voice mail messages, and the list of next steps from your last meeting, it's tempting to 'clear the decks' before you start your own work. When you're up-to-date, you tell yourself, it will be easier to focus."[16] But these tasks will tend to multiply. As you get them done, you'll see more things that need to get done or refined or improved. You'll find yourself on a self-perpetuating path. This is not bad in itself—it is a great way to get a lot done. The problem is that it is taking you away from your important but not urgent work.

Beyond that, McGuinness rightly points out: "The trouble with this approach is it means spending the best part of the day on *other people's priorities*. By the time you settle down to your own work, it could be mid-afternoon, when your energy dips and your brain slows."[17] And then the cycle repeats the next day. You get stuck in reactive workflow, failing to move forward the work that is *most* important for you to get done.

The solution is to reverse this order and do creative work first, and then the reactive work second. McGuinness testifies to the transformation this brought to his life: "I used to be a frustrated writer. Making this switch turned me into a productive writer. Now, I start the working day with several hours of writing. I never schedule meetings in the morning if I can avoid it. So whatever else happens, I always get my most important work done—and looking back, all of my biggest successes have been the result of making this simple change."[18]

This is also the approach that Stephen King takes to his writing. I don't think I've ever read a Stephen King fiction book, but a leadership coach I sometimes work with recommended his book *On Writing*. It is fantastic. King talks not only about how to write well, but also how to make the writing *process* work well for you. Regarding his own schedule, he writes, "My own schedule is pretty clear-cut. Mornings belong to whatever is new—the current composition. Afternoons are for naps and letters. Evenings are for reading, family, Red Sox games on TV, and any revisions that just cannot wait. Basically, mornings are my prime writing time."[19]

That's creative work first, reactive work second. And note that there is plenty of time left over for the reactive work, which does matter (and can be very energizing). The point is not to eliminate all reactive work, as if it doesn't matter. The point is to put it in its proper slot so that it can get done without causing you to compromise your other type of work—important but not urgent deep work activities.

If you take a journalistic approach to deep work, looking to slot deep work into your schedule wherever you can, I recommend making your first-thing, early morning slot be deep work activities for ninety minutes (a key length for achieving concentration). Then go about the rest of your day and slot in additional time for deep work as you can.

This takes discipline, but note that almost all of us have more freedom here than we might recognize. McGuinness rightly notes, "If you want to create something worthwhile with your life, you need to draw a line between the world's demands and your own ambitions. Yes, we all have bills to pay and obligations to satisfy. But for most of us there's a wide gray area between the have-tos and want-tos in our lives. If you're not careful, that area will fill up with e-mail, meetings, and the requests of others, leaving no room for the work *you* consider important."[20]

Take the space between the have-tos and want-tos and use it intentionally on the want-tos, using deep work to get them done well.

Four Hours of Deep Work per Day Is Enough

How much time should you—can you—spend engaged in deep work each day?

I would often make a mistake here, going for twelve to sixteen hours of deep work a day. I reasoned that since deep work is so crucial (I didn't call it that at the time, but that was the concept), then the more the better.

There were two problems with this. First, this approach was not in sync with a realistic energy capacity. As a result, I would often get into a planned marathon deep work session and be completely unable to accomplish what I was hoping. Sometimes it would feel like I was spinning my wheels all day. Was this Parkinson's Law exerting its full force? (Parkinson's Law is the notion that work expands to fill the time available.) That may have been part of it, combined with failing to set sufficiently small goals along the way during the day (see the next section). But more than that, the problem was simply that this goal was not realistic. You can work a sixteen-hour day if you then take time the next day (and probably two) to recharge. But you can't do it day after day.[21]

The second problem was that this approach was not in sync with my context. I had reactive work to do, which was also important and needed to get done. The result was that this work would build up, and then I'd feel overwhelmed by that huge pile when I would emerge from deep work to address it.

It is refreshing to remember that Drucker points out (as we saw earlier) that an executive is fortunate and able to be effective if he or she can just pull together two to three hours of time each day for focused work. That's just ten to fifteen hours per week. And you can accomplish an amazing amount of work—enough to be effective and accomplish your agenda.

And so my recommendation, in general, is to seek three to four hours per day of deep work. The rest can be used for meetings, administration, Facebook, or whatever else you want. And you will likely be able to be guilt-free in that time if you do your deep work first, knowing that you've accomplished your capacity for deep work for the day.

End Your Day at a Specific Time

Ending your day at a specific time is one of the most important ways to preserve your energy. It is also counterintuitive for many of us. Most of us think that if we keep working into the evening, we will get more done. We will get caught up on what we had to set aside because of a series of interruptions, or we can simply make greater progress on our goals.

The problem with this, however, manifests itself when we recall the productivity equation: high-quality work produced = time spent × level of intensity. To have that intensity, you need to protect your energy. And what happens to your energy when you work long hours and have an unbounded end to your workday?

It goes down. If you work longer tonight, you will likely have less energy for your work tomorrow. And if you work two, three, and four nights in a row, you certainly will have less energy the next days. Deep work requires deep concentration, and so it requires that you give yourself the time to replenish your mental energy reserves. This happens when you give yourself a *full stop* to your work at the end of each day.

Newport gives three very convincing reasons to have a definite end to your workday, doing no work after that point but rather taking the evenings completely off for your family and leisure time. The best thing is that these reasons are based on science and research. Having a definite end to your workday actually enables you to get more done—and with less stress and more time to enjoy the rest of what life has to offer.

Downtime Aids Insights

Dutch psychologist Ap Dijksterhuis's research showed that when making complex decisions with nonlinear factors, large amounts of information, and multiple constraints that are vague or even confusing, your unconscious mind—not your conscious mind—does a better job of untangling things. This is now known as unconscious thought theory (UTT).

Your conscience mind is necessary for decisions involving clearly defined rules and steps, but your unconscious mind has greater capacity for handling the more complex and ambiguous problems and decisions. How do you tap into this? Downtime. Downtime enables the ideas to incubate; your subconscious goes to work on them. By giving yourself a definite end to your workday, you enable this process to operate. The result is that you will likely get more work done, because when you shut down your workday you are "not necessarily reducing the amount of time you're engaged in productive work, but . . . instead diversifying the type of work you employ."[22]

A Decisive End to Your Workday Helps You Recharge

Scientific research on attention restoration theory (ART) proves that a decisive end to your workday helps you recharge your batteries for deep work. Concentration—which is the essence of doing deep work—requires directed attention, and our capacity for directed attention is limited. The result is that we have to develop our productivity strategies in light of this reality, which is called *attention fatigue*. If you do not take attention fatigue into account, you are developing your productivity approach in a way that is out of sync with reality, and which will therefore lead to lower productivity.

Attention restoration theory holds that we need time away from the use of directed attention to replenish our reserves. In particular it holds that time in nature improves our ability to concentrate. The reason is that nature involves stimuli that "invoke attention modestly, allowing focused-attention mechanisms a chance to replenish."[23]

Jonathan Edwards seemed to intuitively make application of this reality, as he frequently went horseback riding and took long walks in nature. A walk in nature is a good way to restore your attention reserves during the day, as the researchers found that even just fifty minutes in nature boosted the subjects' ability to concentrate.[24] The value of this research, of course, goes beyond the literal application of taking walks in nature to restore your concentration. The central issue is that your ability to concentrate is based on a capacity that you have in limited measure—but by taking a break from using it, you restore it.

Time away from work in the evening supplies restoration. Anything that gives you freedom from directed concentration enables you to recharge—making dinner (if you enjoy that!), engaging in conversation, listening to music, playing with your kids, and so forth.

But if you try to insert work in the midst of these activities, such as by checking email after dinner or trying to get back to work for a few hours after the kids go to bed, "you're robbing your directed attention centers of the uninterrupted rest they need for restoration. Even if these work dashes consume only a small amount of time, they prevent you from reaching the levels of deeper relaxation in which attention restoration can occur. Only the confidence that you're done with work until the next day can convince your brain to downshift to the level where it can begin to recharge for the next day to follow."[25] The result is that even if you take just a small amount of time to do some work at night, it might reduce the replenishment of your concentration capacity such that you get less work done the next day.[26]

A Hard End to Your Workday Forces You to Cut Waste and Be More Efficient

A hard end to your workday also forces you to find more efficient ways to work. If every day you postpone certain things on the thought that you can do them later that night, you will be less likely to make rigorous priority decisions about what you will do.

On the other hand, if you have decided that you will end your day by 5:30 (or 4:30 if you can), you then need to work backward to find ways to make the most of the time. You will determine what practices are necessary to stay within that constraint, and thus be more likely to limit your tasks to the truly important rather than allowing yourself to be consumed by the trivial.

Newport points out that according to conventional wisdom, this approach should fail. Many high-powered places of work, such as first-tier research institutions, Wall Street, and so forth, tend to have the mind-set that success requires working excessively (often twelve-hour days) and continually. This appears intuitive as well, since it seems logical to conclude that the longer you work, the more you will get done.

But when we look at productivity from the perspective of research and science, as opposed to simply our first-level intuitions, we find this idea to be mistaken. For it does not take energy levels and decision-making practices into account. Instead, the findings we have examined above show that working longer will not necessarily result in getting more done but may actually result in getting less done.

What an unfortunate thing that is, as not only are you getting less done, but by working so much, you are missing out on other important things, such as family and leisure time. The typical high-powered places of work would do well to reconsider their culture and approaches to work in light of these findings.[27]

Understanding these strategies has enabled me to feel good about not working all the time. I used to constantly feel the pressure to work because I had so much to do. This was not only stressful in itself, but any activity or commitment in my personal life began to feel like it was taking away from my work life, making me feel more behind and making ordinary daily activities feel like they imposed an extremely high cost.

STRATEGY #3: Fight Distractions by Understanding Brain Science

One of the biggest obstacles to deep work is distraction. American writer E. B. White is recorded as saying "Creation is in part merely the business of forgoing the great and small distractions." But forgoing distractions is hard, and our environment more and more *encourages* us to be distracted and *penalizes* us when we don't give in. Focus is an "underrated mental asset" in our current society.[28]

To overcome obstacles to undistracted focus, one of the most helpful tactics I've found is not just to avoid them, but rather to *understand* why they are so bad. That gives me the motivation and know-how to minimize them.

So why aren't all the distractions that come our way just to be considered small? Why can't you do just this one thing right now? Why can't you check email continually so that you can give an immediate response?

Because as Cal Newport has said so well, "the constant pin-prick of small things is not negligible." They may seem harmless in isolation "but aggregate to serious injury."[29] There are psychological reasons, demonstrated by scientific research and based in how we are designed, for why this is. We need to understand these reasons so that we are fully convinced of the importance of working without distraction and so that we have a ready response for those who annoyingly act as if their distractions won't make a difference.

Why Are Distractions So Bad?

Distractions and interruptions are two of the key things that get us stuck. Not only do they take us away from the important, but they also take us out of the ultra-productive state of concentration required for deep work. "The more distracted we are, the more shallow our reflections; likewise, the shorter our reflections, the more trivial they are likely to be."[30]

Why do distractions and interruptions have such a negative effect? It is encouraging to learn that there is scientific evidence behind what distractions do and why they have such a powerful effect. If we want to be most productive and engage in deep work, we have to avoid distractions and interruptions *completely* during this time, for distractions kill the flow state. Recall the "intensity" variable of the productivity equation. Distractions reduce the intensity with which you are working as well as the time you are working. The lost time should be the least of your worries. The big problem with distractions is that they reduce your focus and intensity of work—and this effect continues even after they are over, for you have to rediscover the flow you had before you were disturbed.

Two concepts help to explain the distraction problem.

ATTENTION RESIDUE

Most of us have experienced the basic reality that "it takes time to ease into a state of concentration."[31] So right away we can begin to see why interruptions and distractions hinder deep work—they prevent you from having the time it takes to get into a state of focus. This holds true even if the interruptions are very short. Let's say it takes twelve minutes to get into a state of focused concentration. If you have even a thirty-second distraction five minutes in and another forty-second distraction ten minutes in, you won't achieve your full concentration. A mere seventy seconds are having an out-sized effect on your productivity.

Interruptions don't simply eliminate this ramp you need to get into focus. They can also open a Pandora's box that keeps on giving. Glancing at an alarming email on a Saturday morning and having its implications haunt your thoughts all weekend is an example of an ongoing distraction. Or even opening your email to deal with just one item can easily lead to seeing another that you want to address, and then another, and then another. Researchers at Microsoft found that after an interruption, people tended to take *an additional twenty minutes* to get back into a task.[32] In other words, just one interruption often sets you on a trajectory into several other interruptions or distractions that take you away from the task for much longer than the initial interruption.

Besides the fact that one interruption often leads to a set of self-generated distractions, the fact that we have been interrupted may itself reduce our focus. This is due to a scientifically recognized reality called *attention residue*.

Cal Newport summarizes this concept: "When you switch from some Task A to another Task B, your attention doesn't immediately follow—a *residue* of your attention remains stuck thinking about the original task. This residue gets especially thick if your work on Task A was unbounded and of low intensity before you switched, but even if you finish Task A before moving on, your attention remains divided for a while."[33] The chief study on this, by Sophie Leroy of the University of Minnesota, showed that those who experienced attention residue performed more poorly on the next tasks.[34]

We can see from this study that staying focused on a single project for a long period of time is efficient and effective because doing so reduces the effects of attention residue. If, however, you change tasks frequently, going from one thing to the next, you experience the effects of attention residue, thus reducing the cognitive capacity you have for those tasks and therefore reducing your intensity. Once again we see the productivity equation proving true.

A study by a team at Central Connecticut State University led by Laura Bowman found that students who used instant messaging while reading a textbook "took about 25 percent longer to read the passage (not including the time spent on IM), compared with students who simply read."[35] As Gloria Mark, professor of informatics at University of California, Irvine, puts it, "An interruption, even if short, delays the total time required to complete a task by a significant fraction." So activities that you do not do with a single focus take longer—even *after* accounting for the time spent on the interruption. The only explanation for this is that the interruptions reduce your focus and thus make the time spent on the task less effective, in turn requiring more time.

The Zeigarnik Effect

The Zeigarnik effect describes "the ability of incomplete tasks to dominate our attention."[36] For example, if you stop a task right in the middle or have many open loops at the end of the day, the unresolved obligations in your mind will keep battling for your attention. This will deplete your energy and create a nagging feeling. To reduce the Zeigarnik effect, you don't have to complete all the tasks (which would be impossible), but instead just designate a plan for how you will complete them.

The Zeigarnik effect can also be positive: because incomplete tasks continue to pull at our attention, stopping in the middle of a task can actually aid memory. This is likely because of the importance of *rehearsal* to encoding something in memory. Because unfinished tasks continue to pull at your focus much more than completed tasks, your mind ends up rehearsing them, which results in better memory.

One of the best uses of this rehearsal effect is *spaced repetition* for things you have to learn. Many experiments show (though some have not reproduced this effect) that you learn something better if you deal with it over at least two sessions, as opposed to just one.

The Zeigarnik effect can also be utilized to fight procrastination. Since unfinished tasks pull at your attention, you are less likely to keep procrastinating once you have begun a task. Starting a task can be done in a very rudimentary way even if the task itself is not simple (which is why you are procrastinating).

However, when you have too many unfinished tasks pulling at you, the pulls overload your cognitive capacity and reduce your ability to focus.[37] This is related to the Ovsiankina effect, which is the inclination to resume an interrupted action.[38] Picking up the interrupted task again becomes a semi-need, even if you have no other incentive to complete it. As you have more interrupted tasks, your sense of stress increases.

The stress of dealing with multiple unfinished tasks reinforces the value of working on one thing at a time, and working to a complete stopping point before doing something else—even dealing with an interruption from your boss. "While it feels easy enough to put one task on hold to start another, studies like this are a reminder that we find it very difficult to let go of unfinished challenges. They continue to draw on our mental resources even after we think we've switched focus. What's more, attempting to ignore this mental tug drains us even further."[39] By working on one thing at a time and finding a stopping point, we achieve mental closure that allows us to have full energy for what's next.[40]

BUT WHAT ABOUT THE EXCEPTIONS?

Jack Dorsey cofounded Twitter. Cal Newport notes that Dorsey does not spend a lot of time in a state of deep work. He has management duties and believes in making himself serendipitously available. How do successful people like Dorsey thrive without deep work? How can someone be distracted yet do well?

Dorsey is an executive of a large company. For people in these types of jobs, going too far in controlling your time and scheduling can actually hinder your productivity. As John Kotter has noted in his excellent article "What Managers Really Do," interruptions are a large part of the *actual work* of many managers because they are opportunities for managing influence. As summarized in the Harvard Business Review Pocket Mentor book *Managing Time: Expert Solutions to Everyday Challenges*, "Managers who limit their interactions to orderly, focused meetings actually shut themselves off from vital information and relationships. Kotter shows how seemingly wasteful activities like chatting in hallways and having impromptu conversations and gatherings can in fact be remarkably efficient."[41] How can you make the most of these opportunities? Through three main things that Kotter points out: having a flexible agenda, developing broad informal networks, and by being "willing to respond opportunistically to the events around you—but within a clear framework that guides your decisions."[42]

So there are exceptions. But as a general principle, cultivate the habit of deep work and weave it into your schedule. You will find this to be a very powerful tool.

THE UNSTUCK CLINIC

Core Point

To make deep work happen, you need to intentionally work it into your schedule. Fortunately, there are four different approaches to making time for deep work that you can adapt to your specific context: monk mode, the bimodal approach, the rhythmic approach, and the journalistic approach.

Exercise

Reflect on these questions:

1. Have you utilized any of these approaches to deep work before (perhaps without knowing it)?
2. Which approach seems to best fit with the nature of your work?
3. What types of tasks is it best for you *not* to use deep work for?
4. Do you end your day at a definite point? What benefits have you seen when you've done this? What disadvantages have you experienced?

Further Resources

- Roy F. Baumeister, *Willpower: Rediscovering the Greatest Human Strength*
- Jocelyn Glei, ed., *Manage Your Day-to-Day: Build Your Routine, Find Your Focus, and Sharpen Your Creative Mind*
- Cal Newport, *Deep Work: Rules for Focused Success in a Distracted World*
- For authors, I highly recommend Stephen King, *On Writing*

CHAPTER 15

RENEWAL: The Power of Preaching to Yourself

How we develop productive capacity

Renewal is the principle—and the process—that empowers us to move on an upward spiral of growth and change, of continuous improvement.

STEPHEN COVEY[1]

Spend the afternoon. You can't take it with you.

ANNIE DILLARD[2]

One very simple but constantly overlooked reason we get stuck is this: we're tired.

We get tired physically. But we also get tired emotionally, socially, and even spiritually. We have to continually renew ourselves and grow in all four of these dimensions if we are going to stay sharp.

Renewal is about maintaining and developing our productive capacity. Would you run a car for twenty thousand miles without an oil change? Yet we do that sort of thing with ourselves all the time. As our productivity decreases and we become less sharp, we don't even notice it because we've become used to it. Further, renewal is more than just rest. Far more—as we will see.

Taking time for renewal can be hard. We feel as though we can just keep going and going. But taking time for renewal is an investment in productivity capacity. By increasing your capacity to produce, you end up producing more than if you had not taken that time. Beyond that, however, time for renewal is simply good and right in itself, for it is how we are designed.

THE FOUR AREAS OF RENEWAL

We need to renew ourselves in four areas. All four are essential because we are holistic beings. To renew ourselves in only one area but not the others will have negative effects. We need *balanced* renewal, which comes by addressing all four areas.[3] As we renew ourselves in one area, it will spill over and benefit the others because they are so closely interrelated.[4] The four fundamental needs are (1) physical, (2) mental, (3) social/emotional, and (4) spiritual.

Much has been written about physical renewal. New research is showing the central importance of sleep to our productivity. And the value of exercise has been known for a long time. Learning is a key component for mental renewal. Forming relationships and journaling are helpful tools for social/emotional renewal. But what I want to focus on in this chapter is an often neglected tool in the *spiritual* dimension of renewal.

THE CENTRALITY OF SPIRITUAL DISCIPLINES

The spiritual dimension is our relationship with God. It is having him at the center of our lives, getting to know him, and walking with him in life.

We walk with God in many ways—by doing all that we do in conscious reliance on him, praying without ceasing as we go through the day (1 Thess. 5:17), meditating on his Word (Ps. 1; John 15:7), and seeking to live according to justice and grace, trusting in his promises.

Beyond our ongoing life of communion with God, the *spiritual disciplines* are especially foundational. The two disciplines we tend to think of most are prayer and meditating on the Scriptures. These are indeed at the core. But interestingly, there are many more disciplines as well.

Don Whitney has a great discussion of multiple spiritual disciplines in *Spiritual Disciplines for the Christian Life*, including not just Scripture and prayer but also worship, evangelism, serving, stewardship, fasting, silence and solitude, journaling, and learning. I highly recommend his book, as well as David Mathis's *Habits of Grace: Enjoying Jesus through the Spiritual Disciplines*.[5]

One of the most important things you can do to grow in your faith and keep your spiritual life anchored is to spend thirty to sixty minutes every day praying and reading the Bible and reflecting on it. I have said much on this elsewhere, so I won't add to it here other than saying: do it.[6] I will, however, add two disciplines to the ones that Whitney lists.

PREACHING TO YOURSELF

The first additional discipline you should practice is preaching to yourself. When you are stuck in anxiety, hopelessness, or despair, this can be an extraordinary antidote for getting unstuck.

We see it in Psalm 43:5: "Why are you cast down, O my soul, and why are you in turmoil within me? Hope in God; for I shall again praise him, my salvation and my God."

Martyn Lloyd-Jones elaborates on this passage and what it means to preach to yourself in his book *Spiritual Depression: Its Causes and Its Cures*:

> Have you realized that most of your unhappiness in life is due to the fact that you are listening to yourself instead of talking to yourself? Take those thoughts that come to you the moment you wake up in the morning. You have not originated them, but they start talking to you, they bring back the problems of yesterday, etc.

Somebody is talking. Who is talking? Your self is talking to you. Now this man's treatment was this; instead of allowing this self to talk to him, he starts talking to himself. "Why art thou cast down, O my soul?" he asks. His soul had been depressing him, crushing him. So he stands up and says: "Self, listen for a moment, I will speak to you." . . .

The main art in the matter of spiritual living is to know how to handle yourself. You have to take yourself in hand, you have to address yourself, preach to yourself, question yourself. You must say to your soul: "Why art thou cast down"—what business have you to be disquieted?

You must turn on yourself, upbraid yourself, condemn yourself, exhort yourself, and say to yourself: "Hope thou in God"—instead of muttering in this depressed, unhappy way. And then you must go on to remind yourself of God, who God is, and what God is and what God has done, and what God has pledged Himself to do.

Then having done that, end on this great note: defy yourself, and defy other people, and defy the devil and the whole world, and say with this man: "I shall yet praise Him for the help of His countenance, who is also the health of my countenance and my God."[7]

Preaching to yourself is massively powerful for getting unstuck. It acknowledges that you don't have to be the victim of negative, anxious, self-defeating thoughts. You can stop listening to yourself and start preaching to yourself instead.

EDUCATING YOUR CONSCIENCE

The second often overlooked discipline that I want to highlight is educating your conscience. Your conscience functions along with your intuition to enable you to make decisions in the moment. The more your intuition is tuned and your conscience is educated, the better your decisions will be. You educate your conscience chiefly through Scripture. You observe God's commands and promises, reflect on your decisions and actions, and see how they align. Then you identify adjustments to make—things you need to stop doing and things you need to start doing.

This is especially important because Ephesians 5:7–17 teaches us that God does not typically whisper from heaven what decision we should make. He wants *us* to choose because that requires the growth of wisdom, maturity, and conscience. We are to choose on the basis of biblical principles and spiritual expedience. That is, where the Scriptures do not require a particular way of action, we are free to choose our own course on the basis of what seems best and our own desires.[8]

The process of choosing is not merely analytical; there is a discerning to it. This is what Ephesians 5:10 speaks of: *"Discern what is pleasing to the Lord"* (cf. Phil. 1:9–11; Col. 1:9–11). As we meditate on Scripture and get to know God better, our conscience and discernment are educated, and we become more able to make spiritually edifying decisions in the everyday.

THE UNSTUCK CLINIC

Core Point

You can't get everything done by sheer force of will. You also have to build capacity. Renewal is one of the key activities that builds that capacity. For spiritual renewal, two of the most powerful tools (beyond prayer and Scripture) are preaching to ourselves and educating our conscience.

Helpful Quote

"If we let our type A instincts take over, we will . . . be swallowed up whole. We will burn out too early. We need to be as strategic with ourselves as we are with our careers and our businesses. We need to pace ourselves, nurture ourselves, and give ourselves fuel to explore, thrive, and perform."—Greg McKeown[9]

Exercise

What are some of the areas of greatest anxiety for you? Which promises in the Scriptures address those anxieties?

Preach those promises to yourself!

Further Resources

- Stephen Covey, "Sharpen the Saw," in *The 7 Habits of Highly Effective People*
- Tim Keller, *Prayer: Experiencing Awe and Intimacy with God*
- Jim Loehr and Tony Schwartz, *The Power of Full Engagement: Managing Energy, Not Time, Is the Key to High Performance and Personal Renewal*
- David Mathis, *Habits of Grace: Enjoying Jesus through the Spiritual Disciplines*
- Greg McKeown, "Play: Embrace the Wisdom of Your Inner Child" and "Sleep: Protect the Asset," in *Essentialism: The Disciplined Pursuit of Less*
- Andy Naselli and J. D. Crowley, *Conscience: What It Is, How to Train It, and Loving Those Who Differ*
- Tom Rath, *Eat, Move, Sleep: How Small Choices Lead to Big Changes*
- Don Whitney, *Spiritual Disciplines of the Christian Life*

—— PART 4 ——

SPECIAL OBSTACLES

The Laser

Getting Unstuck from
Unexpected Circumstances

The last component of getting unstuck has to do with overcoming all the various unique and unexpected obstacles that come our way. This element is what I call "the laser" (or sometimes "the sledgehammer").

The list of unexpected obstacles (many of which can become routine) can be long. We are going to focus on six cross-functional skills that can help you with these specific obstacles. First we will look at a basic approach to getting unstuck from any problem you encounter. For in one sense, getting unstuck is a form of problem solving. Next we will summarize what an adaptive approach to time management looks like for occasions when our plans and schedules get thrown off by the unexpected. We will then look at building your willpower, organizing space, and getting projects unstuck. And finally we will examine leadership. These are areas most of us deal with and which we can use in many ways to get unstuck.

CHAPTER 16

A BASIC APPROACH TO GETTING UNSTUCK FROM PROBLEMS

To get unstuck from any problem, ask the following questions:

- What is the problem?
- Where do I want to be?
- If I have a hard time defining where I want to be, why is that?
- Why am I having the problem—that is, why am I stuck? What is in the way?
- What might help me?
- Who could provide some legitimate insight to help?

USING THE SCIENTIFIC METHOD TO GET UNSTUCK

Developing hypotheses and testing them can also be very powerful. Use the following scientific method:

1. Observe what is going on.
2. Create a hypothesis for why things are the way they are.
3. Make a prediction based on the hypothesis about what can change things.
4. Act.
5. Observe the results; refine the hypothesis and repeat.

SWITCH THINGS UP

Sometimes you just need to switch things up. Work hard on a problem, then step away for a bit. "When you're at the problem-solving stage or you need to generate new ideas, psychologists have shown that taking your mind off-task briefly can help your subconscious find links between disparate concepts."[1]

CHAPTER 17

TAKING AN ADAPTIVE TIME-MANAGEMENT APPROACH

Execution is especially plagued by two difficulties: many tasks overflow their boundaries, and unexpected things come up. Executing is about making your priorities happen in spite of these obstacles.

The unexpected should not be looked at as something rare. It should be built into the way we conceive of execution from the start. Hence, I advocate what I call *adaptive time management*, which draws its concepts from adaptive project management and agile approaches to technology projects.

THE ADAPTIVE APPROACH

You have to create a plan—both at the macro level and at the weekly level—but you also have to be able to adapt because things will happen that you cannot anticipate.

Beyond this, you have to be aware that some situations are *especially* unpredictable, with high uncertainty and high ambiguity. You have to take a different approach to such situations. Using the same management approach in all situations simply will not work. It's like using the same approach to white-water rafting as floating smoothly down a calm river.

Because project requirements differ, smart managers do not place their chief emphasis on being on schedule with large projects.

Such thinking is an outmoded and inaccurate approach to large projects with high ambiguity and uncertainty. The proper approach in these circumstances is to keep the focus first on *quality*. If the result isn't good, it doesn't matter whether the project is on time or within budget, so enable workers to have the flexibility to adapt to the unknown as they go along.

Many managers who prioritize timelines often treat unmet deadlines as personal failure on the part of the project manager and team. *Managing Projects Large and Small* perfectly captures the types of words that often come out of such managers' mouths (which I myself have heard): "You agreed at the very beginning that you could get the job done in six months if you had a $300,000 budget and a team of five people. So why isn't the job finished?"[1] This is simply not an appropriate way to treat people.

The traditional approach to managing projects is linear. You define the outcomes, organize and plan the work, execute, and close. There is opportunity for things you learn in a later phase to enlighten an earlier phase through feedback loops, but the fundamental approach is linear. The assumption is that you know the work that needs to be done and can estimate the time and costs accurately. This works well for projects that involve known entities with things you have done before.

But if you are doing something that involves new technology or materials, that involves tasks you haven't done before, that has a great deal of uncertainty, or that is larger than you've had experience with, you will encounter a lot of unexpected things during the execution process. Your planning will be insufficient. This is not a personal fault but is merely the nature of the situation. In such cases, an adaptive approach works best.

THE CHARACTERISTICS

An adaptive approach has the following characteristics:

Use Tasks as Experiments

Since you do not know the full answer yet of what will work best, you have to embed learning the best approach into the process itself. This means learning through experience, which involves trial and error. The scientific method is the best approach for this. When you are dealing with an unknown area of the project, make an educated guess of what will work best, and try that. See what happens, then try a different approach or adapt your process based on what you've learned.

Take an Iterative Approach to Tasks

Using tasks as experiments means taking an iterative approach—letting what you do affect what you do next, based on what you've learned from the action. This may mean trying several different options, which will require finding a way to do them quickly and at low cost.

Have Fast Cycles

In addition to learning from each task and using that knowledge right away, you need to keep your planning blocks small. Most teams using an agile approach plan weeklong sprints and then evaluate and replan for the next week's sprints. If you have long lead times, on the other hand, you won't be able to adapt what you do to the things you are learning in the moment.

Deliver Value Frequently and Early

Don't seek to complete the whole project and then unveil it all at once to the stakeholders. Make each deliverable along the way something that delivers value already, which will also build momentum and energy. This is not simply a good thing for adaptive methodologies; even Gutzon Borglum, who led the sculpting of Mount Rushmore, realized the project could die through lack of enthusiasm if he waited until the very end to unveil the full sculpture. Instead, he had a ceremony to highlight the completion of each of the faces on the mountain, thereby perpetuating interest and enthusiasm.

Build the Team with People Who Are Curious and Open to Learning

Because learning and flexibility are central to the adaptive approach, it will not work if the people on the team are closed to learning and uncomfortable with ambiguity.

Additional Applications

The adaptive approach can also adapt to different contexts. For example, the funding for a project can be reconceived in an adaptive way. Instead of approving the full budget at the beginning, as is done in typical approaches, the funding is given by stage. Upon the successful completion of a stage, plans for the next stage (including budget) are refined based on what actually happened and what was learned. Then the funding is adapted and granted for the next stage. This ties funding to ongoing results and can help weed out unworthwhile projects.

CHAPTER 18

BUILDING YOUR WILLPOWER AND GROWING DISCIPLINE

Willpower is a limited resource (see the excellent book *Willpower: Rediscovering the Greatest Human Strength* by Roy Baumeister), but we can help preserve it and increase it by doing the following things:

- getting a good night's sleep,
- exercising,
- minimizing exposure to temptations, and
- alternating between mindful and mindless tasks to give the brain time to process information and restore energy.

GROWING IN DISCIPLINE

Related to willpower is growing in discipline. But discipline goes beyond mere willpower because it anchors willpower in deeper mind-sets and habits, allowing our disciplined decisions to use less of our willpower reserve, and enabling us to remain focused and to better resist the temptation to deviate from our work.

1. **Know what discipline is.** It is "the ability to make and keep commitments." Discipline is "the key to overcoming the pull of the past."[1] Great power resides in the principle of keeping promises and honoring commitments. And

"remember that our personal integrity or self-mastery is the basis for our success with others."[2]

2. **Remember your vision.** Vision enables you to get beyond the "just say no" mentality. "Purpose pulls us in the direction we want to go." In contrast, just saying no is generally not successful "because saying no to something is not as powerful as saying yes to an objective we are passionate about."[3]

3. **Begin small and build.**

   i. Start with small commitments, even made just to yourself, and build up your ability from there. Build momentum through making and keeping smaller commitments, and grow from there.

   ii. Know that you have to do the easier before the harder. Covey points out that many are trying to conquer day four, five, and six problems (such as procrastination, impatience, and pride) without having conquered day one and two problems of getting control over the body (getting to bed early, rising early, exercising regularly, eating in moderation, and working when tired).[4]

   iii. Know that the very process of acting builds discipline and makes it easier. "Active, positive behavior reinforces our good intentions and resolutions. Actions—actual doing—can change the very fiber of our nature. Doing changes our view of ourselves. Our personal behavior is largely a product of such self-made fuel."[5] Resisting the temptation will strengthen you so you are more able to resist the next one.

4. **When your new habit is tested, stop, get control, and rally your resources.** As Covey puts it, "Plumb and rally your resources. Set your mind and heart. Choose your mood. Proactively choose your response. Ask, 'How can I best respond to this situation?' Choose to be your best self, and that choice will arrest your ambivalence and renew your determination."[6]

5. **Be disciplined around principles, not just priorities.**
   Covey captures how surprising—but then obvious—this
   is: "Effective people lead their lives and manage their
   relationships around principles; ineffective people attempt
   to manage their time around priorities and their tasks
   around goals."[7]
6. **See the spillover effect.** Growth in one area often
   results in growth in other areas as well.

Here's another way to express the cycle of getting unstuck and
making change in yourself: learn what you need to do, commit to
doing it, do it, evaluate the results, refine your approach, repeat.

GETTING UNSTUCK FROM BAD HABITS

Related to discipline is eliminating bad habits and replacing them
with new ones.

1. Determine which habit you want to eliminate.
2. Find the cue that is triggering the bad habit.[8]
3. Define the new habit you want to put in its place.
   This should be a core, anchor habit.
4. Create new cues to trigger new behaviors.[9]
5. Start the new habit.
6. Keep going even when tempted to divert, which builds
   endurance.
7. Enlist others to help.
8. Don't try to change too many habits at once.[10]

CHAPTER 19

MAKING YOUR WORKSPACE CLUTTER-FREE

Having become interested in desk and workspace setup as an extension of my Getting Things Done (GTD) practices, I found that they quickly and easily extended further to organizing my whole house. Practicing these principles has saved a lot of time over the years and made it easy to find what we need when we need it. I don't always keep everything perfectly picked up, but I do know where things belong so that it is easy to put everything away.

HOW TO ORGANIZE ANYTHING

I recommend the book *Organizing for Dummies* by Eileen Roth and Elizabeth Miles for learning how to organize your space for optimal efficiency and effectiveness.[1] The authors provide suggestions for organizing every room of your house. Best of all, their system centers on a set of five simple principles based on the acronym PLACE that you can use to organize anything effectively. I've found these principles to be useful time and again. Here they are:

Purge. Get rid of what is unnecessary, especially pens that don't work.

Like with like. This means that you group like things together just as you learned in high school English. This is the central principle to organizing anything.

Access. When you have your groupings determined, place them according to your access needs. This is why, for example, extra supplies go off in a supply closet or other out-of-the-way place rather than in your drawers. You don't want things you don't use often getting in your way when accessing things you do need a lot.

Contain. Don't just let items run loose. Use drawer dividers and other types of containers to organize items.

Evaluate. When you are done organizing, step back and contemplate the results and make sure your new setup works well for you. Make any adjustments.

YOUR WORKSPACE: Creating a High Performing Workflow System

Setting up your workspace and desk well matters for several reasons. First, when you have your desk set up well, you *minimize resistance* so that you can give your focus and energy to doing your work.

Second, you will work better if you have your desk set up well and *know how to use it*. A desk is a *workflow system*; therefore, you ought to approach it with intentionality and purpose. You can be more effective when you *understand your tools* and know how to make the most of them. After all, your desk is the place where you must complete important tasks every day.

Third, when your desk is not set up well, the clutter creates drag and thus drains time, energy, and focus. I like how the authors of *Organizing for Dummies* put it: "You don't need to be an efficiency expert, interior designer, or *feng shui* master specializing in the Chinese art of placement to know that the right work space can set you up for success, while a *whatever* approach to your workplace layout can sap your time, energy, concentration, and creativity."[2]

Or, to say it another way: "Clutter sucks creativity and energy from your brain."[3]

Fourth, when you make it easy to act, you will do more. As Kerry Gleeson, author of *The Personal Efficiency Program*, says, "Most people act when it's easy to do so. The better organized you are, the easier it is to act and the greater the tendency for you to do those things that should be done, when they should be done."[4]

Fifth, you use your desk almost every day, and knowing how to use it is not hard to figure out. So the benefits you get from this are large while the cost involved is minimal.

Sixth, work is more fun when you know how to use your desk. A well-run desk is a work of art!

You can read the full series of how to set up your desk and workspace on my blog.[5] Here are a few key principles:

1. Your workspace should be like a cockpit. You want it to be an effective, efficient home base for dealing with stuff and executing work. Thus it needs to be lean and function with ease. You want to be able to move quickly with minimal drag.
2. You should have fingertip access to the things that you use and do most often, and enough surface area to do your work and create (temporary!) groupings as needed on the desktop (which you clear away when done).
3. Clear space is good. Do not aim to occupy every fragment of space. A desk is for working, not storing things. So *be a minimalist* when it comes to what you keep on your desk permanently.
4. Everything at your desk falls into just a few categories: equipment, supplies, decoration, reference, transient stuff.
5. The desk is for doing work, not storing work or reminding you of work.
6. Creation of centers are necessary. On your desktop, the key centers will likely be the phone center, computer center, tool center, and work center. In your drawers, centers include: writing center, mailing/finance center (if needed), and stapler/filing center. In your files, the major divisions (or centers) are: pending, projects, operations, reference, and archive.
7. Have interchangeable centers at home and work.

FURTHER RESOURCES

- Matt Perman, *How to Set Up Your Desk: A Guide to Fixing a (Surprisingly) Overlooked Productivity Problem* (ebook)

CHAPTER 20

GETTING PROJECTS UNSTUCK

There are lots of reasons projects get stuck, and there are lots of ways to get them unstuck. One of the most powerful ways to getting them unstuck that I've found is applying the "natural planning model" that David Allen outlines in *Getting Things Done: The Art of Stress-Free Productivity*.[1]

The key to this process is first defining your *purpose* for the project. This is how our mind naturally wants to operate (hence, the phrase "natural planning model"). Unfortunately, we tend to default to the opposite approach—we try to come up with a "good idea" before having a clear purpose and vision. Taking this approach almost always creates increased ambiguity and thus stress, because there is no unifying principle to integrate things. The result is that you can easily go off in a thousand directions without ever even hitting on the actions that you really need to take.

But when you define the purpose *first*, it immediately gives you clarity, guidance, and focus. Because you have focus, you save time. Because you have clarity, you are able to determine the actions that will actually work. And because you have guidance, you won't feel lost and confused.

Here is the natural planning model in a nutshell.

THE FIVE STEPS OF THE NATURAL PLANNING MODEL

Purpose and Principles

Step one is defining the "why" of the project. If you are redesigning the website of your organization, for example, why are you doing that? Are you seeking to increase usability, replace an outdated design, or add new functionality? And why are you seeking to do those things? Identifying the steps you need to take on a project is much easier when you know why you are doing it in the first place.

And as Simon Sinek points out in *Start with Why*, starting with the purpose is also the key to motivating and inspiring people. "Those who are able to inspire give people a sense of purpose or belonging that has little to do with any external incentive or benefit to be gained."[2] People who are inspired act because they want to, not because they have to. And this inspiration comes not from external incentives but from purpose.

Principles are the core standards for how you will do things. They are inspiring when they resonate with the core of people and are based on the desire to empower people rather than control them.

Outcome Visioning

After defining the purpose, you then start envisioning what it will be like to achieve success with the project. This is the "what."

For example, to use a wild and crazy idea, if the project is to accomplish a manned mission to Mars, the vision of the outcome might be "Four people have landed safely on the red planet and are ready to walk around and explore; the world is excited by this incredible new step; the visitors will stay for two months and then return."

Or if your company is looking for a new office building, your vision might be "We are in a building with excellent design that is inspiring and doesn't make us feel like we are back in the 1940s; there is enough room for all our employees and many years of growth; the building is near good restaurants and has sufficient parking."

Brainstorming

Envisioning the outcome naturally leads to generating ideas regarding *how* you are going to achieve your goal. What actions do you need to take in order to make it happen? You might need to identify the budget, find a realtor, narrow down the parts of town you want to consider, and so forth.

Organizing

Then these actions need to be organized. Organizing them into groupings of similar components, such as "design," "legal," "search," and so forth can be helpful.

Next Actions

Finally, you determine the very next thing you need to do to get the project going.

UTILIZE THIS PROCESS WHENEVER YOU WANT TO IMPROVE OR CREATE SOMETHING

I was doing a coaching session with an executive recently. When I asked him the main thing in his work or life that he wanted to improve, he said leading his family. That's an excellent decision.

So I took him through this process. We talked about why he wanted to lead his family more effectively. Then we talked about what this would look like and the benefits it would have for his family. Then we talked about what recurring habits and actions would be best to put in place to make this happen.

The number of ideas this process generated and the amount of clarity it brought to the task was amazing. Just by using this simple process, we had a tool for creating powerful change and improvement in this executive's life.

CHAPTER 21

OVERCOMING THE NUMBER ONE STICKING POINT FOR NEW LEADERS

High performers are often elevated to the executive level and then left to figure out on their own how to operate successfully in their new roles.

SCOTT EBLIN[1]

It is possible for a focus on personal productivity to ruin your ability to lead. One of the most helpful books I've read on leading in an organization is Scott Eblin's *The Next Level*. Eblin points out that "40 percent of new executives fail within eighteen months of being named to their positions."[2] That's an incredible statistic.

A typical response might be that this is just the *Peter principle* at work, which states that people have been promoted to their level of incompetence. But I think Eblin is right that this theory actually doesn't make much sense. Most of these people are talented, bright, and motivated. It is unlikely that such a high percentage of them have been promoted beyond their ability.[3]

What is actually going on is that these people are making a classic—but very easy to understand—mistake: when they got into their new leadership positions, they kept doing all the things that got them there. They didn't realize that leadership is a *different sort of thing* than management and, even more significantly, than being an individual contributor. And so they failed. They acted like an individual contributor in a leadership role, and so they ended up doing all the wrong things. They probably even did them extremely well—for it was their capacity for individual contribution that likely got them promoted to a level of more formal leadership—but since they were doing the wrong things, it backfired and undermined their effectiveness in the role.

DON'T CONFUSE THE ROLES OF THE PRODUCER AND THE LEADER

Much of the time, people reach positions of formal leadership because they have proven themselves as fantastic individual contributors. They have done excellent work coding pages for the website (an *individual contributor* task), for example, and so they become promoted to head up the whole web division (a *leadership* task).

The problem is that at the higher levels of an organization, you don't succeed primarily because of your abilities as an individual contributor (that is, because of your abilities to do the work). Rather, your primary role now is to set direction, align your team, and give thought to the direction of the whole organization.

If you keep focusing on doing the work yourself, or acting like another member of the team whose contribution is simply another chunk of work that is the same in kind as what everyone else is doing, you will be neglecting the things you have been put in your position to do. In fact—and this is the key—if you keep trying to do the sorts of things you did as an individual contributor, you simply won't have time to lead at all.

The main takeaway you need to get here is that you have to stop doing some good things in order to lead well. If you keep trying to do your functional responsibilities, you simply won't have time to lead. Your individual contribution tasks will interfere with your leadership tasks.

There is a range here, of course. It's not that the leader has *no* responsibilities as an individual contributor. The leader's *primary* area of focus needs to be leadership tasks, not individual contributor tasks.

LEADERSHIP: Setting Down *Responsibility* for a Few Results and Picking Up *Accountability* for Many Results

Eblin talks about eight core things that you need to stop doing (and eight things you need to start doing) to succeed at the executive level. His most helpful point is that executive leadership requires "setting down responsibility for few results and picking up accountability for many results."[4]

To be "responsible" for something is to be involved in the details. You are either doing it directly or closely involved in directing those who are. Obviously, if you are closely involved with the details of things, you won't have the time to deal with a lot of things.

To be "accountable," on the other hand, is to be answerable for the results that other people (your team) achieve. Since you aren't involved with the details doing things, you can be accountable for many things, which is exactly what any leadership role requires.

Leaders need to accomplish *more* than they did as individual contributors, not less. And that's the precise reason they need to stop acting like individual contributors.

As an individual contributor, your efforts don't scale. But when you lead, your efforts are multiplied through the influence you have on the contributions of others. Thus you need to spend less time on individual projects and more time working across the scope of the organization or, if your role is informal, the movement.

This means, as Andy Stanley has said, that if you are a leader, you need to "spend the majority of your time at the thirty-thousand-foot level while remaining accessible to team members who are closer to the action. Spend more time strategizing and less time problem solving."[5]

HOW GETTING THINGS DONE CAN INADVERTENTLY PREVENT YOU FROM LEADING

How does getting things done inadvertently prevent you from leading? It's simple: the project lists and action lists involved in most productivity approaches (such as GTD) tend to cause your focus to gravitate to your own individual contribution.

When looking at your next actions, for example, it's easy to fall into the notion that "I'd better do these things." Since it's often easier and quicker to do these things ourselves (at first), we end up settling into an individual contributor model when we should be thinking more broadly about our team and the culture of the entire organization.

And this is especially the case if you work for an organization that might be perennially short-staffed, such as a nonprofit or a ministry.

That is exactly what happened to me. At one time I was leading three departments in our organization. I was managing the church and conference bookstores, launching our nationwide radio program, and leading our web department. This was a lot to have going on at once. I was frequently pulling all-nighters (which I actually enjoy—and I disagree with those who say that an all-nighter is a sign that you are inefficient and can't get your work done—not true!), and one week I pulled three all-nighters in a row (my personal record).[6]

The biggest reason for these long hours and all-nighters—aside from the fact that I really enjoyed what we were doing—is that I was doing a lot of work myself. I had a team of a few people in each area but didn't have nearly the number of people I needed. So I filled this gap by doing a lot of the work right along with my team. I even put up a line of slat wall for shelving on the north wall of our bookstore all by myself. (As anyone who has put up slat wall knows, this is a two- or three-person job—doing it by yourself is ridiculous!)

Now, leaders should sometimes, frequently even, pitch in directly by working alongside the people on their teams. But this shouldn't be the main thing leaders do. They need to be setting direction, looking ahead, and aligning people.

I don't want to be too hard on myself here—in a very real sense, due to the small number of people I had to work with, I simply had no other choice. But the size of my team wasn't the only reason for all these hours I was putting it. The other reason was that I simply thought this was what it meant to do my work. I knew that leading my teams was important, but no one had ever told me that to do this well (or, alternatively, keep my sanity!), I had to stop doing so much of the work myself. So I worked eighty- to ninety-hour weeks and pulled these frequent all-nighters.[7]

Utilizing GTD (getting things done) only contributed to my working so many hours. It's certainly not the fault of GTD, but I thought of one hundred next actions and fifty projects as something *I* must do rather than things to delegate. This is not an intrinsic defect of GTD itself. Rather, the fault comes in how we use it. If we aren't aware of this danger, many of us (myself included) are likely to fall into this overwork trap.

So how do we avoid falling into the trap and instead use Getting Things Done to enhance our leadership?

ADAPTING GETTING THINGS DONE FOR LEADERSHIP

There are two main ways to adapt GTD for leadership.

Delegation

The first way to adapt GTD for leadership is to have the right mind-set. We need to avoid overloading ourselves with next actions we need to personally do and projects we need to personally execute. This comes, in part, from making proper use of delegating.

Sometimes this means giving people one-off tasks that come our way. This is an important thing to do, but we need to be careful of allowing this to devolve into *gopher delegation* (just telling people what to do, as opposed to delegating responsibilities).

The most effective approach to delegation for a leader, though, is to delegate entire areas of responsibility rather than one-off tasks as they come. This is much more effective because you don't need to be in the details. It also cuts off many tasks from even coming to you in the first place and needing to be delegated specifically.

By delegation, you can decrease the number of specific tasks you have to deal with, thus keeping more time free for true leadership tasks.

Project and Organizational Dashboard

The second approach is the most exciting. This means instead of just creating a roles checklist for yourself, you create an organizational chart for your department (or, if you are in top management, your whole organization). Then, every week or so, review the organizational chart and consider what actions you can proactively take to keep things going in the right direction or to help make someone more effective, and so forth.

This is the type of thing you are probably doing already in your head anyway, but creating a checklist or visual chart brings a level of proactive intentionality to it. Reviewing the organizational chart visually can be helpful to come up with new ideas and to identify things you might not otherwise have thought of.

To keep this in motion, you can create a weekly repeating task or integrate it into your weekly review.

LEAD WHEREVER YOU ARE

Now, there are many different types of leadership roles, and, as Mark Sanborn has pointed out, you don't even need a title to be a leader.[8] So leadership doesn't equate to having a role on the top leadership team or even necessarily having any formal authority at all. That is a *form* of leadership, and the main form we have been focusing on so far. But it is not the only kind of leadership. Leadership, at its essence, is influence.

And therefore you can lead wherever you are. And the leadership principles I've set forth are still important, even if you are not in a formal leadership role in your organization, because leading where you are involves more than just doing your work. You need to look outward, develop networks, motivate people, and rally them to a better future. You need to do these tasks beyond your individual work if you are an individual contributor—which means you need to be careful about the tendency to get pulled into a narrow focus on your own work.

FIVE TIPS FOR LEADERS

Make the Good of Others Your Primary Aim

The main principle of productivity is to work for the good of others, and leadership has the same aim. Leadership is not about you. It is about serving others, building them up, and making them more effective.

We should lead this way because it is right and it is the way the Scriptures teach us to lead (Matt. 20:25–28; 1 Peter 5:1–3; etc.). Moreover, it is actually the most *enjoyable* way to lead. Inventing ways to help others grow and thrive is far more fun than conceiving plans for your own private advancement. Beyond that, you'll find that serving others makes you more effective as a leader because it unlocks the essential ingredient for true leadership: trust. Mark Sanborn nails this: "When people know you are interested in their best interest, and in helping them meet their needs, they will trust you. It's human nature. And that genuine interest in helping others and making a positive difference is the essence of leadership."[9]

The proponents of servant leadership are not simply contemporary leadership thinkers. Speaking over 250 years ago, Jonathan Edwards wrote:

> Especially will the spirit of Christian love dispose those that stand in a public capacity, such as that of ministers, and magistrates, and all public officers, to seek the public good. . . . It will make them watchful against public dangers, and forward to use their powers for the promotion of the public benefit;

not being governed by selfish motives in their administration; not seeking only, or mainly, to enrich themselves, or become great, and to advance themselves on the spoils of others, as wicked rulers very often do, but striving to act for the true welfare of all to whom their authority extends.[10]

And, on the other hand, Edwards also spoke of the sin of those who, "if clothed with authority, carry themselves very injuriously toward those over whom their authority extends, by behaving very assumingly and magisterially and tyrannically toward them."[11]

Those whom you lead are not there to serve you; you are there to serve them. This is how Jesus himself led (Matt. 20:28); how could you see your role as being any different?

Turn the Work Over to the Team

As we have seen, you cannot give attention to the true tasks of leadership unless you let your team focus on the managing and doing of the work. This is not to say that the leader is to avoid all menial work. Jesus himself showed us that is not the case by washing his disciples' feet before he gave his life on the cross to serve humankind (John 13:12–17). But the primary task of the leader is to set direction, align, and motivate—not primarily create plans and do specific work tasks.

We don't succeed at the executive level because of additional functional strengths. You have to turn the work over to your team even if, at first, they can't do it as well as you.

FOR PASTORS: *DON'T* TURN OVER PREACHING AND TEACHING

It might be tempting for a pastor to think, *Okay, if my primary task is leadership, then I need to hand off more preaching and teaching so I can focus on leading the staff.* This would be a mistake.

The focus of the pastoral role is prayer and the ministry of the Word—not leading the pastoral staff. That does need to happen, but it is not the primary role of the pastor. The primary role of the pastor is to shepherd (lead) the flock. And this is done mainly through—not apart from—preaching and teaching.

The right application of this principle for pastors, then, is not that they should reduce their preaching and teaching load so that they can do more staff leadership and administrative work. Rather, it is that they should *reduce* their administrative work so they can devote *even more* time to preaching and teaching.

Some people think that pastors are an exception to the importance of leadership. They think that a focus on leadership leads to a pastor taking on the CEO model. This is incorrect. Leadership in the pastoral role is practiced primarily *through* the ministry of the Word and prayer. And thus pastors are not an exception to the things I am saying on leadership here; rather, these things actually protect the true nature of the pastoral role.

One nuance here: in large churches, there is often an executive pastor who leads the staff, and other pastors fill numerous other roles (leaders of small group ministries, family discipleship ministries, etc.). I am not saying that's bad. The role of the executive pastor, for example, is mainly to lead the staff. I am talking here about the primary preaching and teaching pastor—which includes the senior pastor.[12] Even so, the executive pastor should place a heavy emphasis on preaching and teaching in his contexts as well.

Take Time to Think

A leader needs to take time to step back, get up on the balcony, and reflect. All good leaders do this. They process what has happened, ponder new and better ways to do things, make sure they keep their eye on the big picture, and just plain *think*. Leadership has a significant reflecting component, and the best leaders tend to be the best thinkers.

You need to find your own way to build reflection into your life as a discipline. For many leaders, virtually all downtime automatically becomes thinking time. They are always musing, always having ideas and reflections and questions running through their heads. You might combine thinking with exercising or, like Jonathan Edwards, go for long walks to spend time in prayer and thought. The key is that you create time to think and do it regularly.

I would also suggest that beyond the ordinary time you take to think during the course of a week that you take a week out every quarter or six months to go somewhere secluded and read and reflect on major issues and across a broad range of topics.

Bill Gates exemplifies this idea with his famous "think weeks," during which he takes "a seven-day stretch of seclusion . . . to ponder the future of technology and then propagate those thoughts across the Microsoft empire."[13] Now that his efforts are turned primarily toward his foundation, I doubt that his focus is still the future of technology. But what better way to contribute to the solutions for large global problems than to spend a week reading and thinking about new and better ways to address them?

And you can do the same for the problems—and, most of all, opportunities—in your organization.

One other word here: Don't merely think. *Draw conclusions.* That's the point of thinking. Those who ponder, ponder, and ponder some more without ever coming to a position on things will be ill equipped to bring much insight and help to others.

Connect!

Leaders need not only time to think but time to connect with people. This should be a top priority for you in your leadership. You need to connect not only with the people in your organization or primary sphere of influence but also with people all across your industry or movement or marketplace or area.

Leaders need to stay in close touch with the people they serve and develop networks of relationships with other leaders. Conferences are a great time to combine taking time to think and connecting with others. And by combing these two areas, they both become more effective because you are able to share your ideas and see how they are refined and built on by others.

And this, in fact, is the purpose of conferences: to connect with others and share ideas.

Some people regard attending conferences as a bonus expense, as something to do if some extra money is in the budget but not worth prioritizing otherwise. I couldn't disagree more. The value that comes from making connections, having time to think, being exposed to great new ideas, and refining your ideas is invaluable. If you work for a nonprofit or a church, you will find that conferences radically expand your ability to accomplish your mission. And if you work in business, a strong case can be made that attending (good) conferences is actually revenue generating.[14]

Don't Ignore the Condition of Your Soul

There are a lot of parallels between productivity and leadership. As we saw above, both should be focused on the good of others. Another parallel is that character is at the heart of both.

Andy Stanley gets this right when he points out that "without character you won't be a leader worth following. Character provides the moral authority necessary to bring together the people and resources needed to further an enterprise. . . . Character is the source of your moral authority."[15] Thus you need to keep your walk with God vibrant and growing. As Stanley says, "To become a leader worth following, you must be intentional about developing the inner man. You must invest in the health of your soul. Nobody plans to fail, especially leaders. But to ignore the condition of your soul is the equivalent of planning to fail."[16]

So don't plan to fail! Be intentional about the condition of your soul, which starts with consistent prayer and reading of the Bible, along with fellowship in a good church.

JOIN THE MOVEMENT

What will happen if you can get unstuck?

You will, of course, be able to get more done with less stress and frustration. You will be able to manage your time more deliberately, increase your energy, and build great momentum in your work and life. You will have greater peace of mind with greater impact.

But don't stop there. Remember the unstuck cycle: the ultimate purpose of getting unstuck is to serve others—especially by helping them get unstuck. This is the most fulfilling way to live, and it is what God calls us to. So use your increased productivity to do good for others in more effective and creative ways. Do this for those in your workplace, your community, and especially your family. Don't just use your increased effectiveness for your own benefit; use it to bring great benefit to others, even through obstacles.

The best way to make this happen is to join up with others. You can't get unstuck alone or use your effectiveness for the greatest good without collaboration, interaction, and friendship with those in a common cause.

The good news is that there is a growing movement of people who are excited about making a difference in their work, communities, and families through greater effectiveness. These people are not just hardworking but are also smart and creative. And they are everywhere.

Find these people—both right around you and online—and join up with them. Work together, share ideas, and collaborate. Get to know these people in your workplace, community, and church who believe in making a difference, and get going on projects together. Share productivity practices. Form groups. Organize initiatives that make a difference.

As you do this in very simple ways with people who share your interests, you join the movement of people who are making a difference in creative, fulfilling ways in the world. And as you join this movement, using your increased effectiveness to make a difference for good *together*, the world can change. You can advance the common good, tackle large global problems like extreme poverty, and further the spread of the gospel.

You can avoid a life that is just marking time and lived for yourself. You can make a difference in a balanced, interdependent way by joining up with the thousands of others who are already learning about getting things done for the good of others. And you can start by talking to just one person.

LEARN MORE AND PASS THIS ON

THE WHAT'S BEST NEXT COMPANY

What's Best Next is a gospel-centered resource, training, and coaching organization based on the methodology outlined in the book *What's Best Next*, founded by me and James Kinnard in 2015. Our purpose is to organize and empower Christians in the world of work, helping them become more effective leaders, managers, and individual contributors in a way that fully reflects the gospel.

As Christians learn to lead and manage their time in a biblical way, people are served and the gospel advances, with the result that God is glorified through our good works (Matt. 5:16) and his glory fills the earth (Hab. 2:14).

OUR WEBSITE

Find us online at http://www.whatsbestnext.com.

At our website you will find hundreds of free blog posts and articles, more books, our availability for online coaching, and a growing collection of online courses and seminars. All of this is to help you do your work in a gospel-centered way for the good of others, your own work, and the glory of God.

THE SOCIAL WEB

Connect with us on Facebook and Twitter:

- Facebook: facebook.com/whatsbestnext
- Twitter: twitter.com/whatsbestnext
- Twitter for Matt Perman: twitter.com/mattperman

TWO OTHER WAYS TO PASS THIS ON AND HELP OTHERS TO BE MORE PRODUCTIVE

- Email people a link to the book:
  o The book page on our website: http://www.whatsbest
    next.com/books/ how-to-get-unstuck
  o The Amazon link: https://www.amazon.com/How
    -Get-Unstuck-Breaking-Productivity/dp/0310526817
- Tweet about the book and share on Facebook!

INVITE MATT TO SPEAK

If you are interested in having Matt speak at your event or do a workshop for your staff, inquire at http://www.whatsbestnext .com/speaking/.

ACKNOWLEDGMENTS

Writing a book always requires the support of many people. First of all, I want to thank the Lord for his grace and for giving me the ability to write this book. May you be honored, Lord, beyond my abilities.

I am grateful to my editor, Ryan Pazdur, who had the initial idea for this book, and the entire team at Zondervan. They are sharp and on the ball. It has been great to work together on a second book.

My agent, Andrew Wolgemuth, has continued to be a consistent encouragement and huge help. Thank you, Andrew.

For part of the time I was working on this book I was also working at Made to Flourish. The team there was such an encouragement and joy to work with. They helped me make the connection between being "unstuck" and "flourishing." The work that Made to Flourish is doing to help pastors connect faith and work is well worth checking out! (www.madetoflourish.org)

I am very appreciative of John Piper for his continued prayers and Glenn Brooke who has now been praying for me for over ten years.

Andrew Kwee read *How to Get Unstuck*, *What's Best Next*, and my forthcoming *Effective in Doing Good* in the short span of just a few weeks and provided excellent feedback as a believer in the business world on real-world application.

Thank you to Danny Jang and everyone at Grace Church, Stamford, for all of your encouragement and support to help me get unstuck during a difficult time. You embody what the church should be!

And once again I'm indebted to my parents and two older brothers who have always encouraged me in my writing.

NOTES

Introduction: We All Get Stuck in Some Way

1. Seth Godin, *Poke the Box: When Was the Last Time You Did Something for the First Time?* (New York: Portfolio, 2015), 3.

2. See, for example, Daniel Coyle, *The Talent Code: Greatness Isn't Born. It's Grown. Here's How* (New York: Bantam, 2009), and chapter 10, "Get the Knowledge You Need," in this book.

3. Seth Godin, preface to *Pick Four: Zig Ziglar's Legendary Goals Program, Updated and Simplified* (The Domino Project, 2011).

4. Stephen Covey, *Principle-Centered Leadership* (New York: Fireside, 1992), 72.

5. Charles Duhigg, *Smarter Faster Better: The Transformative Power of Real Productivity* (New York: Random House, 2016), 8.

6. David Allen, *Getting Things Done: The Art of Stress-Free Productivity* (New York: Penguin, 2015).

7. Matt Perman, *What's Best Next: How the Gospel Transforms the Way You Get Things Done* (Grand Rapids: Zondervan, 2015).

8. I'm following Covey in my use of the terms *compass* and *clock*. The compass and clock, he argues, represent the two fundamental realities in time management—importance and urgency. The "compass" is about knowing what is important—being able to detect importance through a clear mission that is based on principles. In other words, the compass is about *effectiveness*— knowing the right things to do. The "clock," on the other hand, is how we manage our time. It is the realm of schedules and to-do lists and focus. The problem with traditional time management is that it is often "clock only." But to be effective, we must subordinate the clock to the compass. We must manage our time *in light of a greater vision based on what God has said.*

Chapter 1: How We Get Stuck

1. Stephen R. Covey, A. Roger Merrill, and Rebecca R. Merrill, *First Things First* (New York: Free Press, 1996), 18.
2. Dr. Seuss, *Oh, the Places You'll Go!* (New York: Random House, 1990), n.p., emphasis in original.

Chapter 2: What It Means to Be Unstuck

1. Jonathan T. Pennington, *The Sermon on the Mount and Human Flourishing: A Theological Commentary* (Grand Rapids: Baker Academic, 2017), 290, 294.
2. Roy E. Ciampa and Brian S. Rosner, *The First Letter to the Corinthians,* Pillar New Testament Commentary (Grand Rapids: Eerdmans, 2010), 837.
3. John Piper, "You Will Know the Truth, and the Truth Will Set You Free," sermon on John 8:30–36, Desiring God, accessed December 13, 2017, www.desiringgod.org/messages/you-will-know-the-truth -and-the-truth-will-set-you-free.
4. John Piper, *Desiring God: Meditations of a Christian Hedonist* (Colorado Springs: Multnomah, 2011).
5. Martin E. P. Seligman, *Flourish: A Visionary New Understanding of Happiness and Well-Being* (New York: Free Press, 2012), 183.
6. Stephen R. Graves, *Flourishing: Why Some People Thrive While Others Just Survive* (Fayetteville, AR: KJK, 2015), 17.
7. Graves, *Flourishing*, 15.
8. Graves, *Flourishing*, 23.
9. Jim Collins and Jerry I. Porras, *Built to Last: Successful Habits of Visionary Companies* (New York: HarperBusiness, 2004).
10. Jerry Porras, Stewart Emery, and Mark Thompson, *Success Built to Last: Creating a Life That Matters* (Upper Saddle River, NJ: Prentice Hall), 27.
11. Porras, Emery, and Thompson, *Success Built to Last*, 19. And so they encourage people: be careful about working very hard for things that don't matter to you.
12. See also Clayton M. Christensen's excellent message "How Will You Measure Your Life?" *Harvard Business Review*, July–August 2010, https://hbr.org/2010/07/how-will-you-measure-your-life.
13. Seligman, *Flourish*, 16.

14. David Allen, *Getting Things Done: The Art of Stress-Free Productivity* (New York: Penguin, 2015), 18.

15. Stephen Covey, *Principle-Centered Leadership* (New York: Fireside, 1992), 73.

16. Peter M. Senge, *The Fifth Discipline: The Art and Practice of the Learning Organization* (New York: Doubleday, 2006), 7. Interestingly, this makes personal mastery an essential cornerstone of the learning organization. For "an organization's commitment to and capacity for learning can be no greater than that of its members." Nonetheless, "surprisingly few organizations encourage the growth of their people in this manner. This results in vast untapped resources" (7).

Chapter 3: The Unstuck Cycle

1. See Andy Stanley's excellent chapter on what to do when you can't act on a vision right away in Andy Stanley, *Visioneering: Your Guide for Discovering and Maintaining Personal Vision* (Colorado Springs: Multnomah, 1999).

2. Luther's exposition of Psalm 147, quoted in Gustaf Wingren, *Luther on Vocation*, trans. Carl C. Rasmussen (Eugene, OR: Wipf and Stock, 2004), 194.

3. See my summary of the biblical doctrine of sanctification in my outline "The Freedom of Sanctification," What's Best Next, November 28, 1998, www.whatsbestnext.com/1998/11/the-freedom-of-sanctification/.

4. J. Gresham Machen, "Christianity and Culture," *Princeton Theological Review* 11 (November 9, 1913). Online at Made to Flourish, www.madetoflourish.org/resources/christianity-and-culture/.

5. See the excellent chapter "Man Seeking Motivation" in Thomas J. Peters and Robert H. Waterman Jr., *In Search of Excellence: Lessons from America's Best-Run Companies* (New York: HarperCollins, 2004). I love this quote from investment banker Charles Schwab: "I have yet to find a man, however exalted in his station, who did not do better work and put forth greater effort under a spirit of approval than under a spirit of criticism."

6. Emma Seppälä, *The Happiness Track: How to Apply the Science of Happiness to Accelerate Your Success* (New York: HarperCollins, 2016), 125ff.

7. Peter Lewis, *The Genius of Puritanism* (n.p.: Soli Deo Gloria, 1997).

8. David P. Murray, *Christians Get Depressed Too* (Grand Rapids: Reformation Heritage, 2010).

Chapter 4: Recovering Personal Effectiveness as a Force for Good

1. This is the point Marcus Buckingham makes in his book *First, Break All the Rules: What the World's Greatest Managers Do Differently* (New York: Simon & Schuster, 1999), the best book on management I've ever encountered.

2. John P. Kotter, "What Leaders Really Do," *Harvard Business Review* (December 2001), https://hbr.org/2001/12/what-leaders -really-do.

3. See his excellent chapter on leadership in Marcus Buckingham, *The One Thing You Need to Know . . . about Great Managing, Great Leading, and Sustained Individual Success* (New York: Free Press, 2005). See also my blog post summarizing his point, "What Does a Leader Do?" What's Best Next, January 9, 2009, http://www.whats bestnext.com/2009/01/what-does-a-leader-do/.

4. I have grouped Edwards's resolutions into categories, which you can find online at my website: https://www.whatsbestnext.com/2011/ 06/the-resolutions-of-jonathan-edwards-in-categories/.

5. See his thirty-five plus years of resources at http://www.desiring God.org.

6. Bill Hybels, "From Overscheduled to Organized: Harnessing Your Calendar's Power" in *Simplify: Ten Practices to Unclutter Your Soul* (Carol Stream, IL: Tyndale, 2014).

Chapter 5: Understanding Urgency and Importance (for Real)

1. Stephen R. Covey, A. Roger Merrill, and Rebecca R. Merrill, *First Things First* (New York: Free Press, 1996), 36.

2. Covey, Merrill, and Merrill, *First Things First*, 37.

3. Covey, Merrill, and Merrill, *First Things First*, 38.

4. Jonathan Edwards, "Memoirs," in *The Works of Jonathan Edwards Volume 1* (Carlisle, PA: Banner of Truth, 1987), xxxiv, emphasis added.

5. Edwards, "Memoirs," xxxi, emphasis added.

6. Covey, Merrill, and Merrill, *First Things First*, 37.

7. Dan Ariely, "Q&A: Understanding Our Compulsions," in *Manage Your Day-To-Day: Build Your Routine, Find Your Focus, and Sharpen Your Creative Mind*, 99U Book Series, ed. Jocelyn K. Glei (Las Vegas: Amazon, 2013), 45.

Chapter 6: Character: The Great Unsticking Force

1. Stephen R. Covey, A. Roger Merrill, and Rebecca R. Merrill, *First Things First* (New York: Free Press, 1996), 12.

2. Matt Perman, "In Defense of Buzzwords . . . Sort of," What's Best Next, January 6, 2009, http://www.whatsbestnext.com/2009/01/in-defense-of-buzzwords-sort-of/.

3. Covey, Merrill, and Merrill, *First Things First*, 28.

4. Ronald Nash, *Life's Ultimate Questions: An Introduction to Philosophy* (Grand Rapids: Zondervan, 2013), 14.

5. Stephen R. Covey, *The 7 Habits of Highly Effective People*, 25th Anniversary Ed. (New York: Simon & Schuster, 2013), 39–39.

6. Covey, Merrill, and Merrill, *First Things First*, 30.

7. Stephen R. Covey, *Principle-Centered Leadership* (New York: Fireside, 1992), 173–74.

8. Covey, *Principle-Centered Leadership*, 175.

9. Eric Gieger, Michael Kelley, and Philip Nation, *Transformational Discipleship: How People Really Grow* (Nashville: B&H, 2012), 28.

10. For more on this, see my chapter "How the Gospel Makes Us Productive" in Matt Perman, *What's Best Next: How the Gospel Transforms the Way You Get Things Done* (Grand Rapids: Zondervan, 2016).

11. See John Dickson's excellent book *Humilitas: A Lost Key to Life, Love, and Leadership* (Grand Rapids: Zondervan, 2011), and my summary of his message at the 2011 Global Leadership Summit, "The Best Message on Humility I Have Ever Heard" What's Best Next, August 12, 2011, http://www.whatsbestnext.com/2011/08/the-best-message-on-humility-i-have-ever-heard/.

Part 2: Personal Leadership: The Compass

1. I like how John Kotter says this about leadership generally: "The issue of leadership is centrally important because leadership is different from management and the primary force behind successful change is the former, not the later. Without sufficient leadership,

the probability of mistakes increases greatly and probability of success decreases accordingly" (John P. Kotter, *On What Leaders Really Do* [Cambridge, MA: Harvard Business Review, 1999], 10).

2. Stephen R. Covey, *The 7 Habits of Highly Effective People*, 25th Anniversary Ed. (New York: Simon & Schuster, 2013), 51.

3. Also crucial is to develop your mission and values as part of your vision. This is beyond the scope of this book, but more detail can be found in Matt Perman, *What's Best Next: How the Gospel Transforms the Way You Get Things Done* (Grand Rapids: Zondervan, 2016).

Chapter 7: Understand the Power of Vision

1. John Piper, "How I Almost Quit," desiringGod, February 16, 2010, http://www.desiringgod.org/articles/how-i-almost-quit. See the article for the full quote, and Piper's encouragement from it to "beware of giving up too soon. Our emotions are not reliable guides."

2. See especially the great recounting of this story in Sarah Eekhoff Zylstra's article "How John Piper's Seashells Swept over a Generation," The Gospel Coalition, May 20, 2017, http://www.thegospelcoalition .org/article/how-john-pipers-seashells-swept-over-a-generation.

3. James Collins and William C. Lazier, *Beyond Entrepreneurship: Turning Your Business into an Enduring Great Company* (Paramus, NJ: Prentice Hall, 1992), 49, emphasis original.

4. Peter M. Senge, *The Fifth Discipline: The Art and Practice of the Learning Organization* (New York: Doubleday, 2006), 142.

5. Stephen R. Covey, *The 7 Habits of Highly Effective People*, 25th Anniversary Ed. (New York: Simon & Schuster, 2013), 157.

6. Covey, *7 Habits*, 157

7. Stephen R. Covey, A. Roger Merrill, and Rebecca R. Merrill, *First Things First* (New York: Free Press, 1996), 102. Here is how Frankl puts it: "In the Nazi concentration camps, one could have witnessed that those who knew that there was a task waiting for them to fulfill were most apt to survive. The same conclusion has since been reached by other authors of books on concentration camps, and also by psychiatric investigations into Japanese, North Korean and North Vietnamese prisoner-of-war camps" (Viktor E. Frankl, *Man's Search for Meaning* [Boston: Beacon, 2006], 104).

8. Harold Kushner, preface to *Man's Search for Meaning*, ix.

9. Kushner, preface to *Man's Search for Meaning*, x.

10. Mihaly Csikszentmihalyi, *Flow: The Psychology of Optimal Experience* (New York: HarperPerennial, 1990), 92.
11. See Abraham H. Maslow, *Eupsychian Management* (n.p: Irwin, 1965).
12. Simon Sinek, *Start with Why: How Great Leaders Inspire Everyone to Take Action* (New York: Penguin, 2009), 2.
13. Sinek, *Start with Why*, 2–3.
14. Sinek, *Start with Why*, ix. Simon's answer to the question "Why start with why?" is this: To inspire.
15. Csikszentmihalyi, *Flow*, 230, emphasis in original.
16. Csikszentmihalyi, *Flow*, 216, emphasis in original.
17. Csikszentmihalyi, *Flow*, 214.
18. Csikszentmihalyi, *Flow*, 215.
19. Csikszentmihalyi, *Flow*, 217.
20. Csikszentmihalyi, *Flow*, 217.
21. Covey, Merrill, and Merrill, *First Things First*, 116.
22. Andy Stanley, *Visioneering: Your Guide for Discovering and Maintaining Personal Vision* (Colorado Springs: Multnomah, 1999), 13.
23. Covey, Merrill, and Merrill, *First Things First*, 112.
24. Stanley, *Visioneering*, 114.
25. Covey, Merrill, and Merrill, *First Things First*, 116.
26. Covey, Merrill, and Merrill, *First Things First*, 104.
27. Daniel H. Pink, *Drive: The Surprising Truth about What Motivates Us* (New York: Riverhead Books, 2009), 133.
28. Stanley, *Visioneering*, 11.
29. Stanley, *Visioneering*, 10.
30. Covey, Merrill, and Merrill, *First Things First*, 105.
31. Peter M. Senge, *The Fifth Discipline: The Art and Practice of the Learning Organization* (New York: Doubleday, 2006), 194.
32. Stanley, *Visioneering*, 12.
33. James Collins and William C. Lazier, *Beyond Entrepreneurship: Turning Your Business into an Enduring Great Company* (Paramus, NJ: Prentice Hall, 1992), 53.
34. Collins and Lazier, *Beyond Entrepreneurship*, 53–54.
35. Collins and Lazier, *Beyond Entrepreneurship*, 54–55. Emphasis in the original.
36. Charles Duhigg, *Smarter Faster Better: The Transformative Power of Real Productivity* (New York: Random House, 2016), 279. Duhigg goes on to illustrate this with an example: "If my email account says

there are thirty new messages, I know that I should ignore them until 11:30, because that's what the story inside my head tells me to do. If the phone rings and caller ID indicates it's an expert I'm trying to contact, I'll take the call, because the interruption has a place within my mental model." He then summarizes the place of vision (in this case, a short-term vision for the day) in enabling focus: "To stay focused: envision what will happen. What will occur first? What are potential obstacles? How will you preempt them? Telling yourself a story about what you *expect* to occur makes it easier to decide where your focus should go when your plan encounters real life" (279, emphasis in original).

Chapter 8: Be Missional: Understand How Your Faith and Work Relate

1. Tim Keller, *Center Church: Doing Balanced, Gospel-Centered Ministry in Your City* (Grand Rapids: Zondervan, 2012), 284.
2. Keller, *Center Church*, 284.
3. See Keller, *Center Church*.
4. Christopher J. H. Wright, *The Mission of God's People: A Biblical Theology of the Church's Mission*, Biblical Theology for Life (Grand Rapids: Zondervan, 2010).
5. This is also why gospel-driven productivity differs from secular conceptions of work, such as in Timothy Ferriss, *Four-Hour Workweek: Escape 9–5, Live Anywhere, and Join the New Rich* (New York: Crown, 2009), which see work as something you should get done as fast as possible so you can then do what you want and find meaning in that. Instead, in GDP, you find meaning *in* your work, because God values it for his glory and the good of others. *And* you also get it done so that you can do the other things you have to do in life.
6. Hugh Whelchel, *How Then Should We Work? Discovering the Biblical Doctrine of Work* (McLean, VA: Institute for Faith, Work & Economics, 2012), 102.
7. For a brief example of a gospel-centered business approach, see Matt Perman, "The Gospel-Centered Business," What's Best Next, March 17, 2015, http://www.whatsbestnext.com/2015/03/the -gospel-centered-business/.
8. James Davison Hunter, *To Change the World: The Irony, Tragedy,*

and Possibility of Christianity in the Late Modern World (Oxford: Oxford University Press, 2010).

9. See, for example, Daniel Pink's excellent book *Drive: The Surprising Truth about What Motivates Us* (New York: Riverhead Books, 2009). Also see Marcus Buckingham's excellent book *First, Break All the Rules: What the World's Greatest Managers Do Differently* (New York: Simon & Schuster, 1999), and his recent video *Love + Work* at http://www.marcusbuckingham.com/lovework.

10. Simon Sinek, *Start with Why: How Great Leaders Inspire Everyone to Take Action* (New York: Penguin, 2009).

11. For more on how to do this, see Matt Perman, *Effective in Doing Good: Connecting Your Work to God's Work through Gospel-Driven Productivity* (forthcoming from What's Best Next).

12. Hunter, *To Change the World*, 89.

13. Tim Keller and James Hunter, "Getting Upstream to Transform the City," lecture and handout, Redeemer Presbyterian Church, New York City.

14. T. M. Moore, quoted in Whelchel, *How Then Should We Work?* 103.

15. John Stott and Christopher J. H. Wright, *Christian Mission in the Modern World* (Downers Grove, IL: InterVarsity, 2015), 54.

Chapter 9: See Yourself as a Professional (. . . Sort of)

1. Steven Pressfield, "How Pro Can You Go?," in *Manage Your Day-to-Day: Build Your Routine, Find Your Focus, and Sharpen Your Creative Mind*, ed. Jocelyn K. Glei, The 99U Book Series (Las Vegas: Amazon, 2013), 231.

2. Pressfield, "How Pro Can You Go?," 229–30.

3. Andrew Campbell and Laura Nash, *A Sense of Mission: Defining Direction for the Large Corporation*, International Management Series (Boston: Addison-Wesley, 1992), 3.

4. Campbell and Laura Nash, *A Sense of Mission*, 3.

5. See, for example, Daniel Goleman, *Emotional Intelligence: Why It Can Matter More Than IQ* (New York: Bantam, 1995) and *Social Intelligence: The New Science of Human Relationships* (New York: Bantam, 2006).

6. Tim Sanders, *Love Is the Killer App: How to Win Business and Influence Friends* (New York: Three Rivers, 2002), 11.

7. See Tom Rath, *Vital Friends: The People You Can't Afford to Live*

Without, and the Twelve Questions in Marcus Buckingham, *First, Break All the Rules: What the World's Greatest Managers Do Differently* (New York: Simon & Schuster, 1999), which summarize Gallup's research into what makes workers engaged. One of the twelve components is "I have a best friend at work."

8. John Piper, "Ten Principles for Personal Productivity," desiringGod, April 18, 2016, http://www.desiringgod.org/interviews/ten-principles-for-personal-productivity.

9. See Marcus Buckingham, *First, Break All the Rules*, and Curt Coffman and Gabriel Gonzalez-Molina, *Follow This Path: How the World's Greatest Organizations Drive Growth by Unleashing Human Potential* (New York: Warner, 2002).

10. Marcus Buckingham, *The One Thing You Need to Know . . . about Great Managing, Great Leading, and Sustained Individual Success* (New York: Free Press, 2005).

11. John Piper, "Ten Principles for Productivity," at https://www.desiringgod.org/interviews/ten-principles-for-personal-productivity.

12. Robert Brunner and Stewart Emery, with Russ Hall, *Do You Matter? How Great Design Will Make People Love Your Company* (Upper Saddle, NJ: FTPress Delivers, 2009), 74.

13. Henry McKenna, "Bill Belichick Explains What Makes Great Players Great," PatriotsWire, January 20, 2017, http://patriotswire.usatoday.com/2017/01/20/bill-belichick-explains-what-makes-great-players-great/.

14. Keith Ferrazzi and Tahl Raz, *Never Eat Alone: And Other Secrets to Success, One Relationship at a Time* (New York: Crown, 2014), 22.

Chapter 10: Preparation: Get the Knowledge You Need

1. Rudy Giuliani, *Leadership* (New York: Miramax, 2005), 52.

2. Giuliani, *Leadership*, 52.

3. Giuliani, *Leadership*, ix–x.

4. Bobby Knight, quoted in Tim Sanders, *Today We Are Rich: Harnessing the Power of Total Confidence* (Carol Stream, IL: Tyndale, 2011), 178.

5. Sanders, *Today We Are Rich*, 175.

6. Sanders, *Today We Are Rich*, 176.

7. John P. Kotter, "Leading Change," *Leadership Excellence* 22, no. 11 (2005): 5–6.

8. Steven F. Hayward, *Churchill on Leadership: Executive Success in the Face of Adversity* (New York: Three Rivers, 1998), 26.

9. Willie Pietersen, *Strategic Learning: How to Be Smarter Than Your Competition and Turn Key Insights into Competitive Advantage* (Hoboken, NJ: John Wiley & Sons, 2010), 208–9.

10. Liz Wiseman, *Rookie Smarts: Why Learning Beats Knowing in the New Game of Work* (New York: HarperCollins, 2014), 12.

11. Bill Welter and Jean Egmon, *The Prepared Mind of the Leader: Eight Skills Leaders Use to Innovate, Make Decisions, and Solve Problems* (San Francisco: Jossey-Bass, 2006), 173.

12. David Allen, *Getting Things Done: The Art of Stress-Free Productivity* (New York: Penguin, 2015), xii.

13. Jocelyn K. Glei, ed., *Manage Your Day-to-Day: Build Your Routine, Find Your Focus, and Sharpen Your Creative Mind*, 99U Book Series (Las Vegas: Amazon, 2013), 101.

14. Daniel Goleman, *Focus: The Hidden Driver of Excellence* (New York: HarperCollins, 2013), 28.

15. Jeff Brown and Mark Fenske also explain this well in *The Winner's Brain: 8 Strategies Great Minds Use to Achieve Success* (Cambridge, MA: Harvard University Press, 2010). They write, "The more tasks you can automate and the more information you can shift to implicit memory, the lighter the load on the attention systems and the more control you gain over your powers of focus and concentration" (97). And so we see the importance of practicing until you can work on autopilot. Getting tasks on autopilot enables you to focus by freeing up your attention to do so.

16. Goleman, *Focus*, 28.

17. Martin E. P. Seligman, *Flourish: A Visionary New Understanding of Happiness and Well-Being* (New York: Free Press, 2012), 108–9.

18. Seligman, *Flourish*, 109.

19. Seligman, *Flourish*, 112.

20. Goleman, *Focus,* 31. One of the primary themes we have seen over and over is the importance of recognizing our limitations—in this case of our mental energy. Overloaded attention also has implications for the amount of distractions we now have due to our digital lives: "Life immersed in digital distractions creates a near-constant cognitive overload. And that overload wears on self-control" (31). We will see more about this in chapters 13 and 14 on deep work.

21. Justin Menkes, *Executive Intelligence: What All Great Leaders Have* (New York: HarperCollins, 2006), 90.

22. Sanders, *Today We Are Rich*, 177.

23. Sanders, *Today We Are Rich*, 177.

24. Greg McKeown, *Essentialism: The Disciplined Pursuit of Less* (New York: Crown, 2014), 97.

25. For one of the best articles on deliberate practice, see Anders Ericsson, Michael J. Prietula, and Edward T. Cokely, "The Making of an Expert," *Harvard Business Review* (July–August 2007), https://hbr.org/2007/07/the-making-of-an-expert?autocomplete=true. For a short take, see the chapter in *Maximize Your Potential* "Developing Mastery through Deliberate Practice."

26. Sanders, *Today We Are Rich*, 180.

27. Charles Duhigg, *Smarter Faster Better: The Transformative Power of Real Productivity* (New York: Random House, 2016), 88–102.

28. Duhigg, *Smarter Faster Better*, 101.

29. Duhigg, *Smarter Faster Better*, 101.

30. Duhigg, *Smarter Faster Better*, 102.

31. Duhigg, *Smarter Faster Better*, 102.

32. Duhigg, *Smarter Faster Better*, 92.

33. Duhigg, *Smarter Faster Better*, 93. Interestingly, this also helps with getting a job! "The candidates who tell stories are the ones every firm wants. . . . It's a tip-off that someone has an instinct for connecting the dots and understanding how the world works at a deeper level" (93).

34. Giuliani, *Leadership*, 62.

35. Jefferson Bethke, *Jesus > Religion: Why He Is So Much Better Than Trying Harder, Doing More, and Being Good Enough* (Nashville: Thomas Nelson, 2013).

36. Wayne Grudem, *Systematic Theology* (Grand Rapids: Zondervan, 1995); and William Lane Craig, *Reasonable Faith: Christian Truth and Apologetics*, 3rd ed. (Wheaton, IL: Crossway, 2008).

37. Timothy Keller, *Center Church: Doing Balanced, Gospel-Centered Ministry in Your City* (Grand Rapids: Zondervan, 2012).

38. Thomas Sowell, *Basic Economics: A Common Sense Guide to the Economy*, 5th ed. (New York: Basic Books, 2014).

39. Shaunti Feldhahn, *The Surprising Secrets of Highly Happy Marriages: The Little Things That Make a Big Difference* (Colorado Springs:

Multnomah, 2013); and Tim Kimmel, *Grace-Based Parenting: Set Your Family Free* (Nashville: Thomas Nelson, 2005).

40. James Collins and William C. Lazier, *Beyond Entrepreneurship: Turning Your Business into an Enduring Great Company* (Paramus, NJ: Prentice Hall, 1992), 202.

41. Collins and Lazier, *Beyond Entrepreneurship*, 202.

42. Collins and Lazier, *Beyond Entrepreneurship*, 203.

43. Wiseman, *Rookie Smarts*, 136. Quotes in previous paragraph also from Wiseman.

44. Giuliani, *Leadership*, 65.

Part 3: Personal Management: The Clock

1. David Allen, *Getting Things Done: The Art of Stress-Free Productivity* (New York: Penguin, 2015), 7.

2. Annie Dillard, *The Writing Life* (New York: HarperPerennial, 1989), 32.

3. *Managing Time: Expert Solutions to Everyday Challenges*, Pocket Mentor (Cambridge: Harvard Business School Publishing, 2006), 71.

4. Robert C. Pozen, *Extreme Productivity: Boost Your Results, Reduce Your Hours* (New York: HarperCollins, 2012), 1.

5. Allen, *Getting Things Done*, 10.

6. Allen, *Getting Things Done*, 9–10.

Chapter 11: Start with Your Time, Not with Your Tasks

1. James Collins and William C. Lazier, *Beyond Entrepreneurship: Turning Your Business into an Enduring Great Company* (Paramus, NJ: Prentice Hall, 1992), 20.

2. Peter F. Drucker, *The Effective Executive: The Definitive Guide to Getting the Right Things Done* (New York: HarperCollins, 2006), 25.

3. Drucker, *Effective Executive*, 25.

4. Jim Collins has a great discussion of this in *Beyond Entrepreneurship*, 18–21.

5. Drucker, *Effective Executive*, 26.

6. For more on this, see my workshop "The Gospel and Money," The Gospel Coalition, http://www.slideshare.net/mattperman/the-gospel-and-money-1345175 (slides) and https://www.thegospelcoalition.org/conference_media/the-gospel-and-money/ (audio; my portion starts about 25 minutes in or so).

7. Drucker, *Effective Executive*, 26.

8. Jonathan Edwards, "The Preciousness of Time, and the Importance of Redeeming It," in *The Works of President Edwards*, 10 vols. (New York: Carvill, 1830), 6:486.

9. Drucker, *Effective Executive*, 26.

10. John Piper, *Don't Waste Your Life* (Wheaton, IL: Crossway, 2009).

11. Drucker recommends doing it for three to four weeks twice a year in *The Effective Executive*.

12. Drucker, *Effective Executive*, 27.

13. Drucker, *Effective Executive*, 36.

14. Drucker, *Effective Executive*, 37.

15. Drucker, *Effective Executive*, 39.

16. Note that I differ from Drucker on this, in large part, I believe, because of changes in the environment since he originally wrote *The Effective Executive*. There he said that "a work force may, indeed, be too small for the task.... Much more common is the work force that is too big for effectiveness" (43). The symptom of overstaffing, though, is not your subjective sense. Rather, it is if the senior people have to spend more than about 10 percent of their time on human relations problems ("feuds and frictions" and "questions of cooperation"). "In a lean organization people have room to move without colliding with one another and can do their work without having to explain it all the time" (43). That is something I totally agree with. And now with the rise of freelancers (see Daniel Pink, *Free Agent Nation: The Future of Working for Yourself* [New York: Warner Business, 2001]), thanks to the internet, it is possible to have a team with the talent you need and less full-time staff. One of the most helpful rules on when to hire a position on staff is when the knowledge and skills for that position are needed "day in and day out for the bulk of the work" (43).

17. Patrick Lencioni, *Death by Meeting: A Leadership Fable ... about Solving the Most Painful Problem in Business* (San Francisco: Jossey-Bass, 2004), vii.

18. Lencioni, *Death by Meeting*, viii.

19. Lencioni, *Death by Meeting*, viii.

20. Drucker, *Effective Executive*, 45.

21. Drucker, *Effective Executive*, 39.

22. Drucker, *Effective Executive*, 47.

23. Drucker, *Effective Executive*, 49.

Chapter 12: Set Your Priorities: Make Importance Truly Work

1. Sundar Pichai, quoted in Harry Mccracken, "At Sundar Pichai's Google, AI Is Everything—And Everywhere," *Fast Company* (December 2016/January 2017), 74.
2. Peter F. Drucker, *The Effective Executive: The Definitive Guide to Getting the Right Things Done* (New York: HarperCollins, 2006), 24.
3. Drucker, *Effective Executive*, 100.
4. Greg McKeown, *Essentialism: The Disciplined Pursuit of Less* (New York: Crown, 2014).
5. Drucker, *Effective Executive*, 100.
6. Drucker, *Effective Executive*, 101.
7. Charles Duhigg, *Smarter Faster Better: The Transformative Power of Real Productivity* (New York: Random House, 2016), 90.
8. Duhigg, *Smarter Faster Better*, 90.
9. Greg McKeown, *Essentialism: The Disciplined Pursuit of Less* (New York: Crown, 2014), 7.
10. Brian Tracy, *Eat that Frog! 21 Great Ways to Stop Procrastinating and Get More Done in Less Time* (Oakland, CA: Berrett-Koehler, 2017), ix.
11. McKeown, *Essentialism*, 4.
12. Drucker, *Effective Executive*, 110.
13. Drucker, *Effective Executive*, 111.
14. Drucker, *Effective Executive*, 101–2.
15. Drucker, *Effective Executive*, 111.
16. Greg McKeown, *Essentialism*, 60.
17. See part 2 of McKeown, *Essentialism*.
18. McKeown, *Essentialism*, 61.
19. See chapter 13, "Clarifying Your Roles" in Matt Perman, *What's Best Next: How the Gospel Transforms the Way You Get Things Done* (Grand Rapids: Zondervan, 2016), for more on this.
20. Drucker, *Effective Executive*.
21. Drucker, *Effective Executive*, 103.

Chapter 13: Deep Work, Part 1: The New Superpower of Knowledge Work

1. Daniel Goleman, *Focus: The Hidden Driver of Excellence* (New York: HarperCollins, 2013), 2–3.
2. Peter F. Drucker, *The Effective Executive: The Definitive Guide to Getting the Right Things Done* (New York: HarperCollins, 2006), 100.

3. Goleman, *Focus*, 2–3.
4. Mihaly Csikszentmihalyi, *Flow: The Psychology of Optimal Experience* (New York: HarperPerennial, 1990), 267.
5. Goleman, *Focus*, 23.
6. Goleman, *Focus*, 22.
7. Cited in Daniel H. Pink, *Drive: The Surprising Truth about What Motivates Us* (New York: Riverhead Books, 2009), 114.
8. And, interestingly, Csikszentmihalyi's research shows that we are more likely to enter flow at work than in leisure pursuits.
9. Goleman, *Focus*, 22.
10. Pink, *Drive,* 115.
11. Cal Newport, *Deep Work: Rules for Focused Success in a Distracted World* (New York: Grand Central, 2016), front flap.
12. Newport, *Deep Work*, 3.
13. Newport, *Deep Work*, 3.
14. Newport, *Deep Work*, 6.

Chapter 14: Deep Work, Part 2: Put Deep Work into Your Schedule and Overcome Distractions

1. Cal Newport, *Deep Work: Rules for Focused Success in a Distracted World* (New York: Grand Central, 2016), 157.
2. Newport, *Deep Work*, 98.
3. Cal Newport, "Schedule in Time for Creative Thinking," in *Manage Your Day-to-Day.*
4. Newport, *Deep Work*, 102.
5. Newport, *Deep Work*, 108.
6. Newport, *Deep Work*, 108.
7. Newport, *Deep Work*, 110.
8. Newport, *Deep Work*, 112.
9. Newport, *Deep Work*, 113.
10. From the biography of Edwards at the beginning of the Banner of Truth Edition of *The Works of Jonathan Edwards* (Carlisle, PA: Banner of Truth, 1974), xxxix.
11. Newport, *Deep Work*, 113. Newport also makes this great observation: "For a lot of bosses, the standard is that you're free to focus as hard as you want . . . so long as the boss's e-mails are still answered promptly" (113).
12. Newport, *Deep Work*, 115.

13. Newport, *Deep Work*, 115.

14. Newport, *Deep Work*, 116.

15. See Jim Loehr and Tony Schwartz, *The Power of Full Engagement: Managing Energy, Not Time, Is the Key to High Performance and Personal Renewal* (New York: Free Press, 2003), chap. 1, esp. pp. 3–4. Consider two great examples he gives: "You attend a four-hour meeting in which not a single second is wasted—but during the final two hours your energy level drops off precipitously and you struggle to stay focused. . . .You set aside time to be with your children when you get home at the end of the day, but you are so distracted by thoughts about work that you never really give them your full attention" (4).

16. Mark McGuinness, "Laying the Groundwork for an Effective Routine," in *Manage Your Day-to-Day: Build Your Routine, Find Your Focus, and Sharpen Your Creative Mind*, ed. Jocelyn K. Glei, 99U Book Series (Las Vegas: Amazon, 2013), 26.

17. McGuinness, "Laying the Groundwork," 26.

18. McGuinness, "Laying the Groundwork," 26–27.

19. Stephen King, *On Writing: 10th Anniversary Edition: A Memoir of the Craft* (New York: Simon & Schuster, 2010), Kindle loc. 1770–72.

20. McGuinness, "Laying the Groundwork," 26.

21. You might be able to do so for a period of about three to four weeks if you enter that period rested and with good energy. But after about four weeks, your ability to get the most out of those sixteen-hour days will vanish. Most studies show that working much past forty hours ends up diminishing your productivity, and if you work seventy hours, you are actually not getting any more done than if you had quit at forty (due to decreased focus, impaired decision making, and increased errors). I'm also being generous in interpreting these studies—most do not note that this only happens after a few weeks, but act as though it kicks in immediately. I don't find that true to my experience or that of many others. But I do find it true to experience that if you keep up the seventy-plus-hour weeks, the amount you get done per hour decreases substantially. Working fewer hours of greater intensity is more effective *and more fun*.

22. Newport, *Deep Work*, 146. Newport also provides this excellent summary: "Providing your conscious brain time to rest enables your unconscious mind to take a shift sorting through your most complex professional challenges" (146).

23. This comes from Attention Restoration Theory, as theorized by Professor Stephen Kaplan. Quoted in Newport, *Deep Work*, 148.

24. Newport, *Deep Work*, 148.

25. Newport, *Deep Work*, 149.

26. Newport puts it well: "Trying to squeeze a little more work out of your evenings might reduce your effectiveness the next day enough that you end up getting *less* done than if you had instead respected a shutdown" (Newport, *Deep Work*, 149).

27. See Newport, *Deep Work*, 236–42, for Newport's discussion of how having a firm and early end to the workday has resulted in higher productivity in academia for himself and others, in contrast to the common practice of working a punishing schedule that most new academic institutions at tier one follow.

28. Daniel Goleman, *Focus: The Hidden Driver of Excellence* (New York: HarperCollins, 2013), 3.

29. Newport, *Deep Work*, 142.

30. Goleman, *Focus*, 18.

31. Newport, *Deep Work*, 112. I also like Newport's quote from Donald Knuth: "What I do takes long hours of studying and uninterruptible concentration" (101).

32. Glei, ed., *Manage Your Day-to-Day*, 83. Study: Shamsi T. Iqbal and Eric Horvitz, "Disruption and Recovery of Computing Tasks: Field Study, Analysis, and Directions," Proceedings of the Conference on Human Factors in Computing Systems, 2007.

33. Newport, *Deep Work*, 42.

34. See Sophie Leroy, "Why Is It So Hard to Do My Work? The Challenge of Attention Residue When Switching between Work Tasks," *Organizational Behavior and Human Decision Processes* 109 (2009): 168–81.

35. Glei, ed., *Manage Your Day-to-Day*, 82. See the study by Laura L. Bowman, Laura E. Levine, Bradley M. Waite, and Michael Gendron, "Can Students Really Multitask? An Experimental Study of Instant Messaging While Reading," *Computers and Education* 54, no. 4 (May 2010): 927–31.

36. Newport, *Deep Work*, 152.

37. See this helpful summary of the Zeigarnik effect: "The Zeigarnik Effect Explained," Psychologist World, accessed December 14, 2017, http://www.psychologistworld.com/memory/zeigarnik-effect

-interruptions-memory.php. Another article on using it effectively is Alina Vrable, "The Zeigarnik Effect: The Scientific Key to Better Work," Sandglaz, November 5, 2013, http://blog.sandglaz .com/zeigarnik-effect-scientific-key-to-better-work/. See also the discussion of the Zeigarnik effect in relation to GTD in Roy F. Baumeister and John Tierney, *Willpower: Rediscovering the Greatest Human Strength* (New York: Penguin, 2012), 80–84.

38. See the German study: Kurt Lewin, "Untersuchungen zur Handlungs-und Affektpsychologie," *Psychologische Forschung* 9, no. 1 (December 1927), 1–85. https://interruptions.net/literature/ Ovsiankina-PF28.pdf.

39. Glei, ed., *Manage Your Day-to-Day*, 84–85.

40. On the other hand, when stuck in the creative phase of a task, switching things up can be a key strategy to getting unstuck. "When you're at the problem-solving stage or you need to generate new ideas, psychologists have shown that taking your mind off-task briefly can help your subconscious find links between disparate concepts" (Glei, ed., *Manage Your Day-to-Day*, 85).

41. *Managing Time: Expert Solutions to Everyday Challenges*, Pocket Mentor (Cambridge: Harvard Business School Publishing, 2006), 88.

42. Quote from *Managing Time*, 88. See Kotter's article "What Managers Really Do" for an excellent deeper dive.

Chapter 15: Renewal: The Power of Preaching to Yourself

1. Stephen R. Covey, *The 7 Habits of Highly Effective People*, 25th anniv. ed. (New York: Simon & Schuster, 2013), 316.

2. Annie Dillard, *Pilgrim at Tinker Creek* (New York: Harper Perennial, 2013), 269.

3. Covey gives great examples of what happens when organizations neglect one or more of these areas in *7 Habits*, pp. 314–15. This is also the reason that the "human relations" school of management philosophy in the 1950s and '60s did not work. It seemed like it would because it recognized that the economic component of work is not enough, and that people need to be treated well. But it ended up *leaving out* the economic dimension altogether, so that a type of country club management was the result. These organizations ended up performing poorly because the social component was not combined with the economic. Some people, however, wrote off the

importance of managing for the human side altogether because of this, failing to realize that this was simply a reflection of the fact that organizations, like people, are holistic entities. All four dimensions need to be addressed, not just one or two. Thomas J. Peters and Robert H. Waterman Jr. talk about this in *In Search of Excellence: Lessons from America's Best-Run Companies* (New York: HarperCollins, 2004) as well.

4. Just as the characteristics of love are interconnected, as Edwards argues in his sermon "All the Graces of Christianity Interconnected" in Jonathan Edwards, *Charity in Its Fruits: Christian Love as Manifested in the Heart and Life* (Lawton, OK: Trumpet Press, 2014), chap. 13.

5. Don Whitney, *Spiritual Disciplines for the Christian Life* (Colorado Springs: NavPress, 2014); and David Mathis, *Habits of Grace: Enjoying Jesus through the Spiritual Disciplines* (Wheaton, IL: Crossway, 2016).

6. See "The Role of Scripture and Prayer in Our Productivity," the extended version of the chapter from *What's Best Next*, at my website at https://wp.me/P9silk-31c. Also see Keller's book *Prayer* and my message "Prayer as the (Non-Superficial) Power of Entrepreneurship" (forthcoming on WhatsBestNext.com).

7. D. Martin Lloyd Jones, *Spiritual Depression: Its Causes and Its Cure* (Grand Rapids: Eerdmans, 1965), 20–21.

8. See Gary Friessen's classic treatment of this in *Decision Making and the Will of God*.

9. Greg McKeown, *Essentialism: The Disciplined Pursuit of Less* (New York: Crown Business, 2014), 94.

Chapter 16: A Basic Approach to Getting Unstuck from Problems

1. Christian Jarrett, "Banishing Multitasking from Our Repertoire," *Manage Your Day-to-Day: Build Your Routine, Find Your Focus, and Sharpen Your Creative Mind*, ed. Jocelyn K. Glei, The 99U Book Series (Las Vegas: Amazon, 2013), 85.

Chapter 17: Taking an Adaptive Time-Management Approach

1. Harvard Business Review, *Managing Projects Large and Small: The Fundamental Skills to Deliver on Budget and on Time* (Cambridge, MA: Harvard Business School Publishing, 2004), 115.

Chapter 18: Building Your Willpower and Growing Discipline

1. Stephen Covey, *Principle-Centered Leadership* (New York: Fireside, 1992), 73.
2. Covey, *Principle-Centered Leadership*, 77.
3. G. Lynne Snead and Joyce Wycoff, *To Do Doing Done: A Creative Approach to Managing Projects and Effectively Finishing What Matters Most* (New York: Fireside, 1997), 24.
4. Covey, *Principle-Centered Leadership*, 85.
5. Covey, *Principle-Centered Leadership*, 78.
6. Covey, *Principle-Centered Leadership*, 77.
7. Covey, *Principle-Centered Leadership*, 52.
8. See Greg McKeown, *Essentialism: The Disciplined Pursuit of Less* (New York: Crown, 2014), 209–10.
9. McKeown, *Essentialism*, 210–11. See also the discussion of priming in Jim Loehr and Tony Schwartz, *The Power of Full Engagement: Managing Energy, Not Time, Is the Key to High Performance and Personal Renewal* (New York: Free Press, 2003), 177. Rituals work because they function as cues.
10. See especially Charles Duhigg's *The Power of Habit*.

Chapter 19: Making Your Workspace Clutter-Free

1. Eileen Roth and Elizabeth Miles, *Organizing for Dummies* (Hoboken, NJ: Wiley, 2001).
2. Roth and Miles, *Organizing for Dummies*, 183.
3. G. Lynne Snead and Joyce Wycoff, *To Do Doing Done: A Creative Approach to Managing Projects and Effectively Finishing What Matters Most* (New York: Fireside, 1997), 92.
4. Kerry Gleeson, *The Personal Efficiency Program: How to Stop Feeling Overwhelmed and Win Back Control of Your Work* (Hoboken, NJ: John Wiley & Sons, 2009), 4.
5. Matt Perman, "How to Set Up Your Desk: An Introduction," What's Best Next, October 13, 2009, http://www.whatsbestnext .com/2009/10/how-to-set-up-your-desk-an-introduction/.

Chapter 20: Getting Projects Unstuck

1. David Allen, *Getting Things Done: The Art of Stress-Free Productivity* (New York: Penguin, 2015).

2. Simon Sinek, *Start with Why: How Great Leaders Inspire Everyone to Take Action* (New York: Penguin, 2009), 6.

Chapter 21: Overcoming the Number One Sticking Point for New Leaders

1. Scott Eblin, *The Next Level: What Insiders Know about Executive Success*, 2nd ed. (Boston: Nicholas Brealey, 2011), 6.

2. Eblin, *The Next Level*, xii.

3. In fact, I'm not sure I agree with the Peter Principle at all. It simply doesn't make much sense to me. People can be promoted outside of their strengths. But to say they've been promoted "beyond their ability" implies that that the person has only a certain amount of ability that can only take them so far. In contrast, I believe that people can keep learning and growing and rise to the occasion if they truly desire to. The issue is that the higher role may not be a good fit for what they are most highly motivated and gifted to do. But the problem here is not that the role is higher and they can't somehow handle the responsibility; the problem is one of *fit*. There may be other roles of even greater responsibility that are a good fit, and in which the person would excel.

4. This is the title to one of the chapters in Eblin's *The Next Level*. It is said very well!

5. Andy Stanley, *Next Generation Leader: Five Essentials for Those Who Will Shape the Future* (Colorado Springs: WaterBrook Multnomah, 2003), 19.

6. The thing about all-nighters, by the way, is that you also have to work the next full day; otherwise you defeat the purpose. If you are going to stay up all night and then go to bed at 6:00 a.m., why not just go to bed at night and get up early?

7. Interestingly, another factor here was that because I was working for a ministry, I really believed in and loved what we were doing as an organization. I don't think I would have done this if I was working at a for-profit organization. It would have been much more natural for me to say, "We have to hire more people, or we just can't do this stuff." This is one of the great things about working at a ministry—but also one of the dangers. The work was so meaningful that I really loved what I was doing and didn't begrudge these

all-nighters. But precisely because I loved what I was doing, it was easy to overlook the fact that I was doing too much.

8. See Mark Sanborn's excellent book *You Don't Need a Title to Be a Leader: How Anyone, Anywhere, Can Make a Positive Difference* (Colorado Springs: WaterBrook, 2006).

9. Sanborn, *You Don't Need a Title to Be a Leader*, 64. Keith Ferrazzi and Tahl Raz get this as well: "Do you understand that it's your team's accomplishments, and what they do because of you, not for you, that will generate your mark as a leader?" (Keith Ferrazzi and Tahl Raz, *Never Eat Alone: And Other Secrets to Success, One Relationship at a Time* [New York: Crown, 2014], 57). What they do *because* of you rather than simply *for* you is a critical difference. Sanborn adds, "I realized that my long-term success depended on everyone around me. That I worked for them as much as they worked for me" (58).

10. Jonathan Edwards, *Charity in Its Fruits: Christian Love as Manifested in the Heart and Life* (Lawton, OK: Trumpet Press, 2014), 170–71.

11. Edwards, *Charity in Its Fruits*, 169. Note that servant leadership is not a recent innovation in leadership theory. It is taught and modeled in the Bible, and writing more than two hundred years ago, one of the greatest theologians the church has ever produced affirmed it.

12. I know some people say the concept of "senior pastor" is not in the Bible. And I do believe, as Alexander Strauch argues in *Biblical Eldership: An Urgent Call to Restore Biblical Church Leadership* (Colorado Springs: Lewis & Roth, 1995), that all elders are equal in authority. But as Strauch also points out, one elder typically stands out as "first among equals," and different reporting relationships may exist within the pastoral staff.

13. Robert A. Guth, "In Secret Hideaway, Bill Gates Ponders Microsoft's Future," *Wall Street Journal*, March 28, 2005, https://www.wsj.com/articles/SB111196625830690477.

14. See my post "Is Attending Conferences an Unnecessary Expense?" What's Best Next, March 1, 2010, http://www.whatsbestnext.com/2010/03/is-attending-conferences-an-unnecessary-expense/.

15. Stanley, *Next Generation Leader*, 12.

16. Stanley, *Next Generation Leader*, 153.

What's Best Next

How the Gospel Transforms
the Way You Get Things Done

Matt Perman

Do work that matters.

Productivity isn't just about getting more things done. It's about getting the right things done—the things that count, make a difference, and move the world forward. In our current era of massive overload, this is harder than ever before. So how do you get more of the right things done without confusing mere activity for actual productivity?

When we take God's purposes into account, a revolutionary insight emerges. Surprisingly, we see that the way to be productive is to put others first—to make the welfare of other people our motive and criteria in determining what to do (what's best next). As both the Scriptures and the best business thinkers show, generosity is the key to unlocking our productivity. It is also the key to finding meaning and fulfillment in our work.

By anchoring your understanding of productivity in God's purposes and plan, What's Best Next will give you a practical approach for increasing your effectiveness in everything you do. This expanded edition includes a new chapter on productivity in a fallen world and a new appendix on being more productive with work that requires creative thinking.

Available in stores and online!